Jews and the New American Scene

*"An intier [entire] new scene will open it self,
and we have the world to begin againe."*

Mordechai Sheftall, 1783

~ *Jews* ~
and the New American Scene

Seymour Martin Lipset and Earl Raab

Harvard University Press

Cambridge, Massachusetts, and London, England, 1995

Library of Congress Cataloging in Publication Data

Lipset, Seymour Martin.
Jews and the new American scene /
Seymour Martin Lipset and Earl Raab.
p.   cm.
Includes bibliographical references and index.
ISBN 0-674-47493-7
1. Jews—United States—Identity.
2. Jews—United States—Social conditions.
3. Jews—United States—Politics and government.
4. United States—Ethnic relations.
I. Raab, Earl.   II. Title.
E184.J5L745   1995
305.892′4073—dc20   94-32358
CIP

Designed by Gwen Frankfeldt

For Kassie and Sydnee

⁓ Acknowledgments ⁓

Our obligations to others are many. They extend particularly to both the Russell Sage Foundation, which supported Lipset's research for a year in New York City and also provided a grant for subsequent work, and the National Endowment for the Humanities, which awarded a fellowship to Raab for a year's freedom to harvest some of the materials that ended up in this book. The Wilstein Institute for Jewish Policy Studies contributed much to our resources, as did the Mandel Institute for the Advanced Study and Development of Jewish Education. We are especially grateful to the Hoover Institution, where Lipset, as a Senior Fellow, did much of his writing, and to the Perlmutter Institute at Brandeis University, which gave Raab the free time to pound away on his computer.

Mordichai Rimor of the Louis Guttman Institute for Applied Social Research in Jerusalem provided us with analytic tables from the 1990 National Jewish Population survey that underlie many of our conclusions, although the statistical analyses are not detailed in the body of this book. Some are presented in Lipset's *The Power of Jewish Education,* published by the Wilstein Institute in 1994. We owe a debt of gratitude to those who conceived and carried through the population study and made the data tapes available to the scholarly world, in particular Barry Kosmin and Sydney Goldstein.

We would also like to acknowledge a few of the many colleagues who contributed to our knowledge in conversations and who freely offered commentary on written work: Robert Merton of the Russell Sage Foundation; Shmuel N. Eisenstadt of Hebrew University; Arnold Eisen of the Jewish Studies program at Stanford University; Seymour Fox and Annette Hochstein of the Mandel Institute in Jerusalem; David Gordis of the Wilstein Institute; Bernard Reisman, Jonathan Sarna, Lawrence Sternberg, and the late Marshall Sklare of Brandeis University; Don Kash of George Mason University; and Daniel Bell and Nathan Glazer of Harvard University. For research assistance we have relied on the many and varied contributions of Scott Billingsley, Jeffrey Hayes, Marcella Ridlen Ray, Chris Winters, and Steve Wuhs.

At Harvard University Press, Aida Donald was steadfast in her encouragement and support during critical stages of the book's publication. Last, but very far from least, is our debt to Susan Wallace Boehmer, whose editing improved the flow of our analyses and kept us on our toes by challenging some of our interpretations of biblical and theological issues.

Seymour Martin Lipset
Earl Raab
September 1994

~ Contents ~

Jews and the New American Scene

∼ *Introduction* ∼
America's Tribal Dilemma

In his novel *The Rise of David Levinsky*, the chronicler of American Jewish life at the turn of the twentieth century, Abraham Cahan, described the following scene in a Catskills hotel. The musicians were having trouble rousing a dining room full of successful Jewish immigrants. "Finally, [the conductor] had recourse to what was apparently his last resort. He struck up the 'Star-Spangled Banner.' The effect was overwhelming. The few hundred diners rose like one man, applauding. The children and many of the adults caught up the tune joyously, passionately . . . There was the jingle of newly-acquired dollars in our applause. But there was something else in it as well. Many of those who were now paying tribute to the Stars and Stripes were listening to the tune with grave, solemn mien. It was as if they were saying: 'We are not persecuted under this flag. At last we have found a home.' Love for America blazed up in my soul. I shouted to the musicians, 'My Country,' and the cry spread like wildfire."[1]

In their extravagant style, these immigrants were applauding America for providing a new order of freedom, status, and opportunity for Jews. But today, at the turn of another century, that same kind of underlying exuberance is not to be found. American Jews enjoy much more opportunity and freedom than ever before, and yet American Jewry is beset by great uncertainty about its future in the new millennium.

In the 1990s Jews were elected to Congress by their fellow Americans in numbers more than three times their proportion in the population. But during the same period, anti-Semitic vandalism was reported by some Jewish agencies to be on the increase, and the majority of Jews told pollsters they were worried about anti-Jewish hostility. While American Jewry seems to be at the peak of its organized strength, as measured by membership and monetary contributions, the evidence is clear that increasing numbers of Jewish young people are dissociating themselves from family traditions that their parents and grandparents held dear. Further, the emergence of the state of Israel, though a watershed for a renaissance of American Jewish life, has, with the passage of time, required American Jews to paper over significant disparities in their emotional and philosophical attachment to Israel for the sake of politically supporting that beleaguered state. If peace agreements reached with the PLO and Jordan are successful, relationships between American Jews and Israel may become more problematic.

These uncertainties have come to a boil in the American Jewish community, particularly within its leadership circles. Fear about the loss of "Jewish continuity" has risen to the top of the agenda, forming in its wake countless new committees, conferences, and studies. These activities were accelerated by a definitive 1990 sample survey of the Jewish population which put statistical flesh on many skeletons that everyone already knew were in the closet. Causing the greatest concern was the finding that most marriages involving Jews in the past decade have been with non-Jews, and that the majority of the children from these marriages are unlikely to receive a Jewish education. Conferences and committees about the vagaries of Diaspora–Israel relations have also proliferated, at a rate second only to those on Jewish continuity. And at the annual conclaves of Jewish public affairs agencies from around the country, debates still rage about whether anti-Semitism is or is not a continuing danger. Controversies also arise about whether the traditionally liberal political orientation of American Jews is still in their best interest, given their current socioeconomic status.

American Jewish life seems riddled with conundrums like these; and not surprisingly, given the Jewish love affair with words, books on the state of American Jewry have multiplied. Most of them have been valuable, but many have been written from the inside out. Like the institutional committees and conferences, they have tended to ask, "What is wrong with American Jewry?" Sentimentality and ideology often skew the answers.

Putting the issue of assimilation and decline this way places the onus solely on Jewry, when in fact the answers are to be found in the dynamic between American society and the Jewish community. The relationship between the two is, in many ways, unique, as we shall see, owing to the congruence between the values and characteristics of the Jewish people and those of the larger society.

The most celebrated analyst of American culture, Alexis de Tocqueville, noted in his great book *Democracy in America* that the United States is "exceptional"—that it is qualitatively different from other nations in a variety of respects. Almost every country with the exception of the United States and the now-deceased Soviet Union is a historically defined nation, united by a common history, not a political doctrine. Though immigrants may acquire citizenship almost everywhere, the meaning of being English, French, German, or Russian is predominantly a birthright status. As a new nation legitimated by a revolutionary ideology, America differed from all these other countries, and the meaning of being an American was different.

Americanism is an *ism* or ideology in the same sense that communism, fascism, or liberalism are *isms*. Its evolving creed can be defined by four words: antistatism, individualism, egalitarianism, and populism.[2] As the self-conscious center of liberal revolutions from 1776 into the twentieth century, the United States has been open to new citizens who are willing to accept the creed. Conversely, one may be proscribed as un-American, regardless of birth, by rejecting the doctrine, by accepting an alien one.

The exceptional character of America entailed norms of universalism and equality that were conducive to individualism and the development of capitalist markets. The United States began as a new society, making it the one major industrialized country that is not postfeudal. Apart from the situation of blacks and, to some extent,

Native Americans, the United States lacks the experience of fixed social status groups—caste-like structures that in English are sometimes referred to as estates or, in German, *standen*. Feudal and aristocratic systems required the explicit exhibition of deference to superiors. They rejected the values linked to social mobility, and instead emphasized particularistic factors, including family and ethnoreligious background, as sources of social status and the rights of citizenship.

As emphasized by much of the nineteenth-century foreign traveler literature, including the *Baedeker Guides,* America's major difference from Europe was that social status, as well as wealth, could be secured by achievement. One did not have to be born into a high position to receive the respect of others. In Europe, by contrast, the new class—the middle class—did not automatically secure greater prestige as its members gained economic resources.[3]

As Friedrich Engels, Antonio Gramsci, Max Weber, and other social theorists pointed out, America is the purest example of a bourgeois society, one that has followed capitalist norms. These norms assume universalism, the notion that everyone is treated according to the logic of the marketplace, that is, without reference to inherited traits. Individuals should be hired because they are the most competent employees available, regardless of background, whether they are black or white, Jew or Christian. Ideally, discrimination linked to ascribed characteristics rather than competence would, in the long run, injure the bigot in his competition with those who are not prejudiced. The perception of America as a meritocracy, an open society, implies that it is more open to the talented, the efficient, the competent.

Universalism is the broadest, perhaps the most radical principle underlying the ideology of liberalism, directly implying the equality of humankind. Equality itself, however, is a more complicated liberal idea. What substantive equality means and who is to be included as an equal have been contested throughout history. Equality in the American sense, though, has never meant equality of economic outcome. Rather, as noted by Tocqueville, it has had two distinct meanings: equal opportunity and equal respect.

The latter entails the notion that the most important attribute defining social relations is an individual's status as a human being (although in Tocqueville's time this egalitarianism defined relations only among white males). Unlike postfeudal Europe and Japan, in America all individuals were to be shown respect, regardless of where they stood in the economic or power structure, or whether they were Christian or Jewish. That ethos of egalitarianism was part of the pre-revolutionary consciousness. The *Pennsylvania Journal* wrote in 1756, "The people of this province are generally of the middling sort, and at present pretty much upon a level . . . the meanest among them thinks he has a right to civility from the greatest."[4]

Owing to all of these exceptional American circumstances, for the first time in the history of the Diaspora since the dispersal from Roman Palestine, Jews in the United States became free to partake in the society and polity as equals with everyone else. Of the many ethnic and religious minorities that have immigrated to these shores in search of liberty and opportunity, Jews in particular have benefited greatly from America's openness, its egalitarianism, and its social heterogeneity. The pariah status they experienced in Europe and the Islamic world has had no parallel in the New World. As Edward Tiryakian states:

> At the heart of American exceptionalism concerning Jews . . . is that, while, for Jews, the United States is not and cannot be ontologically and existentially "the Land" the way that Israel is, it has been more of a rewarding and accepting home than any other setting outside Israel itself . . . What makes the American case different from the others?
>
> I would propose that Jews in America have not been marginalized as "wholly other" by virtue of their religion; there has been no historical ghetto experience, no pogroms. In fact because of a deep-structure affinity of Calvinist Puritanism for Judaism, it is in America that Jews have increasingly found full societal and cultural participation and acceptance, symbolized by widespread acceptance in recent years of the term "Judeo-Christian."[5]

In the nineteenth century, in some parts of Western Europe, the imperatives of middle-class society began to open new political opportunities for Jews, including the right to vote and hold office. But there was a qualitative difference with America. As Todd Endelman pointed out, privileges for English Jews at the time were " 'bought' rather than freely dispensed [and] when the [British] Board of Jewish Deputies decided in 1829 to seek political emancipation, it was the wealth and government connections [of Rothschild and Goldsmid] that gave them entree to the ministry in the first place."[6] By contrast, in America, Jewish men were granted the suffrage along with the rest of the white male population, and many years before they had the vote elsewhere, they were able to rise to positions of political prominence. America has provided the most supportive environment that Jews have experienced since they left Palestine in the first and second centuries. And in response to these new freedoms and opportunities, Jews have become the prototypical Americans, achieving extraordinary success in intellectual, economic, and political life.

Yet American exceptionalism has been a double-edged sword. The same factors that encouraged Jews to partake of America's abundance have undermined traditional Judaism and encouraged Jews to integrate into the majority society. In the experience of all immigrants to the United States, success and assimilation have gone hand in hand. The great majority of the small groups of Jews who arrived in colonial times and in the early years of the republic drifted away from Judaism, largely as a result of intermarriage. The pattern was repeated for the much larger, predominantly German immigration of the pre- and post-Civil War era. Numbering a quarter of a million, this group sought to Americanize their religion, to make it resemble a middle-class Protestantism or Unitarianism. As with the earlier immigrants, intermarriage rates were high. Later still, the massive wave of millions of Eastern European Jews, which began in the late 1880s and continued into the immediate post-World War I years, refurbished Jewish religion and culture. The East Europeans repeated the German Jewish story of upward economic and social mobility, eventually ascending to the middle and upper rungs of business, academic, and political life in contemporary America. But again today, the future of Jewry is being undermined by assimilation.

Most American Jews are not willfully abandoning their identity in the way that some did in other times and places, particularly in Europe, in order to avoid oppression and disadvantage. The erosion of identity is mainly a natural product of living in America. But if Jews are not doing anything "wrong," neither is America. The problem is that American society has been doing what most people think is right: providing citizens with individual freedom to achieve success and status on the basis of their capacity, unencumbered by ancestral background.

That, of course, is the American *ideal*, slow to be fulfilled for many ancestral groups, still in process for some, especially those who came as slaves rather than as immigrants. It remains, however, an ideal whose progress toward realization is inexorable because of the very nature of the society. To that extent at least, American Jewish identity is captive to the same exceptional characteristics in this culture which affect other ancestral groups, whether Irish, Italian, Chinese, Latino, or African. Except for blacks, all are blending within the powerful melting pot.

All such groups, including the Jews, can be characterized as *tribal*, a term which in its most generic meaning refers to a cohesive ancestral group with particular customs, traditions, and values—religious, linguistic, and otherwise. Life in America presents each group with a tribal dilemma in the form of an antagonism between individualism, which most ancestral group members value, and group identity, which they also cherish. In the ensuing conflict, tribal cohesion tends to lose out, despite all sentimental denials and institutional investments to the contrary. Identification with the tribe no longer provides members with a life meaning that can compete with the fruits of individual accomplishment.

We contend that the conundrum of individual Jewish success amidst the dissolution of the Jewish community can best be explained by examining the relationship between American exceptionalism and Jewish exceptionalism. American exceptionalism refers to the unique historical conditions under which the nation was founded, and to the unprecedented national ideology they spawned. Jewish exceptionalism addresses the extraordinary history of the Jewish people and the extraordinary zeal with which American Jews have adopted the American creed and subsequently achieved economic, political, and social success. Only by exploring the dynamic between these two exceptionalisms can we gain insight into historical developments that have led up to the recent sense of crisis in the Jewish community.

To that end, the ensuing chapters will attempt to answer a series of questions. What is it about Jews that has made them so successful in America, as compared with so many other ethnic groups (Chapter 1)? Conversely, what is it about America that has allowed Jews to experience such unprecedented personal freedoms (Chapter 2)? In what ways do the very achievements of American Jews carry with them the seeds of the radical diminution of their tribal identity (Chapter 3)? Since the final layer of glue that has held ancestral groups together is defensiveness in the face of perceived disadvantage, why have American Jews, despite their favorable socioeconomic status, remained insistently defensive? And to what extent is anti-Semitism still in fact a serious problem (Chapter 4)? What is the role of Israel in American Jewish identity, and what will happen to that identity if Israel is no longer viewed as threatened (Chapter 5)? Why have Jews remained politically liberal when all other comparably successful groups in America have become politically conservative (Chapter 6)? And finally, what light does the past experience of other ancestral groups cast on the future of American Jews, and what factors in the future might affect the diminution of the Jewish community, change its character, or inspire a rebirth (Chapter 7)?

In 1783, on the occasion of the official suspension of hostility between Great Britain and the United States, Mordechai Sheftall, a second-generation Jew in Georgia who had been active in the Revolution, summed up the feeling of Jews about America when he wrote to his son, "An intier [entire] new scene will open it self, and we have the world to begin againe." A little more than two hundred years later there is continuing corroboration that America is exceptional, but there are also signs that another "new scene" is faced by American Jews—and by other ancestral groups—with consequences not envisioned at the start of American independence.

∾ 1 ∾

An Old People in a New Land

There was no Statue of Liberty, but Benjamin Sheftall and his forty-two Jewish companions encountered something more important to their future as their ship approached the American land mass in July 1733. They could smell the dense virgin forests; some seamen reported that they could detect that thick aroma a hundred miles off shore.

Sheftall, a refugee from Germany who had been living in England, became the head of one of Georgia's first prominent Jewish families. He was not a student of John Locke. He knew little if anything about "the rights of man" or philosophic concepts of political freedom. He anticipated no new or independent nation, no Constitution or Bill of Rights. The theoretical constructs and hypothetical potential of an exceptional America did not draw him. But as a practical matter, he knew, as the aroma of the vast uncut forests suggested, that Georgia was a *new* territory, with the consequent promise of a new kind of opportunity, a new beginning. Sheftall concluded his last will and testament in 1765 with a prayer of thanks: "Thou has *rescued* me, O Lord God of truth."[1]

Without benefit of theory, Sheftall and other early Jewish immigrants learned that America was the first nation in their experience in which it was largely possible for economic success and social status to be achieved by individual effort rather than ascribed by ancestral history. Moreover, they were able to see the practical benefits of early America's marked ethnic heterogeneity. By 1790 there were five major nationality groups in the country, and dozens of smaller ones. Over half of the white population south of New England was non-English. Virtually all who came were eligible for citizenship. Alone among the nations of the world, the new United States made it easy for the foreign-born to become citizens. "Being American" was not based on a birthright or bloodline status.

For most of its history, of course, immigration was heavily restricted to European countries, and for several troubled decades in the twentieth century, America substantially narrowed its welcome even to them. But the doors were opened wide again in midcentury, and, more recently and radically, the country began to draw heavily on settlers from Third World countries.

Economic opportunity has been the major magnet for most immigrants to America, especially given the much greater hindrances in the labor market for lower status persons in Europe. The degree to which these new immigrants can achieve equality of results in the marketplace has, however, always depended on the state of the economy. It is no accident that the flow of immigration has usually followed the curve of economic expansion and contraction in America. But under all conditions, immigrants have generally seen equal access to the economic market as symptomatic of a free and achievement-oriented society.

Economic opportunity was not the only incentive for immigrants. As Tocqueville stressed, America also offered an unusual degree of freedom and respect for both individuals and groups, regardless of their economic achievements. Mary Antin wrote about her immigrant father at the turn of the twentieth century:

> It is true that he had left home in search of bread for his hungry family, but he went blessing the necessity that drove him to America. The boasted freedom of the new world meant to him far more than the right to reside, to travel and to work wherever he pleased; [it meant also] the freedom to speak his thoughts, to throw off the shackles of superstition,

to test his own faith unhindered by political or religious tyranny. He was only a young man when he landed—32; and most of his life he had been held in leading strings, he was hungry for his untasted manhood.[2]

Depending on world and homeland conditions, the pushes and pulls that brought people to America varied. Sometimes they blessed the economic necessity that brought them inadvertently to freedom. Sometimes, religious or political freedom was the primary motivation of refugees. But more often the two incentives were inextricably intertwined.

For the Jews, the centuries-old pariahs of Europe, both economic opportunity and civic liberty in America were grounded in religious freedom. Their religious identity, seen also as their ethnic image, was, after all, the perceived source of their oppression. But their ability to compete equally and to succeed in the marketplace was a prime index of their acceptance, as well as the chief medium through which they were integrated into the American mainstream.

Jews in the Colonial Economy

The careers of the Sheftall family illustrate the way Jews and early America responded to each other. Benjamin prospered reasonably well in Georgia, at his death leaving a house, land, and other property. At the age of twelve, his younger son, Levi, borrowed money from his father to go into the business of dressing deerskins. At the age of eighteen, with the money he had accumulated, Levi went into the butcher business with a Christian partner. He and his brother Mordechai were constantly engaged in a variety of mercantile activities. In one transaction, they traded tobacco, indigo, and deerskins for about 2,000 pounds of goods from England. At various times Mordechai operated a warehouse, a wharf, sawmills, and a tannery. Levi once owned a schooner, *Beggar's Benison,* which carried goods up and down the coast. The brothers were also engaged in land transactions. Once they took a second mortgage on one of the Georgia sea islands owned by Button Gwinnett, later a signer of the Declaration of Independence.

There were Jewish artisans as well. Isaac Moses, a skilled gold and silver refiner, was shipped to Georgia from Hanover in 1758 and sold as an indentured servant for three years in payment of his passage. Mordechai Sheftall redeemed him within a year, and he was able to practice his trade.

But for the most part, the hundreds of Jewish families in the colonies in the first decades of the eighteenth century were, like the Sheftalls, engaged in the mercantile activities so important to the colonial economy. Between 1730 and 1770, exports and imports in both Pennsylvania and New York increased about fourfold. Jews were mainly gathered around some of the leading port cities: New York, Newport, Philadelphia, Charleston, and Savannah.

By and large, Jews did not arrive in America with greater economic resources than any other immigrant group, but they did come with a different historical experience that shaped certain distinctive characteristics and values. Some of these make up that elusive quality known as "achievement drive," which Jews have exhibited in abundance in comparison with other ethnoreligious groups in the United States.

The sources of this so-called Jewish achievement drive have been attributed to: (1) a religiously inspired emphasis on education, which, secularized, has been linked to disproportionate intellectual preoccupations since the early Middle Ages; (2) a history as urbanites par excellence, which has given Jews an advantage in the centers of business, professional, and intellectual life; (3) a greater socialization in middle-class norms and habits, and a greater capacity to defer gratification; and (4) long-term experience with marginality, which has taught them how to form new social relations in different class environments.

The new American society, lacking an aristocracy, showed more respect than did the Old World for the trading occupations that ambitious Jews had followed in Europe. For their part, early Americans recognized that commercial skills and energies necessary to drive the economy were in short supply. Benjamin Franklin endorsed the emphasis on achievement through trade when he said that he did not want his son William "to be what is commonly called a gentleman. I want to put him to some business by which he may, with care and industry, get a temperate and reasonable living."[3]

The American playwright Joseph Addison wrote in 1712 that the Jews were "the pegs and nails in a great building, which, though they are but little value in themselves, are absolutely necessary to keep the whole frame together."[4] George Mason said the Jews "were not only noted for their knowledge of mercantile and commercial affairs, but also for their industry, enterprise and probity."[5] The needs and talents of the European Jews and the requirements of a burgeoning America were a perfect fit. They continued to mesh, in different and sometimes more difficult patterns, as America developed and changed.

Jews have done uncommonly well in America because Jewish characteristics and values, including their achievement drive, have been especially congruent with the larger culture. These traits strongly resemble the modal national pattern set by the New England Protestant sectarians. Writing in the 1920s, the sociologist Robert Park suggested that Jewish history and culture be taught in the schools so that other Americans can learn what America is. Park argued that the Jews were quintessentially American.[6]

Supporting such assumptions is Max Weber's analysis of the relationship between the Protestant ethic and the spirit of capitalism in America. In his classic work on the subject, Weber, in explaining the economic success of the United States, emphasized that the Puritans— being Old Testament Christians—brought with them the religiously derived values conducive to capitalism: rationality, hard work, savings, and a strong achievement drive. "The spirit of capitalism," he wrote, "was present [in America] before the capitalistic order."[7] Weber noted that "Puritanism always felt its inner similarity to Judaism . . . The Jews who were actually welcomed by Puritan nations, especially the Americans . . . were at first welcomed without any ado whatsoever and are even now welcomed fairly readily."[8]

Weber's principal examples of a secularized capitalist spirit were drawn from the writings of Benjamin Franklin.[9] He quoted extensively from Franklin's works as prototypical of the values that are functional for the emergence of an industrialized free market system. And, indeed, Franklin's American values found an enthusiastic audience in Eastern Europe among Jews, to whom those values also resonated as consistent with their religious beliefs and secular culture. Franklin's writings were translated into Yiddish around 1800, were read devoutly, and were discussed in Talmudic discourse fashion by young Jews in Poland and Russia after they had completed their daily religious studies in yeshivas.[10]

In Frontier America

The first large-scale migration of Jews to America began in the 1830s as conditions worsened in Germany. Governments in that country continued to curtail Jewish rights; anti-Jewish riots recurred in the streets of many cities; and opportunities for Jews were limited. In some cases, the Jews Toll had been imposed, taxing Jews on entering and leaving certain cities and obstructing economic activities. In reaction to such conditions, a group of German Jews wrote to Mordechai Noah, a major Jewish political leader, that "the better part of the European Jews are looking with the eager countenance of hope to the United States of North America, happy once again to exchange the miseries of their native soil for public freedom."[11]

Between 1820 and 1860 the American Jewish population had increased ninefold, to about 150,000. Most came with little capital; peddling and trade on the frontier were ways to accumulate it. Their colonial predecessors had settled largely in the few cities of the new land, but the early German Jews tended to scatter over the frontier.

Much of America was literally frontier country—on the edge of expansion, in the process of development, little controlled by state or institution, urgently needing channels of trade. The expanding American frontier had always offered economic opportunity. The records of the Richmond, Virginia, firm of Cohen and Isaac contain a receipt from Daniel Boone for 6 pounds in return for the sale of 10,000 acres of newly surveyed Kentucky land, "Resit fun Kornel Bon far 10,000 agir lant" [Receipt from Colonel Boone for 10,000 acres of land].[12] But it was the commercial peddlers out on the advancing frontier who provided a lifeline of trade for the far-flung settlers.

The Jews did not create frontier peddling, an old Yankee pursuit. John Jacob Astor, a decidedly non-Jewish immigrant, was selling doughnuts, tea, and novelties to the Indians in the 1780s, on his way to amassing a fortune. But peddling became predominantly a Jewish occupation as the immigration of business-minded German Jews began to swell. In Easton, Pennsylvania, for example, more than 60 percent of the gainfully employed Jews were peddlers in 1855.[13]

Both Benjamin Bloomingdale and Adam Gimbel emigrated from Germany in the early part of the nineteenth century. Bloomingdale started his career by peddling a variety of goods around Kansas and across the Great Plains. Gimbel began by peddling up and down the Mississippi River, with an oilcloth pack and a rifle, and then opening a dry goods store on the banks of the Wabash River in Indiana. They both ended up with department store empires, and their names became synonymous with merchant success.

Most Jewish peddlers did not become Gimbels and Bloomingdales. Frontier trade was hard and dangerous. Louis Nathan, Henry Levy, and Isaac Goldstein were reportedly scalped by Indians. Sigmans Schlesinger reported a contrary outcome, writing in his diary that after he and a party had fought off 700 Sioux and Cheyenne Indians, he had "scalpt 3 Indians."[14] Adolph Kohn was captured by the Apaches and then traded by them to the Comanches, with whom he rode on war parties for about two years.

But even short of such extreme encounters, the life of the itinerant trader was always hard and often fruitless. Rabbi Isaac Meyer Wise reported the definitive account of a peddler's life by one Stein in the latter part of the nineteenth century:

Our people in this country may be divided into the following classes: (1) the basket peddler, he is as yet altogether dumb and hopeless; (2) the trunk-carrier, who stammers some little English and hopes for better times; (3) the pack-carrier, who carries from 100–150 pounds upon his back, and indulges the thought that he will become a businessman someday. In addition to these, there is an aristocracy which may be divided into three classes: (1) the wagon-baron, who peddles through the country with a one- or two-horse team; (2) the jewelry-count, who carries a stock of watches and jewelry in a small trunk, and is considered a rich man even now; (3) the store-prince, who has a shop and sells goods in it.[15]

Of the 20,000 itinerant traders in America on the eve of the Civil War, the majority were German Jews. Few accumulated great wealth, but many of them became "store princes" in one degree or another. It became part of the folklore that when asked why they stopped in some particular locale to set up a store, former wanderers would say, "That's where the horse died."

The economy changed, manufacturing soared, and as frontiers stabilized so did the economic status of Jews. In Albany, New York, for example, more than half of the peddlers licensed annually between 1842 and 1850 were Jewish. By 1870 the percentage was down to less than 10 percent, as itinerant Jewish tradesmen and their offspring became stable merchants and, occasionally, professionals.[16]

Jews were not as successful at penetrating the large new industrial establishments. In the 1870s the one hundred top leaders in textiles, railroads, and steel were all Protestant.[17] Some Jews did graduate into mining and finance, however. Joseph Seligman (who was to be the first wealthy Jew to be notably denied access to a posh resort) started with dry goods and clothing shops in Pennsylvania and Alabama in the 1830s and eventually established one of America's leading banking houses, with branches in Europe.

The brothers Joseph and Emanuel Rosenwald also became wealthy bankers as well as merchants. As they made their way up the economic ladder, they had this kind of adventure on one of many standard businessmen's caravan trips from the East to California:

We bought 2 ox wagons fully equipped and one mule wagon, sufficient groceries in Texas and started down to the Arkansas river, where Fort Wise [Colorado] was building at the time. Joe drove one wagon and I drove the second ... We took the remainder of our stock from here to Pike's Peak. On our way up we were followed by a band of Indians ... We however escaped them. We traded our entire remaining stock for potatoes, took them to Denver, peddled them out and after finishing our sale sold our oxen wagons and started in our mule wagon for Wyandotte, Kansas.[18]

Henry Lehman, an Alabama peddler, eventually created one of the great investment houses in the nation. The Guggenheim brothers prospered in mining in Colorado. In California, Anthony Zellerbach and his brothers established a pulp and paper empire, and two decades after he arrived, Isaac Friedlander was exporting three quarters of the state's wheat crop.

Taking stock of its commercial resources in 1864, the Salt Lake City *Telegraph* noted only Jewish names. "The Ransahoffs are expecting a rich and heavy stock. Siegel & Co., a new house, has got an early advance and are opening up to wholesale trade. When Bodenberg and Kahn ... come in with their huge piles, we will most assuredly have enough [goods] to last a while."[19] Across the country, from banker to store prince, in large cities and small, Jewish immigrants, mostly but not all German, built in this half-century an unprecedented record of commercial accomplishment and a widely dispersed influence network.

Politicians noticed. In 1885 the mayor of Albany, helping to lay the cornerstone for a new synagogue, said, "Tax records show that your people bear a very large proportion of the public burdens. I estimate the taxable property of the city of Albany at $670 for each inhabitant, while I find that the taxable property belonging to your people amounts to $1323 for every man, woman and child of the Israelitish community."[20]

American public officials and newspapers continually made reference to the productive mesh between the middle-class qualities of the country and of the Jews, as in this 1872 editorial in the Philadelphia *Evening Telegraph*, the most widely circulated newspaper in the country:

Wherever there is a chance for enterprise and energy, the Jew is to be found. Go to whatever land and into whatever city you may, and he will be met with. In this country he has made strong footing. The peculiar advantages it offers to his characteristic abilities render America his favorite home. And Americans should be glad that such is the case, for the Jew as a citizen is to be highly esteemed. He brings into every community wealth and qualities which materially assist to strengthen and consolidate its polity . . . He takes care of himself and his own . . . He is sober and industrious.[21]

Anti-Semitism did exist and sometimes was a hazard to Jewish achievement. In the 1850s some insurance companies warned against insuring itinerant peddlers or Jews, at that time almost synonymous terms. Right after the Civil War, the decision by some insurance companies to refuse to sell policies to Jews set off protest meetings and a boycott movement in the Jewish community. Dun & Company tended to assign poor credit ratings to Jews unless the investigator noted that the businessman in question was "a white Jew," or "an Israelite of the better classes." In the general community, there was open opposition to such bigoted behavior. A Philadelphia newspaper editorialized in 1867 that such discriminatory practices were groundless, divisive, and "contrary to the interests of the country," and condemned "in the strongest terms the insulting action of a portion of the New York insurance companies."[22]

These biased practices eroded in the marketplace of that period, where individual achievement, not ethnicity, was the prevailing measure of men. Isidor Strauss, whose father's peddling career in Georgia ended with the establishment of Macy's, wrote that one paid creditor saw in his father "a demonstration of the keen sense of integrity which . . . was the reverse of what his . . . prejudice had led him to expect."[23]

In Industrial America

The scenario changed with the influx of Eastern European Jews, the closing of the frontier, and the advent of industrialization. When Jacob H. Schiff emigrated to America from Germany in 1865, the son of a

Rothschilds' broker, he joined a prosperous German-Jewish brokerage firm in New York. When Morris Hillkowitz came from Eastern Europe two decades later, in 1887, he worked as a cuffmaker in New York's garment sweatshops. Hillkowitz was one of over a million and a half East European Jews—about a third of the Jewish population in that region—who arrived in America between 1881 and 1910.

Despite the contrast in their backgrounds, the lives of Hillkowitz and Schiff would eventually cross paths in the "Great Revolt" of 1910, a historic labor-management confrontation primarily between Jewish workers and a garment industry whose leadership was dominated by Jews. But neither their roles in trade unions nor their life courses in America were as confrontational as their economic circumstances might have suggested. Morris Hillkowitz had by 1910 become Morris Hillquit, an attorney, one of the founders of the American Socialist Party and a vocal opponent of the capitalist system. And Jacob Schiff had become one of the country's most eminent capitalists, a millionaire banker who handled a billion dollars in the financing of the Pennsylvania Railroad.

The East European Jews came with no more money in their pockets than other immigrants, but with a different background than most. Partly because of their exclusion from European agricultural life, about seven out of ten Jews had been associated with a commercial or industrial occupation prior to migrating, as compared with about one out of ten non-Jewish immigrants.[24] In the old country, some of the Jews had been storekeepers, peddlers, middleman merchants in grain and other products, and small factory owners—but they were typically on the fringe of the society and of business activities. When Eastern Europe's agricultural economy declined rapidly in the latter part of the century, so did the position of the Jews.

In Vilna, a cultural flagship for East European Jews, a newspaper reported that Jews "live in miserable hovels, dirty and badly ventilated . . . In the same dwelling may be found four, five or even six families, each of them having a number of children of tender age . . . Meat is an unknown luxury, even on the Sabbath. Today water and bread, tomorrow bread and water, and so on day after day."[25] The vast emigration of Jews can be traced to that growing poverty, and to the accompanying anti-Semitic backlash.

But despite their extreme impoverishment, most East European Jews came to America with craft backgrounds. At the turn of the twentieth century, two out of three male Jewish immigrants had working skills in one of several dozen different trades, although they were most heavily concentrated in the garment trade.[26] Many such skilled craftsmen had simultaneously been small businessmen in Europe: independent artisans, butchers, bakers, and tailors. But by the time they immigrated to America, the industrial economy here had no place for that combination of skill and entrepreneurship. Some of these craftsmen turned to peddling, but most of them had to find work in factories.

In the 1880s more than half of American Jewish businessmen were engaged in some aspect of the clothing business. Over 95 percent of the clothing manufacturers in New York were Jewish.[27] The ready-to-wear garment industry was new. The sewing machine, invented shortly before the Civil War, created an unprecedented demand for manufactured clothing. It was the kind of marginal industry to which Jewish businessmen flocked. As measured by capital investment, the garment industry, initially dominated by German Jews, more than tripled between 1880 and 1900.[28]

Because of the demand for the kinds of labor skills that the Jews tended to possess, East European Jews turned to the garment industry for work. At one point, over half of the employed residents of New York's Jewish ghetto were garment workers. By 1897 about 60 percent of the New York labor force was employed in making clothes, and about 75 percent of those workers were Jewish.[29] In most cases, life was hard. In 1900 the average wage for male garment workers was about $12.00 a week, for females about half that, and for children about half that again. For those wages—scarcely enough to pay for the bare essentials—the garment makers typically worked ten hours a day, six days a week, in miserable working conditions. Living conditions were no better. In the lower East Side, the density rate by 1910 was 730 persons per acre, exceeded only by Bombay, India.[30]

Immigrant dissatisfaction with their economic life in America was no less than it should have been. As one mother in a novel by Michael Gold, a radical chronicler of the ghetto, said, "It is a good land but not for the poor. When the Messiah comes to America, he had better come in a fine automobile with a dozen servants. If he comes here on a white horse, people will think he is just another poor immigrant. They may set him to work washing dishes in a restaurant."[31]

However, for younger people especially, the ghetto on the lower East Side was qualitatively different from the Vilna ghetto. Here, there seemed to be the possibility of getting out. One observer at the turn of the century noted, "I have met very few wage-workers among Russian Jewish people who regard it as their permanent lot in life to remain in the condition of laborers for wage. Almost all are bending their energies to get into business or to acquire an education so that they may fit themselves for some other calling than that of the wage worker of the ordinary kind. More of our boys and girls who have attended the public schools enter stores and offices than shops and factories."[32]

Meanwhile, the older German Jewish immigrants had, as a whole, done spectacularly well, even those who had come with less economic panache than the financier Jacob Schiff. By the time the East European Jews came en masse, the German Jewish peddlers had virtually disappeared. Between 1860 and 1900 the number of Jewish firms worthy of commercial ratings rose from 374 to over 2,000.[33] At the end of that period, it was reported that Jewish millionaires, such as Schiff, constituted about two and a half times their proportion of the population, extending "from banking to pork-packing, from realty to dry goods, from distilleries to cotton."[34]

The German Jewish population's relatively unimpeded movement to middle-class status, though never easy, was simpler for them than it would be for the East European Jews. For one thing, the East Europeans arrived in larger numbers and clung to the cities. When the mass of East European immigrants was settling down, the American frontier was closing. There was still plenty of room for business, but business required more and more capital. The age of the independent artisan/entrepreneur was ending, and the corporate world was in sight. It had been simpler to move from peddler to storeowner to financier than from industrial worker to factory owner, even though a number of East European Jews did just that, especially in the garment industry.

The most direct route to independent middle-class status for Jews at the turn of the century was by way of becoming "a professional man." It was also a way to avoid hiring bias. Education was the key to professional status, as well as to other white-collar jobs, and Jews were particularly well suited to rigorous study. The special educational drive of the young Jewish immigrant was noted by other Americans. The New York *Evening Post,* on October 3, 1903, wrote that at the public library "lines of children reaching down two flights may not infrequently be seen at the Chatham Square branch . . . The Jewish child has more eagerness for mental food, it is an intellectual mania . . . No people read so large a proportion of solid reading."

The intellectual mania of the young Jewish immigrants has often been laid to the fact that they were "the people of the book." The reference, of course, is to the study of the Bible and rabbinic commentary which traditionally occupied so many Jews. The customary pattern of individual reading and subsequent discussion maintained a high level of literacy, even though their intellectual pursuits were often severely limited to religious texts. During the period of the Enlightenment, this literacy and propensity for discussion were often easily transferred to secular subjects. Though the religious factor cannot be altogether ignored, it must be linked to Jews' understanding that education was a way out of the working class. In 1908 a study of 77 institutions of higher education found that more than 8 percent of the students were Jewish, although Jews comprised less than 2 percent of the population. Most of those Jewish students were preparing to become pharmacists, lawyers, dentists, and teachers.[35] In the 1890s a Russian journalist, investigating the fate of Russian Jews in America, found only a few dozen Russian Jews in medicine and law and hardly any in the teaching profession. By the first decade of the 1900s there were 400 to 600 Russian Jewish physicians in New York, along with several thousand in teaching, and many in other professions.[36] By 1930 in New York City, where Jews were one fourth of the population, they comprised 55 percent of that city's physicians, 64 percent of its dentists, and 65 percent of its lawyers—all by way of professional education.[37]

As one Italian American wrote with some sorrow about the typical Italian immigrant who came here with a different background: "He has not yet learned the lesson which the American Jew could teach him so well; that in America the child of uneducated parents has not only the right but the duty to rise to the highest rungs of the educational ladder, and thus achieve the success which his uneducated father failed to achieve."[38]

It was among those in the labor movement that the achievement drive was most dramatically exhibited. At the end of 1909, 20,000 garment workers, mostly Jewish women, went on strike, ushering in what came to be known as the Great Revolt. The period that followed was marked by much strife and violence throughout the industry. In September 1910 a "protocol of peace" was signed between labor and management, which, while not ending labor unrest, achieved a historic new plateau for organized labor. That protocol of peace brought in the union shop, accepted shop chairmen as the voice of the union in each establishment, and set up grievance committees, a board of sanitary control, and a board of arbitration on which the public was to be the third party. The labor movement was never again to be the same; it had become a legitimate force.

This historic agreement was engineered by Louis Brandeis, then a Boston lawyer, supported by Jacob Schiff. They were brought in partly because the "uptown" Jews were disturbed by the image of public strife between Jewish workers and Jewish factory owners. But Schiff and Brandeis were also moderates by philosophy and temperament, and they had a middle-class distaste for class struggle. Schiff had long supported the concept of peaceful collective bargaining.

Many Jews in the labor movement mirrored this concern for moderation, in spite of the fact that the East European environment had bred a legendary farrago of Jewish radicals—socialists and anarchists of various stripes. These immigrants seemed to dominate intellectual life on the lower East Side and were active in labor organizations and radical movements. Eventually, however, many of them began to take a reformist tack. Morris Hillquit, a party on the union side to the "protocol of peace," had himself made the ascent, by way of night school, from penniless garment worker to prosperous attorney, from the lower East Side to fashionable Riverside Drive. William Haywood, the Industrial Workers of the World (IWW) leader, attacked the middle-class tendencies of many New York socialists, saying that they "feel immensely flattered when they are invited, as Morris Hillquit was recently, to perform at pink teas at Fifth Avenue mansions."[39]

Hillquit eventually abandoned the concept of a convulsive class struggle and became an evolutionary socialist, a gradualist. Whether or not this personal change was partly a result of his own success, as his more radical enemies charged, it probably had at least as much to do with the "achieving" temper of the Jewish workers with whom he came in contact. Hillquit once complained that while the Jewish workers came together in a crisis, they were normally difficult to organize. They were more interested in making money at piecework than in achieving a reduction in hours and higher fixed wage rates. An immigrant guidebook noted that "impoverished Jews earned 50 cents a day, spent 10 cents for coffee and bagels, saved 40 cents."[40] Jacob Riis remarked in 1893 that "over and over again, I am met with instances of these Polish or Russian Jews deliberately starving themselves to the point of physical exhaustion while working night and day at tremendous pressure to save a little money."[41]

They wanted to save money in order to get their families out of the sweatshops and into more middle-class occupations. At times, the Jewish workers organized and fought hard against oppression in the shop, but they did not constitute a revolutionary labor force. Despite their dramatic labor struggles, they did not even constitute a steadfast base for labor unions. Owing to the strong motivation among Jews to achieve, the Jewish labor movement was largely a one-generation phenomenon. As the historian Henry L. Feingold noted, "The Jewish worker was neither the son of a worker nor would he produce a son who was a worker. Middle-class aspirations required that he earn more."[42]

But, as in earlier days, higher earnings was only one of the Jews' middle-class aspirations. In the American environment, "middle class" denoted social status as well as earnings, and both could, in theory, be achieved through hard work.[43] The "right to civility from the greatest," as the *Pennsylvania Journal* had written in 1756, was a middle-class right.

All white-collar jobs are usually considered middle-class, even though some portion of them do not pay more than many manual jobs.[44] Because of such status implications, the disproportionate growth of white-collar and professional jobs in the economy inherently produced upward social movement. Between 1870 and 1940, while the population increased by little more than three times, the number of technical, managerial, and professional employees multiplied thirteen-fold.[45] In addition, the percentage of clerical workers in the workforce increased by more than 300 percent between 1900 and 1940, compared with a population growth of 75 percent, while the percentage of manual workers remained virtually the same.[46]

Many workers—Jewish and others—were radicalized by the deep depression of the 1930s and the heightened level of labor–management confrontations. Still, young Jews were able to achieve a disproportionate niche in the middle-class sectors of the economy. In New York in 1935 they comprised three out of ten youths in the general population; but roughly six out of ten young proprietors, managers, or officials were Jewish, and about four out of ten in professions or clerical and sales work had the same ethnoreligious background.[47]

After World War II

The great expansion in the higher education and professional sectors of the economy after World War II provided enormous opportunities in law, medicine, scientific research, academics, real estate, government, and eventually the corporate world. Certain kinds of traditionally Jewish entrepreneurship, such as department-store ownership, became less important as discriminatory barriers against Jews fell and they moved into these other occupations. Before World War II, Jewish comedians could have raised loud laughter by suggesting that one

"Irving Shapiro" would become the head of Du Pont de Nemours, a company whose aristocratic name and mainstream economic power seemed inaccessible to the children of immigrant Jews. But that is exactly what happened in 1973, when the son of an immigrant pants-presser, who was publicly forthright in proclaiming his Jewish identity, was made head of that company. Shapiro was later elected chairman of the Business Roundtable, the most prestigious collection of corporate heads in the country.

Nor was Irving Shapiro's ascendancy a singular event. Studies of national origin and religious groups, using census and sample survey data, find that Jews achieve higher levels of education, professional status, and income than all other subgroups. A national survey of American Jews and non-Jews completed for the American Jewish Committee in April 1988 by Steven M. Cohen concluded that per capita Jewish income is almost double that of non-Jews. More than twice as many Jews as non-Jewish whites report household incomes in excess of $50,000, whereas almost twice as many non-Jews as Jews indicate incomes of less than $20,000.[48]

A 1982 analysis of the four hundred richest Americans, as reported by *Forbes* magazine, finds that sixteen of the wealthiest forty are Jews (40 percent), as are 23 percent of the total list.[49] They have moved into high positions in banking and the corporate world. In 1986 Jews, who make up less than 3 percent of the nation's population, accounted for 7.4 percent of senior executives in the nation's largest businesses and 13 percent of executives under the age of forty.[50] Data gathered for an American Leadership Study in ten major sectors in 1971–72 indicated that Jews make up over 11 percent of the overall sample, whereas they constitute only 3 percent of the national population. No other group did as well.[51]

An analysis of those listed in *Who's Who in America* as of the mid-seventies found that over 8 percent were Jewish, up from 2 percent in 1944–45. From the early 1920s on, Jews have been over-represented in *Who's Who*, as compared with all other ethnic groups except the English. By the mid-1970s they were far ahead of those of English descent as well. During the last three decades Jews have made up 50 percent of the top two hundred intellectuals, 40 percent of American Nobel

Prize winners in science and economics, 20 percent of professors at the leading universities, 21 percent of high level civil servants, 40 percent of partners in the leading law firms in New York and Washington, 26 percent of the reporters, editors, and executives of the major print and broadcast media, 59 percent of the directors, writers, and producers of the fifty top-grossing motion pictures from 1965 to 1982, and 58 percent of directors, writers, and producers in two or more primetime television series.[52]

Those figures paint a dramatic picture of the position of the Jews in the American melting pot, not just in terms of wealth but even more profoundly as judged by acceptance and integration in the economic mainstream. The disproportion is less startling when the successful Jews in question are compared with others having the same educational attainment (about twice the proportion of Jews as non-Jews are enrolled in higher education). But the cold figures do attest to the lack of obstruction in the economic and educational marketplaces which mark the new integration of Jews.

The elite universities are the golden gateways to economic achievement. Less than half a century ago, Jews were severely limited by quotas from entering these prestigious institutions as students or faculty. At the beginning of the 1990s, 87 percent of college-age Jews were enrolled in higher education, as compared with 40 percent for the population at large. And, like the Jewish faculty, they are heavily located in the schools with higher academic standards. An American Council on Education survey of college freshmen found that those of Jewish parentage had significantly higher secondary school grades than their non-Jewish counterparts, in spite of the fact that a much larger proportion of all Jews than of others go on to college. Moreover, Jews seemingly perform better as undergraduates; by a considerable margin, they are disproportionately elected to Phi Beta Kappa.[53]

In sum, the scions of the German Jews who immigrated in the nineteenth century and the East European Jews who came later have been able to become the best educated, the most middle-class, and, ultimately, the most affluent ethnoreligious group in the country. No other immigrant group has evinced such rapid and dramatic success.[54]

All of these data reveal a level of economic success that even

Abraham Cahan's ecstatic Catskills revelers could not have dreamed of at the turn of the twentieth century. Jews are often wary of drawing attention to their financial status, which has sometimes served as a provocation for anti-Semites. In America, however, the economic achievement of Jews paralleled their deep integration into the society.[55] But what explains this beneficial meshing? In order to answer this question, we must turn to aspects of the larger American religious experience, in particular the heterogeneity and openness that has characterized the society throughout its history.

∽ 2 ∽

The Promise of Double Freedom

An excited fifteen-year-old Jewish boy named Naphtali Phillips marched in the greatest parade this country had seen to date, on July 4, 1788, in Philadelphia. It was held to celebrate the ratification of the Constitution by the requisite number of states. A crowd of thousands cheered a procession of floats dramatizing such themes as "Independence," "Union," and "Federal Roof." Blacksmiths walked behind a large bellows representing the passion to keep alive the flame of liberty. Other occupational sections included clergymen and rabbis, arm in arm, as well as shoemakers, hairdressers, and school children.

Phillips, one of those school children, later described the intoxicating event in a letter, making special mention of the food served the marchers at the end of the parade: "There was a number of long tables loaded with all kinds of provisions, with a separate table for the Jews who [for religious reasons] could not partake of the meat from the other tables; but they had a full supply of soused [pickled] salmon, bread and crackers, almonds, raisins etc. This table was under the charge of an old cobbler named Isaac Moses."[1]

The flaunting of a kosher table at this patriotic extravaganza suggested America's exceptional promise of "double freedom," of both religious belief and group cultural difference. It further implied a unique acceptance of religious Judaism itself.

The favorable position of Judaism in early America was a function of the special character of American Christianity. The sectarianism of the religious sphere is an important dimension of American exceptionalism, contributing, as we shall see, to a genuine religious pluralism that allowed Jews to meet with the kinds of successes detailed in Chapter 1.

Religion in an Open Society

The European and Latin American nations have historically been dominated by *churches*—Anglican, Catholic, Lutheran, Orthodox. The overwhelming majority of Americans were and are adherents of Protestant *sects:* Baptists, Methodists, and hundreds of other smaller denominations. Churches have been state-established and hierarchical. Sects have never been state-related; they have always been voluntary institutions, and most of them have been congregational rather than hierarchical.

As Edmund Burke, Tocqueville, and latter-day students of American religion and society have emphasized, Protestant sectarianism, which stresses the personal relationship of individuals with God unmediated by church or hierarchy, has contributed to the strength of American individualism. Burke noted that American Protestantism is "of that kind most averse to all implicit submission of mind and opinion . . . It is the dissidence of dissent, and the Protestantism of the Protestant religion."[2] Tocqueville saw in the voluntary character of religion in America both the secret of the country's greater religiosity and the stability of its democratic order.

And as the twentieth century comes to an end, survey data support Tocqueville's impressions. Today, more people in America believe in God, attend church, and accept Biblical statements about the existence of Heaven and Hell than in any other country in the Christian world, except for a few like Ireland and Poland where religion and the struggle against national oppression have been interlinked. But no one in the United States is expected to adhere to any dominant religious creed. Voluntary denominations encourage allegiance and participation and are conducive to the formation of a host of mediating organizations positioned between the citizenry and the state. They inhibit the tendency of the state to monopolize power, a propensity which, according to 1992 opinion polls, most Americans still feel is inherent in governmental institutions.

The competition among the numerous Christian denominations enabled the Jews to fit in from the start of the republic as one religious entity out of many, rather than as the only or principal deviant group. That early America resounded with Old Testament references is often seen as testimony to the compatibility of Puritan Protestantism with Judaism, beyond the achievement drive common to both. In fact, most Protestants tended to view Roman Catholics more harshly, more negatively, than they did Jews. Catholicism was seen by many sectarians not as a different set of religious beliefs but as an alien conspiracy seeking to undermine the American Protestant way of life, and therefore outside the pale.

A certain indifference to sectarian religion prevailed among the Revolutionary forefathers themselves. Thomas Jefferson and John Adams both said they expected that Jews, along with most Christians, as reasonable men, would eventually become nondenominational Unitarians. Nevertheless, American Jews adapted their religious practices to the dominant Protestant pattern. They developed a congregational style, eschewing the organized communal or hierarchical structures that have characterized Jewry in many European countries.[3]

European Jews were governed by *kehillahs,* communal organizations that included the entire population, or by grand or chief rabbis, whose status has resembled that of bishops or archbishops. Canadian Jewry, living in a country that places greater emphasis on the solidarity of ethnic and religious communities than does the United States, is organized into one group, the Canadian Jewish Congress, which resembles a European *kehillah.* American Jewry has no chief rabbis or disciplined communal bodies. An effort to form a *kehillah* in New York before World War I failed.[4] Judah Magnes, who played a major role in creating it in 1909, was to note a decade later that the "European notion of a uniform . . . all-controlling . . . *kehillah* cannot strike root in American soil . . . because it is not in consonance with the free and voluntary character of American religious, social, educational, and philanthropic enterprises."[5]

On the European continent, the rise of ethnic nationalism typically led to an intolerance of cultural separateness. This occurred even in those countries such as France where the new spirit of individual freedom and an anticlerical opposition to religious tyranny made citizens relatively open to individual religious differences. Clermont de Tonnere said so clearly in the French Assembly, as he rose to champion the cause of Jewish emancipation after the French Revolution: "To the Jews as individuals, everything; to the Jews as a nation, nothing." Similarly, Edward Von Hartmann championed religious freedom for individual Jews in Germany, at the same time that he deplored "Jewish tribal solidarity."

The question was not so much whether the Jews were good Christians, but whether they were good Frenchmen or Germans. Napoleon brought a conclave of Jewish notables together to ask them to settle that question. With an obfuscation honed through the ages, they assured Napoleon that their group loyalty was purely French. Napoleon's resentment over the seeming desire of French Jews to remain socially distinct from others was an emotion foreign to American society.

The nativist thrust of some of the modern European countries, and their imperative for cultural homogeneity, became a new and fateful source of antipathy for Jews, finally outweighing traditional religious bigotry. The nativist edge which gave force to the modern anti-Semitism of Europe—from the Dreyfus case to Hitler—was mitigated in America, owing to the country's religiously pluralist origins.

Religious Pluralism in the Early Republic

In his message to the Jews of Newport in 1790, Washington stated that in the new republic "all possess alike liberty of conscience and immunities of citizenship." Even more significantly, at a time when Jews lacked citizenship rights everywhere else, Washington emphasized that the patronizing concept of "toleration . . . of one class of people

... [by] another" has no place in America, that Jews are as much Americans as anyone else. Astonishingly, given what was happening in Europe, Washington recognized that "tolerance" denotes second-class citizenship.[6]

The next three presidents—Adams, Jefferson, and Madison—also noted that America was different from Europe, and that the discrimination against Judaism prevailing there did not exist here, where, in Jefferson's words, all are "on an equal footing." He approved of the presence of Jews in America because they would contribute to the social heterogeneity which he believed was the best defense of liberty.[7]

Public congratulations and self-congratulations flew back and forth between the Jews and the founders of the new nation. Only a few days after the inauguration of George Washington in 1789, Benjamin Sheftall's son Levi, then head of the Savannah congregation, sent a letter of congratulations to the president. A similar letter from Jacob Cohen, head of the congregation in Charleston, said that the Revolutionary events and proclamations had "raised us from the state of political degradation and grievous oppression to which partial, narrow, and illiberal policy and intolerant bigotry has reduced us in almost every other part of the world."[8]

Washington responded to Levi Sheftall that a new "spirit of liberality" was abroad, and hoped "that your brethren will benefit thereby in proportion as it shall become still more extensive."[9] Later, on acknowledging the receipt of a sermon at the consecration of the synagogue in Savannah in 1820, Thomas Jefferson wrote that he was excited by "the gratifying reflection that [my] country has been the first to prove to the world two truths, the most salutary to human society, that man can govern himself and that religious freedom is the most effectual anodyne against religious dissension."[10] James Madison acknowledged the receipt of the same sermon at Savannah with the comment that "among the features peculiar to the political system of the United States is the perfect equality of rights which it secures to every religious sect."[11] It was a heady concept—that every American was to get equal privilege, not because of a benevolent toleration, nor even because of practical necessity, but because it was due them.

Equal religious status for Jews did not come easily or at once, despite the enthusiasms of George Washington and other founders. The Constitution applied to the national government only. Religious obstacles persisted well into the nineteenth century in some states. Many were originally set up in the European style, with a religious establishment, or at least a religious bias. At the time of the Constitutional Convention in 1787, most of the thirteen states still had laws that prevented Jews from holding office or otherwise participating in the political process if they did not take Christian, notably Protestant, religious oaths.

For example, the North Carolina State Constitution, adopted in 1776, proclaimed that there would be "no establishment of any one religious church or denomination," nor would any person "be compelled to attend any place of worship contrary to his own faith." But it also stated that no person who denied "the truth of the Protestant religion" could hold any public office. Similarly, the Massachusetts Constitution of 1780 affirmed the right of everyone to worship "in the manner and season most agreeable to the dictates of his own conscience," and then required a belief in "the Christian religion" as a qualification for officeholding. In 1818 Connecticut disestablished the Congregational Church—at which time Jefferson wrote to John Adams that "protestant popedom is no longer to disgrace the American history and character"—but until 1843, the state constitution still withheld public office from all but Christians.[12]

The Jews were not the main targets of these edicts, if only because there were so few Jews in America at the time of the Revolution. There is no record of such a law being addressed by name to the Jews, although the Christian tone of the laws was naturally disadvantageous to them. Jews were just automatically included in those colonial acts specifically directed at religious minorities, most pointedly at Catholics, who were popularly referred to as "Papists."

The practical result was that, while the colonial laws varied considerably, Jews typically were taxed to support an establishment church, forced to close their businesses on Sundays, often formally disqualified as voters, and uniformly barred as officeholders. On religious matters

American society was divided between the devout and the secularists, although some of the former, particularly the Baptists, were as dedicated to religious freedom as any Jew or agnostic.

Christianizing America in the Nineteenth Century

The nineteenth-century frontier period brought a new religious zeal which attempted to affect public policy. Revivals called "Great Awakenings" followed the frontier, stimulated by the growth of evangelical denominations. In 1843, having returned from a long visit to Europe, the Reverend Robert Baird reiterated Tocqueville's observation that "in no other part of the world, perhaps, do the inhabitants attend church in a larger proportion than in the United States."[13] Paul Schaff, a Swiss theologian visiting America, said a decade later, "There are in America probably more awakened souls, and more individual effort and self-sacrifice for religious purposes, proportionately, than in any other country, Scotland alone perhaps excepted."[14]

Much evangelical effort was directed toward making America an explicitly Christian country. The Reverend Ezra Stiles Ely expressed one clerical viewpoint in a July 4 sermon in 1827, saying that "we are a Christian nation: we have the right to demand that all our rulers in their conduct shall conform to Christian morality."[15] In 1829 Supreme Court Justice Joseph Storey attacked the religious indifference of the earlier Jeffersonian era and said that "one of the beautiful boasts of our municipal jurisprudence is that Christianity is a part of the Common Law."[16]

Laws enacted by states and cities to prohibit work and other activities on Sunday exemplified the municipal jurisprudence that Justice Storey hailed. These local laws were customarily supported by the state courts. The Nebraska Supreme Court ruled in 1892 against Sunday baseball, saying that "Christianity is woven into the web and woof of free government." The Supreme Court of Illinois had said in 1883 about Sunday laws that "when the great body of the people are Christians in fact or sentiment, our laws and institutions must necessarily be based upon and embody the teachings of the Redeemer of mankind."

However, three major kinds of constraints interfered with these local and state laws: marketplace imperatives, which took precedence over religious discrimination; the sheer diversity of American religious life; and the federal culture of religious freedom. In colonial America, the formal religious restrictions on the law books had often been treated with scofflaw indulgence under the practical lenity of an economically oriented society. For example, Mordechai Sheftall, one of Benjamin's sons, was appointed by the Georgia governor and legislature as port inspector, although the Georgia law stated that all those who were appointed to office must take a Christian oath, a requirement that Mordechai did not fulfill. Similar episodes occurred throughout the late colonial period. Although Rhode Island would not give voting rights to Jews who refused to take the oath "upon the true faith of a Christian," 10 of 78 Newport residents who, as citizens, signed a petition for fairer tax assessments in 1762 were Jews who had not taken such an oath.[17]

Jewish achievement itself contributed to the relaxation of political restrictions. A so-called Jew Bill to remove test-oath provisions from the Maryland Constitution was introduced in that state in 1819; and although initially defeated, it passed a few years later. Much opposition to the initial failure of the bill was expressed by the press. Although the sponsor of the bill, Thomas Kennedy, favored an amendment that would abolish *any* religious test, the legislature would only agree to a "specific" one that only extended voting rights to Jews. A Baltimore Jew, Solomon Etting, was asked by a legislator for information about the Jews in America. His written reply, which was used to gain backing for the bill, noted that there "were some 150 Jews in the state and some 6,000 in the United States, possessing, respectively, by rough estimate, half a million to six million dollars in wealth, thus making a vital economic contribution. Jews had served in both the American Revolution and the War of 1812, they currently occupied high federal positions as diplomats and military officers, and none could doubt their patriotic contribution."[18]

Religious tolerance flowed in part from the practical necessity of making the social enterprise work in the face of America's exceptional diversity. The Virginia legislature was presented in 1846 with a petition asking for aid to Christian sects. One William S. Plumer, a Presbyterian minister, successfully testified against this proposal, pointing out how divisive such legislation would be, since he calculated that there were about twenty different religious denominations in Virginia.[19]

This need to accommodate diversity occurred even where there was something less than respect for Jews or Judaism. William Lloyd Garrison often expressed his distaste for the Jews as a class and once said that they deserved their "miserable dispersion in various parts of the earth."[20] But Garrison supported religious freedom for the Jews as a leader in the 1848 anti-Sunday law convention, which stated that if a legislature could pass laws so binding Americans, it could also determine "a peculiar faith which they shall embrace and thus entirely subvert civil and religious freedom."

Often added to these practical considerations was intense anti-statism. Many of the denominational groups in America had suffered from the intolerance of established state churches in European countries, and they opposed any centralized authority, even in their own sects, for that reason. Moreover, the religious doctrines of most religious sects in the United States were congregational, not hierarchical, and emphasized an individual rather than a church-mediated relationship to God. Therefore, in 1828, when the Moral Reform Society of Painesville, Ohio, brought criminal charges against eight residents for the violation of state morality laws on temperance, over a hundred residents gathered the next day to proclaim "that in this land of independence and liberty, it is advisable that every man should be the guardian of his own conduct and not subject to the whims or peculiarities of any sect or denomination."[21] When the attempt was made, nevertheless, to prosecute the eight erring citizens, the majority of the townspeople proceeded to march upon the courthouse and beat up the county sheriff.

If heterogeneity was a consideration for individual states, it was much more so for national policymakers. In 1810, after Congress enacted a Sunday mails law—which provided that a certain number of post offices be kept open on Sunday, so that the mail could be delivered—churchmen, in reaction, formed a General Union for Promoting the Observance of the Christian Sabbath, whose main purpose was to close the post offices on Sunday. The congressional rejection of these lobbying efforts was epitomized in an 1836 Senate Committee report on the matter, endorsed by Congress and written by the senator and future vice-president Richard M. Johnson:

> The Constitution regards the conscience of the Jew as sacred as that of the Christian ... If a solemn act of legislation shall in *one* point define the God or point out to the citizen one religious duty, it may with equal propriety define *every* part of divine revelation and enforce *every* religious obligation, even to the forms and ceremonies of worship ... It is the duty of this government to affirm to *all*—to the Jew or Gentile, Pagan, or Christian—the protection and the advantages of our benignant institutions on *Sunday,* as well as every day of the week.[22]

In this statement, Johnson, who was also the head of the American Baptist Union, was not only enunciating the formal responsibility of the federal government, he was also reinforcing the legitimacy of constitutional principles in the general political culture.

Efforts to formally and more comprehensively Christianize America were consolidated on a national scale in 1861, when many moderate as well as fundamentalist Protestant groups joined to establish a National Reform Association, proposing that the following words be included in the Constitution: "Recognizing Almighty God as the source of all authority and power in civil government, and acknowledging the Lord Jesus Christ as the Governor among the nations, His revealed will as the supreme law of the land, in order to constitute a Christian government."[23] When a petition for such an amendment was presented to Congress in 1869, not one congressman spoke in its behalf.

In opposing religious discrimination, American Jews were quick to draw on the language of the founders, the First Amendment, the Declaration of Independence, and similar grand proclamations by various states, even if there were conflicting statutes on the books. Jews encouraged scofflaw attitudes toward restrictive statutes by quoting from the loftier documents and attitudes of the time, and were able to win a number of battles involving their rights. In 1845, when the city of Richmond increased penalties for Sunday violators, the Jews protested, saying that such penalties, applied to Jews, were "the beginning of a revolution backwards, to abridge the rights of individuals, which has been opened as wide as the gates of mercy, by the sages of the Revolution."[24] The Richmond ordinance was revoked, the Virginia legislature in 1849 excused Jews from being penalized on this account, and exemptions for them were gradually put into place around the country.

While the North Carolina Constitution requiring that all officeholders swear a Protestant oath was not altered until 1868, a Jew, Jacob Henry, had been elected to that state's House of Commons in 1808 without taking such an pledge. In 1809, when someone challenged his election on those grounds, Henry protested that the state's 1776 Declaration of Rights had consecrated "certain great and fundamental rights and principles which even the [state] Constitution cannot impair."[25] The House of Commons affirmed Henry's right to be elected, although the state constitution said otherwise for another half century.

In the 1850s, when Uriah P. Levy, a graduate of the first Naval Academy class at Annapolis, was dismissed from the Navy along with about two hundred other officers, presumably for inefficiency, he was convinced that he had been discharged because he was Jewish. He told a naval board of inquiry convened to hear his case: "My parents were Israelites, and I was nurtured in the faith of my ancestors. In deciding to adhere to it, I have but exercised a right, guaranteed to me by the constitution of my native State, and of the United States. [But after I had gained my lieutenancy] I was forced to encounter [from some fellow officers] a large share of the prejudice and hostility by which, for so many ages, the Jew has been pursued."[26] The board came to the same conclusion after listening to some testimony from the secretary of the Navy and others. Levy was restored to duty, and in 1860 was put in command of the Mediterranean fleet with the rank of Commodore.

Religious Equality in the Twentieth Century

It was only in 1942 that the U.S. Supreme Court clearly established the principle that state and municipal governments were constrained by the First Amendment. It ruled unconstitutional the expulsion of Jehovah's Witness children from schools all over West Virginia because they refused on religious grounds to salute the American flag. By the 1960s the U.S. Supreme Court ruled that Bible reading, recitation of prayers, and other sectarian religious practices in schools were unconstitutional in all states across the nation. Before that decision, about three dozen states still formally allowed or required religious exercises in the public schools, and school districts in a majority of the states still practiced Bible reading. After the Supreme Court ruling, the banned practices rapidly diminished in most local jurisdictions. Although over a hundred resolutions have been introduced in Congress calling for legislation or amendments that would overturn the Supreme Court's position, they all have failed.

Despite a lot of fine-tuning since then, no basic judicial or legislative retreat from the ban against government imposition of sectarian religion has occurred. Indeed, laws have generally been extended to specifically accommodate the religious needs of Jews. The civil rights legislation that has flowered since the 1960s places the burden on both public and private employers to adjust schedules so that Jewish employees can be absent on religious holidays. In one case, the Court ruled that Jewish applicants could not be disqualified for unemployment insurance merely because they did not look for work on a Jewish holiday. In another case, Congress passed a bill designed to permit Jewish soldiers to wear a yarmulke on duty, in exemption from the dress code of the armed services.

After the Supreme Court ruled that the use of drugs in a Native American religious ritual could be outlawed in the larger interests of society, Congress passed the Religious Freedom Restoration Act, which made it more difficult for government to encroach on the free exercise of religion by diverse groups. Then, in 1993, the Supreme Court ruled that it was unconstitutional to prohibit animal slaughter in connection with an ancient West African religious ritual practiced by thousands of Caribbean immigrants.

Among white Protestant Americans, at least 20 million adults today qualify as evangelical—not only having a fundamentalist belief in the literal word of their Bible but also having a commitment to convert others, certainly including Jews, to their form of Christianity. Activist evangelical groups created a stir in the 1980 electoral campaign. One of the country's most prominent evangelical ministers, Jerry Falwell, formed an organization called the Moral Majority to mobilize support in the public arena on behalf of "Christian values." The Reverend Falwell proclaimed that "what's happening to America is that the wicked are bearing rule." Another evangelical political group proclaimed in that same year, "We believe that America, the last stronghold of faith on this planet, has come under increasing attack from Satanist forces in recent years . . . that the standards of Christian morality . . . are now under the onslaught."[27]

This kind of religious-right political thrust was primarily directed toward certain social issues, particularly abortion and homosexuality, which were coming to a policymaking crisis in the public arena, but they were also redolent of the old attempts to designate Christianity as the official American religion. Lacking broad national support, Falwell's Moral Majority collapsed and went out of business. During the 1992 presidential campaign, the socially conservative Catholic journalist Pat Buchanan, who echoed evangelical sentiments in saying that there was a "religious war" in America, failed badly as a candidate for the Republican presidential nomination.

The mobilization of the religious right continues to have some effect in certain local and regional political arenas. That movement was given some credit for helping to elect Republican George Allen as governor of Virginia in 1993, although his more explicitly evangelical running-mate was defeated. In 1994 one news service reported that "religious conservatives" have "seized outright control of the [Republican] party in a half dozen states." As we will see in Chapter 6, this activity of religious activists within the Republican Party has mainly affected the ability of that party to win national elections, and has further strengthened Jewish voters' affinity for the Democrats.[28]

However, unlike the situation in Poland, Ireland, and certain other ex-Communist regimes, the major cultural debate now is not about establishing Christianity or any denomination thereof, or about specific Christian practices. While state support of denominational schools still exists in countries as disparate as Canada, France, Germany, and Great Britain, the complaint put by the militantly devout in America is that religion in general has been so banished from public life that a kind of irreligious "secular humanism" has taken its place as the official creed.

The backlash against a perceived relaxation of moral standards has strengthened this concern about secular humanism and has extended it beyond the religious right. There was much applause in some quarters for the Supreme Court when it ruled in 1993 that while public schools could not permit clergymen to offer prayers at graduation ceremonies, students could do so. Later that year, the Supreme Court affirmed the right of religious groups to use school facilities after hours on the same basis as other community groups.

But the barrier against sectarian religious domination remains firm in official national politics because of an ideology buttressed by such pragmatic factors as denominational heterogeneity. Sectarian control, once dominant in the colonies and early Republic, is clearly no longer officially tolerated. In the culture generally, the "civil religion" that largely pervades America typically includes Judaic participation. Controversy about religious symbols in public places continues, but wherever crosses are permitted, so are menorahs. When public ceremonies require clergymen, rabbis are typically called upon along with Christian ministers. Politicians, even Pat Buchanan, are usually careful to invoke "Judeo-Christian values."

The American approach to religious pluralism was reaffirmed in very explicit fashion on April 20, 1994, by Rudolph Giuliani, New York mayor and a devout Catholic. He noted that

I will work hard to protect someone's right to believe in God as he or she sees fit—or not to believe in God—because I realize my right to practice my religion depends completely on my commitment to defend someone else's right to practice theirs or to practice no religion at all.

The condition of diversity—the condition most obvious to anyone looking at New York—mandates that we live in respectful disagreement. It makes that demand because the alternative is that we cannot live at all.[29]

While America's "Christian culture," and indeed America's "secular humanist" culture, has some effect on the internal quality of American Jewish life, the first-class status of Jews as a religious people is safe, even safer than it was when George Washington proclaimed it.

Conclusion

Some might say that the beneficent situation Jews enjoy in America today—equal economic opportunity and equal religious status—result from an unprecedentedly low level of popular anti-Semitism in America. The level of popular anti-Semitism *is* markedly lower in America than it has ever been. But that is largely the *result* of the favorable conditions for Jews that have existed in America since its inception.

In distilling the unique qualities of America as they affected the Jews—its achievement-oriented marketplace and its egalitarian political structure—there is always the danger of idealizing the American Jewish experience. The actualization of those qualities has often been tortuously hit-or-miss. America has not been a trouble-free sanctuary for Jews. But with all the negative events in the past and the necessary wariness about the future, the benign exceptionalism of America has withstood many assaults and changes, and still withstands them, perhaps more strongly than ever, as we approach the twenty-first century.

In 1783, when Mordechai Sheftall put it prophetically that for Jews there was an "entire new scene" in America, he was referring to the linked promise of equal economic opportunity and equal civil status for Jews. But there was another aspect of America's double freedom which he could not foresee: that it would be so open and egalitarian that second and subsequent generation Jews would enter the larger society and drop away from involvement in their ancestral community.

Even at the beginning of the twentieth century, the hazard of assimilation was noticed. The David Levinsky who celebrated America so exultantly ended by reflecting, "My past and my present do not comport well. David, the poor lad swinging over a Talmud volume at the . . . synagogue, seems to have more in common with my inner identity than David Levinsky, the well-known cloak-manufacturer."[30]

That kind of identity crisis, brought on by the pressure to assimilate—also a function of exceptional America—is today more threatening than ever to Jews.

～ 3 ～

The Downside of Exceptionalism

In 1791 Rebecca Samuels of Petersburg, Virginia, wrote in a letter to her German parents, "One can make a good living here, and all live in peace ... As for the Gentiles, we have nothing to complain about ... Jew and Gentile are as one. There is no *galut* here ... You cannot know what a wonderful country this is for the common man ... [but] Dear parents, I know quite well you will not want me to bring up my children like Gentiles. Here they cannot become anything else. Jewishness is pushed aside [by the Jews] ... I crave to see a synagogue to which I can go."[1]

Samuels was foreshadowing the dilemma to be posed by the open American society. It was not hostility which threatened Jewish existence, but the absence of enmity, along with the paucity of Jewish population at the time. Much has happened in the ensuing two centuries, including major waves of immigration and spells of increased hostility. But today, the concern is greater than ever that Jewishness is being pushed aside by Jews.

As of the 1990s, more than half of young Jews are marrying outside the faith, and conversions of the non-Jewish partners are in a distinct minority. Jewish knowledge and education are, for most Jews, thin at best and becoming thinner. Some religious customs, such as attendance at an annual family Passover seder dinner, continue to be observed by as many as three out of four Jews, but rituals are often driven more by nostalgia and familial attachment than by deep religious commitment. Even those practices can be expected to diminish as older generations disappear and as intermarriage rates increase even further. Meanwhile, traditional religious observance and synagogue attendance are decreasing.

The Jewish birthrate is low and declining. The completed fertility rate for Jewish women aged 45–49 is 20 percent below that of Jewish women of the same age twenty years ago, almost 20 percent below that of all American white women, and 10 percent less than the level needed for population replacement.[2] According to demographic projections, the Jewish proportion of the population will drop below 2 percent within the next century, the lowest it has been since the turn of the twentieth century.[3]

The fears concerning demographic decline may be partially counterbalanced by the continued attractiveness of America to foreigners, including Jews. The United States is still by far the world's largest receiver of refugees and other immigrants. The upswing since the 1970s has included a renewed Jewish influx, a phenomenon not generally publicized since it implies a rejection of Israel as a place to settle or live. According to Hebrew Immigrant Aid Society (HIAS) reports, between 1967 and 1980 the agency assisted in settling over 125,000 Jews in the United States. HIAS records do not include the large number of Jewish immigrants from Latin America, Canada, South Africa, and Iran, nor do they list the well over 100,000 Israelis who have come here.[4] Further, many more from the former Soviet Union entered in the late eighties and early nineties.

However, there is little prospect of a swell of immigration to match that of 1880–1920, and while that immigrant flood did mitigate the weakening of Jewish identity taking place in the last half of the nineteenth century, it obviously did not hold off the erosive forces of Americanization. In examining Jewish continuity, we must look with an unsentimental eye at the ways in which American exceptionalism may threaten the future of the Jews even more than did the anti-Semitic hostilities of the past.

Such prophecies of doom have often been made in the 2000-year history of the Diaspora and in the three-centuries-long existence of

American Jewry. Some analysts protest against them, pointing out both that some American Jews are intensifying their religious observances and education, and that many others are not so much disappearing as just changing to less stringent forms of observance and group cohesion, as are many Christians.

In fact, no one is saying that American Jewry will vanish, or that some core of strongly committed Jews will not remain. But current evidence suggests that group identity and cohesiveness are severely eroding for the large majority. And the Jews are not alone in experiencing this collective malaise. The unique and otherwise benevolent qualities of America which are largely responsible for the loss of Jewish identity have similarly affected most other ethnic and ethnoreligious groups. Thus, America's historical openness may be seen as a double-edged sword, hacking away at disadvantage, and, on the backstroke, cutting away at identity, Jewish or otherwise.

A History of Dissolution

In several periods since Rebecca Samuels articulated the dilemma, Jews have feared for their continuity in America. The colonial Jews had basically vanished by 1800. By 1880 the German Jews were in the process of disappearing. Fewer than one third of Jewish schoolage children were receiving even the most rudimentary Jewish education, and ten years later less than 10 percent of American Jews were affiliated with synagogues.[5] These facts, and the growing prevalence of intermarriage, naturally led to concerns about Jewish erosion.

That prophecy was temporarily derailed first by a massive Eastern European immigration and then, in this century, by a period of heightened anti-Semitism that raised the consciousness of the Jewish community. But the doomsday prophecy was revived again after World War II when Jews reached new heights of acceptance and achievement. In May 1964 *Look* magazine featured a cover story about "The Vanishing American Jew."

Again, events soon joined to confound the prophecy. In 1967 a largely delayed positive reaction to the emergence of the state of Israel occurred when that country seemed seriously threatened by a multination invasion. This defensive response, together with an apparent revival of general ethnic consciousness in America, led to a renaissance of Jewish life. The force of those developments eventually faded, however, as Jewish success and integration in the open American society again lessened group defensiveness, cohesion, and identity.

In 1990 the National Jewish Population Study dramatically documented that, despite some limited trends to the contrary, the erosion of Jewish identity in America was proceeding apace. Answers to questions about intermarriage (fewer than a fifth saying they would oppose it, even "somewhat," for their children), as well as to statements about attachment to Israel and feelings about Jewish identity, all indicated declining group cohesion.[6]

The poll results, which suggested that something more than a benign transformation to fit modern reality was taking place, produced near-panic among the community's leadership. Much of the Jewish establishment became preoccupied as never before with the problem of "Jewish continuity," as it was indelibly and somewhat misleadingly named. But many of the proposed remedies tended to be tautological complaints rather than solutions: Jews would be more involved if only they were better educated, or if only they were more religious. In short, they would be better Jews if only they would pull themselves together and became better Jews.

The source of the problem is not a lack of will, however. The well-meaning culprit—not just for Jews but, in different ways and degrees, for most ethnic and ethnoreligious groups in this country—is the very openness of American society. Part of America's inherent promise has been that ethnic separateness and open integration into the larger society can exist side by side. The American experiment, particularly under the conditions we face at the end of this millennium, is testing whether that is possible, as it has proven not to be in the world generally. The effort has already failed for most European immigrant groups in America. It may eventually fail for the majority of Jews.

There is, however, at least one apparent difference between Jews and other immigrant groups which are defined by ethnicity, culture, and language. The central core of Jewish identity has been religion, even though an ethnic culture is built into that religion. That religious core provides a special base for Jewish survival.

Many believe that Jewish group cohesion will fade as a substantial majority moves from a religious identity to the kind of ethnic feeling that has characterized other identity-diminished immigrant groups. Indeed, the National Jewish Population Study (NJPS) indicates that more American Jews today see themselves as members of an "ethnic" group than of a "religious" group. But the meaning of that distinction is anything but clear-cut. In general, the word "ethnicity" has become too imprecise to describe what is happening to Jews and other ancestral groups in America.

The "Tribal" Dimension

A typical modern dictionary definition of the term "ethnic" refers to "a group sharing a common and distinctive culture, religion, language or the like." In earlier dictionaries, one was likely to find the term primarily defined as "nations not Christian or Jewish," that is, heathen or pagan, with perhaps a secondary definition "pertaining to race distinctions."[7] The new meaning of the word has become particularly useful in multicultural societies such as America where "nationality" is no longer applicable.

In practice, the term "ethnic" has been used to refer to national origin or racial groups, and as these have become increasingly more politicized, so has the term itself. In recent years, "ethnic" has often served as a code word in public discourse for disadvantaged racial groups. In defensive reaction, some groups of European origin have tried to reassert their identities as white ethnics in the United States. But such efforts only reveal the extent to which "ethnic" has become a tepid and indistinct concept when applied to the practices of the groups themselves.

In the later Middle Ages, court ladies, dressed in peasant costumes, would often go out on picnics and eat peasant food. After an afternoon of such nostalgic dalliance harking back to a simpler time, they would return to the palace. The ethnic practices of older immigrant groups in America are in the same mold, still maintaining some patterns of association and some turns of mind, but mainly celebrating old-country food, music, and snippets of language.

Nathan Glazer and Daniel Patrick Moynihan, describing contemporary dinners in the prosperous ambience of the Society of the Friendly Sons of Saint Patrick, note that while the dinners start and end with fancy non-Irish dishes, there is an obligatory "middle course of boiled bacon, Irish potatoes, and kale, a wistful reminder of those far-off cabins in Roscommon. No one touches it."[8] Food habits are leveling out even in the concentrated Italian neighborhoods of Boston. Fewer younger Italian Americans know how to prepare "Italian dishes," or eat them nearly as often, as did older generations.[9] And the most common Italian dishes have been coopted by the general American population.

Pockets of ethnic cohesion for older immigrant groups—in less affluent Boston and Chicago areas, for example—can still be found, infused sometimes with new immigration. By and large, however, these populations have been folding into the general society. The rates of intermarriage for many of them are higher than for Jews. The Irish Historical Societies have been waning, as have afterschool Italian-language classes.

The use of an alternative designation, "tribal," is useful to deromanticize the pervasive term "ethnic." For this purpose, following generic dictionary definitions, "tribal" means "strong feeling for a social group comprising numerous families or generations claiming common descent, although often accepting adopted strangers, and typically characterized by some developed set of customs and traditions." There is nothing special about the term "tribal"; it just describes the more cohesive rather than the nostalgic edge of ethnicity. But it is precisely the cohesive "strong feeling" that is noticeably dwindling in so many of the earlier immigrant groups, along with the drying up of specific customs and traditions. Both the words "ethnicity" and "tribalism," as applied to groups, are on a continuum from the cohesive to the merely nostalgic. Certain elements of "identity" can linger long after they no longer have much meaning for the individual or the group. The use of "tribal" often shocks and draws resistance just because it so starkly signifies group solidarity and particularism.

Resistance to the tribal concept was expressed in the early 1900s by the American Jewish philosopher Morris R. Cohen in voicing his opposition to Zionism. He saw Zionism as the epitome of a possible future in which the world would be "Balkanized—that is, organized on a tribal basis as it was in the Dark Ages. But whether tribalism triumphs or not, it is none the less evil, and thinking men should reject it as such."[10]

The evils of combative tribalism are generally acknowledged, and have been strikingly demonstrated in post-Cold War developments in Eastern Europe, former Yugoslavia, sub-Saharan Africa, and South Asia. Cohesive ethnicity has been especially tainted for those who believe that intergroup hatred and international war will not cease until all particularistic national loyalties disappear. But it has been an article of faith in America—and the hypothesis of one of America's experiments—that different ethnic groups should exist, and can exist, together benignly. And some serious form of particularism, of ingroup solidarity and mutual support, is exactly the quality that enables ethnic groups to endure.

When a group no longer serves an important and unique need, it begins to lose its cohesive, if not yet its nostalgic, force. That cohesive feeling exists as long as the group serves three kinds of needs: (1) the need to mount group defense against disadvantage; (2) the need to belong to a familiar and accepting community, marked by "a developed set of customs and traditions"; and (3) the need to draw on such customs and traditions to give unique form, meaning, and direction to personal life. When an ancestral group loses these three functions, it ceases to exist as a cohesive or enduring unit, despite cherished traces of ethnic identity.

The perceived need for solidarity against both strangeness and danger once heavily affected the identity of Irish and Italian Americans, for example, and still heavily marks African Americans and relative newcomers such as the Chinese and Vietnamese. The defensiveness has been inspired not only by discrimination but also by the objective disadvantages of being new and different. The ghetto serves as an important way-station for many immigrant groups, allowing them to speak their own language and feel comfortable in their own ways while they venture into the outer world. Mutual help in finding jobs or capital has always been a notable aspect of immigrant neighborhoods.

Long after an ethnic group has fulfilled its function as a support group against disadvantage, it can have a cohesive significance of its own. Ancestry groups have distinctive cultural characteristics, such as language, food, and life traditions, which enable their members to feel communally "at home." The role of their leaders and intellectuals has been to articulate that sense of personal meaning and to translate some of those cultural patterns into higher values unique to the group.

A distinctive family style is typically proclaimed as one of those traits. When Richard Gambino writes about "the core of the Italian American ethnicity," he lists family as first among the "unique" components of Italian ethnicity. Andrew Greeley does the same for the Irish, prominently citing "cultural patterns in family structure."[11] A strong family bond marks other ethnic groups as well, including Jews, Hispanics, and Asians. When we questioned a number of San Franciscans why they chose to be Jews, they answered in these terms: "I like the strong family feelings ... the people are warm ... I feel at home ... It's like an extended family."[12]

Other positive values, normally transmitted by the family and neighborhood at an early age, are also mentioned by the various enthusiasts for particular ethnicities. Greeley emphasizes a distinctive Irish "world view," dating from ancient Celtic origins, allegedly related to a "modified dualism" which forces the Irish "to oscillate on many emotional continua." In a similar vein, Gambino suggests that Italians have a uniquely "complicated personality."[13]

However, the main value of these cultural elements lies in the fact that they are, for group members, *their* communal traditions. Asked why being Jewish was important to them, most of our survey respondents gave such answers as, "It is my culture," "It is my way of life," "It provides me with a tie to other Jews." When other centrifugal pressures diminish, it often becomes clear that the distinctiveness of those feelings is not vital.

Strong ethnically related family traditions have dissipated in open America, which, in Russell Jacoby's words, has a "multiculturalism that undercuts multiculturalism."[14] In the dedication to his book on Italian Americans, Richard Alba tellingly writes, "For Michael, so that he may know what he could never learn on his grandfather's knee." Alba has documented the growing convergence of family and other cultural attitudes and practices between younger generations of Italian Americans and Anglo-Americans.[15] In the long run, cohesive ethnicity in America requires something more than family values or other existential community beliefs in order to endure.

The decline of ethnicity into nostalgia among earlier immigrant groups has always been marked by a growing rate of intermarriage, which Milton Gordon called "the keystone in the arch of assimilation."[16] Intermarriage is, after all, the definitive evidence of diminished group cohesion. Only one fifth of husbands and wives born in the United States after 1950 came from the same ethnic ancestry; outside the South the number is only 15 percent.[17] In the case of Italian Americans, to take one example, fewer than one out of ten aged 65 or older in 1979 had mixed Italian ancestry, as compared with four of ten Italian Americans aged 35 to 44 and eight of ten aged five or younger. The intermarriage rate of younger Italian Americans was well over 70 percent.[18]

Special cohesive factors, as we will see, come into play with non-European tribal groups—African Americans and the various groups customarily lumped together as "Latinos" and "Asians." But these ancestry groups will eventually be subject to the same American conditions that have detribalized older immigrant stocks. Already, about half of third-generation Japanese Americans are intermarrying, most often with whites.[19]

Given their low level of religious commitment and practice, if Jews are to prove even a partial exception to the almost inexorable American pattern of decline in tribal cohesion, they will presumably need some cohesive factor beyond defensiveness on behalf of themselves or Israel.

As a result of the high and growing rates of intermarriage, the organized Jewish community is becoming desperate to explicitly identify characteristics of "Jewishness" which have an intrinsically particularistic quality and are not interchangeable in the general cultural marketplace. In other words, they are trying to fill the third need we listed above: to draw on customs and traditions to give unique form, meaning, and direction to personal life.

Jewish Tribal Values

Some commentators want to believe that an intrinsic aspect of Jewish life consists of such universally benevolent "Jewish social values" as equality, social justice, and world peace. In a *Los Angeles Times* 1988 survey many more Jews were likely to choose pursuit of equality and social justice rather than religion or Israel as the most important Jewish value for them.[20] These emphases within the Jewish community have become most explicit when some of the main streams of American Christianity, usually the higher status denominations, have exhibited a moralistic rather than a theological cast and espoused the "social gospel." But this liberal social gospel fits the needs of American Jews particularly well.

By taking on a public orientation similar to Christian denominations, Judaism runs the danger of appearing more Americanized and less particularistic. Of course, a case can be made that Judaism provided the original base for these social beliefs, as they emerged in America, Christianity, and Western society generally. But however original they may be to Jewish culture and however strongly they may be held by Jews, in their general import most of those social values are no longer unique to Jews and have clearly not provided the glue that will keep the Jewish community together.

If social values are not the glue, what are the other candidates? Those who believe that American Jews are just changing the forms of their Jewish commitment to fit modern life take great stock in the fact that Jews tend to congregate in the same occupational and educational cohorts. For example, Calvin Goldscheider and Alan Zuckerman write that "the American Jewish community has moved rapidly and thoroughly from large proportions with low levels of education and blue-collar employment to college education and professional and managerial positions. This transformation implies internal cohesion . . . Jews share similar social and economic positions in the general society, thereby maintaining high levels of interaction. Structural factors tie most Jews to other Jews."[21]

These kinds of associational patterns certainly contribute to group cohesion in the short run. But distinctive educational and occupational gaps between Jews and the host population will not likely persist. The rate of college attendance, for example, has risen rapidly for the general American population; and it is on the university campus where the most significant assimilationist interactions between Jews and non-Jews often take place. In any case, whether these associational patterns persist or not, they do not in themselves speak to any distinctive intrinsic quality, if that is what it will take to keep the Jewish community indefinitely cohesive.

The search for a special Jewish trait inevitably leads back to religion. Religious belief is the source of the customs and traditions that give unique form, meaning, and direction to Jewish personal life. Of course religion is not unique to Jewish ethnicity. It has played a role in the cohesion of those other ancestry groups, which are often described as "ethnoreligious." Both Greeley and Gambino talk about religious identities as central positive attributes of Irish and Italian Americans. (The Irish Protestants, who are as numerous as Irish Catholics, are not considered "Irish" except in census reports.) Other European ethnic groups in America such as the Poles and the Russians are also marked by a distinctive religious orientation.

But one of the homogenizing effects of America has been to heavily de-ethnicize Christianity—to replace ethnic group commitment with religious group loyalty. Between the turn of the century and the civil rights explosion of the 1960s, people gradually identified themselves more readily as Catholics or Methodists or Mormons than as Irish, African, or Anglo-Americans.[22] Judaism has never been de-ethnicized, however. While history has led the cultures of some other ancestry groups to be linked to a particular religion, at its root the Jewish religion cannot be separated from the Jewish people. One can theoretically join a "universal" religion by a commitment of personal belief, but one cannot "join" Judaism without enlisting in the tribe. After all, the religious component of Judaism is formally built around a specific relationship between God and the Jewish people as a whole. That religious commitment is presumably the most durable core of Jewish tribal identity, but itself has been subject to America's shaping forces.

The Jewish Religious Mode

Forecasting "the uncertain future" of the American Jewish community, Rabbi Arthur Hertzberg cites a meeting between Secretary of State Henry Kissinger and many high-level representatives of the largest Jewish groups in the country. As the discussion with Kissinger drew on, one of Hertzberg's fellow rabbis became anxious to participate in a traditional afternoon religious service, called *Mincha*, in which he would say a memorial prayer for his mother. A company of ten Jews was needed for the short service, but that did not seem to be a problem since all those prominent Jewish leaders were present.

However, it was quickly discovered that the three rabbis in the group—and Henry Kissinger, of European upbringing—"were the only four people in the room who knew which end of *Mincha* was up!" Hertzberg ascribes the weakness and decline of the Jewish community to this disappearance of traditional Jewish learning ("except for a minority of about 15 percent").[23]

Those Jewish leaders were meeting with the U.S. secretary of state for the ultimate purpose of defending Israel and the status of American Jews. If there were no longer any need to be concerned about the security of Jews anywhere in the world, what kind of a Jewish community—if any—would be reflected by leaders so deficient in traditional Jewish learning? What, if anything, would take the place of defensiveness?

When early American Jews pushed aside their Jewishness, in Rebecca Samuels's words, they did not do so to deliberately escape the yoke of

Jewish observance. Benjamin Sheftall, when he came to Georgia on the *William and Sarah,* took a circumcision kit with him. His companions brought a Torah scroll and an Ark. On disembarking, they immediately began to hold religious services, and several years later constructed a *mikvah,* a ritual bath. And when Benjamin Sheftall's grandson went into apprenticeship to learn the "art, trade and mystery" of the law for three years, the Christian attorney to whom he was apprenticed agreed that he would not be required "to attend to any business or to do or perform anything appertaining to the study or profession of the Law, on the Jewish Sabbaths, or any other Days consecrated to that religion."[24]

The earlier Jewish immigrants tended to think of their Jewish identity in traditional religious terms. In most frontier towns in the nineteenth century, every handful of Jews set up Jewish religious institutions. From St. Joseph, Missouri, came word in 1860 that "the twelve Jewish families . . . had acquired burial grounds."[25] Writing from Pike's Peak in the recently opened Jefferson Territory, "some fifteen Israelites" reported that they had organized themselves into a congregation called Beth Elohim Bamidbar, "the House of the Lord in the Wilderness."[26] One Jewish soldier in the Army of the Potomac wrote that "we are quite satisfied to fight with our Christian comrades for one cause, one country and THE UNION," but indicated that he fasted on Yom Kippur while engaged in battle, and met together with other Jews on the edge of battle for Sabbath worship.[27]

The movement away from traditional practice was initially a result of objective circumstance rather than of philosophical choice. In some Indian tribes on the frontier, Jews came to be known as "the egg-eaters" because so many of the Jewish peddlers trading with them refused to eat their unkosher meat. But one Jewish peddler wrote that "leading such a life, none of us is able to observe the simplest commandment . . . thousands of peddlers . . . have given up their religion for the pack which is on their backs."[28]

Under the free conditions of American life, Judaism was ripe for more deliberate and systematic adjustment. The Reform movement which eventually adapted Jewish religious practice to the dominant modern culture came out of Germany and was endorsed by the majority of American Jews and their rabbis during the late nineteenth century. Yet it caused a conflict in the minds of many Jews, as expressed by Mordechai Noah, one of the most prominent Jews in early nineteenth-century America:

> The Jewish religion should never change its original form or type. Reforms create schisms and promote divisions, besides impairing the unity of our faith ... [But] I must confess that I should like to see some changes in our ritual and ceremonies. While admiring the beauty and the sublimity of the Hebrew language, I should still be gratified if we could introduce in our prayers a portion of the language of the country in order that we may better comprehend the great responsibilities of our faith. We might also curtail many repetitions and introduce some beneficial changes; but where are the limitations and boundaries to these reforms, when we once introduce the pruning knife?[29]

Noah struggled with this religious dilemma in his personal life. He ate only kosher meat at home, but, like many latter-day Jews, when dining out he also ate oysters with delight. He publicly disapproved of Jewish storekeepers who violated the Sabbath, but he wrote that his children "are making arrangements to hang up their stockings for Christmas tonight."

Modernization and Reform

In the 1840s and 1850s several "reform societies" were established to modernize religious customs. In some synagogues, men and women were no longer separated. English began to be used more often in the services. But an 1869 conference of rabbis in Philadelphia is considered the first statement of the Reform position in America, involving a change in theology, not just in practices. Article I of the resolutions passed at the 1869 conference dropped the biblical concept of "the chosen people," the election of Israel, by renouncing the messianic goal of the restoration of Israel. The substitute objective was "the unity of all rational creatures."[30]

The more renowned Pittsburgh Platform of an 1885 rabbinic conference repeated and elaborated on that theme. It said that "we hold that all such Mosaic and Rabbinical laws as regulate diet, priestly purity and dress originated in ages and under the influence of ideas altogether foreign to our present mental and spiritual state." And it added that "we no longer consider ourselves a nation, but a religious community."[31] However altered some practices and customs, the Reform movement still presented itself and its Jewish identity in religious terms.

Some thought that the Reform movement was going too far, even before the 1885 statement. Two years earlier, on the occasion of the first graduation of the Hebrew Union College in Cincinnati, a dinner was held at the Highland House, a well-known resort. A Jewish caterer had been hired to serve the dinner. In the words of one of the graduates, David Philipson, "Terrific excitement ensued when two rabbis rose from their seats and rushed from the room. Shrimp [one of the forbidden foods, *terefa*] had been placed before them as the opening course." The Highland House dinner came to be known as the "*terefa* banquet."[32]

The incident precipitated the formation of the Conservative movement in America, whose purpose was to adapt to the new society while preserving many of the traditional forms which Reform seemed ready to abandon. The great East European immigration at the end of the nineteenth and beginning of the twentieth century brought with it a renewed impulse toward traditional religious observance. In fact, the term "Orthodox" was a modern invention, describing an explicit traditional reaction to what was seen as galloping religious modernism on the part of the Reform and Conservative movements.

That immigration also brought to America a stream of secular Judaism, a particular product of radical political ideology and general "enlightenment" which flourished among many East European Jews. In New York City, early in this century, scoffingly nonreligious Jews threw pieces of ham at families solemnly walking to synagogue on Holy Days. Less dramatically, they established systems of secular Yiddish schools for children sponsored by radical associations, such as the

Workmen's Circle. They sought to celebrate the history and ethnic quality of the Jews, often strained through a political prism, while rejecting the religious substance of Judaism; that is, they wanted to preserve Jewry as a national and tribal, rather than a religious, group.

But the formal secular Jewish movement did not thrive in America much past the generation which brought it here, although some organized strands of Jewish humanism still exist. Among the reasons for the eventual failure of this movement were the decline of both political radicalism and Yiddish, and the sobering effect of Hitler. But most of all, explicit secularism, especially espoused by a group generally perceived as religious, did not fit the American style.

This country has consistently been perceived by its citizens as religious, and from the beginning most non-Jewish Americans have *wanted* to see Jews as a religious group. In 1784 a letter appeared in a Philadelphia newspaper, signed by "A Protestant," probably the Reverend Charles Crawford, complaining about Christian indifference as compared with Jewish commitment: "I cannot help being extremely shocked when I observe the day of our blessed Saviour's death (Good Friday) . . . treated by all ranks of people with . . . unchristianlike levity . . . The Jews set us the example; who, at the time of their Passover . . . refrain from the tempting lucre of gain during the course of almost a week."[33]

Even as the evidence grew in the twentieth century that Jews spend much less time in synagogue than other Americans spend in church, and keep their stores open on most Holy Days, the American public continues to cherish the religious image of Jewish identity. Most Americans still identify Jews in such terms, rather than as an ethnic entity—unlike the Jews themselves, more of whom tend to identify themselves as cultural or ethnic rather than religious.[34] Strengthening that perception are the many pervasive Jewish lifestyle patterns which are seen by American Christians as religious in nature.

About half of American Jews say that they fast on Yom Kippur, a religious obligation on what is generally considered the most solemn of Jewish Holy Days. About the same proportion of Jews say they always participate in a Passover seder; another quarter say that they usually or sometimes participate in such a ceremonial dinner. An equal portion say they always light candles on Hanukkah.[35] The observance of these home rituals has increased since the fifties.[36]

On the other hand, synagogue attendance, never very high among modern Jews, seems to have decreased even more since midcentury. Four out of ten Americans overall, but only one of ten American Jews, claim to attend services weekly.[37] But three quarters of American Jews say they attend services at least once a year, mostly on one or several High Holy Days. More than a third of American Jews say they belong to a synagogue.

In short, about three quarters of American Jews indicate that they participate somehow, at home or at synagogue, in some kind of religious service. Even if the figures are exaggerated, which they surely are, presumably they are inflated in recognition of the significance of religious observance to Jewish identity.

On the other hand, according to Hertzberg's estimate, only 15 percent of American Jews "know which end of *Mincha* is up." Actually, slightly less than 15 percent queried by the NJPS say they attend services at least several times a month; even fewer report they keep the dietary rules of *kashreth,* or refrain from handling money on the Sabbath, or believe that the Bible is the actual word of God.

The lamenters within the community tend to interpret the diminishing religious tradition as a defensive effort to avoid clashing with the American culture. When Hertzberg wrote that Judaism could survive only by "emphasizing what is unique to itself," he said that "this, however, means something radically different than our contemporary Jewish 'religion' which is itself a form of institutional assimilation to the prevailing American modes."[38] There is clearly such an adaptive mode among Jews. Marshal Sklare found that those rituals engaged in by the majority, such as the Passover seder, correspond to specific rituals within the religious culture of the larger community and do not demand social isolation.[39]

There may well be an element of defensiveness in the history of such Jewish adaptation, especially in periods of anti-Jewish hostility. More probably, an overarching and less deliberate process is at work. In suggesting what has come to be known as Heine's Law, Heinrich Heine proposed that to understand the Jews in any one country, it is first necessary to study the Gentiles, since the social and religious behavior of Jews varies from country to country depending on the customs of the Gentiles; that is, Jews adapt to the dominant modes in the host society.[40]

In America, this kind of adaptation is not unique to Jews. Christian denominations have also been shaped by American conditions. Early in American history some Catholics attempted to elect their own bishops, in a kind of American congregational mode. This effort was rebuffed, but activities within the American Catholic Church have often been a thorn in the side of traditional European Catholics, including the Vatican.[41] The conflict they face is familiar: to what extent does integration in the American scene breach the separatist values essential to survival? As one historian described the conflict between "Americanized" and more traditional Catholic clerics and laity at the end of the nineteenth century:

> The conflict was so acute that it frequently broke into print on the front pages of the nation's daily newspapers . . . [The religious conservatives] wanted to hold all other religious groups at arm's length, sometimes refusing even minor courtesies . . . When they saw Catholics participate with non-Catholics in civic meetings, they feared that each handshake betokened a conspiracy and that each statement of common interest represented a scandalous concession to unbelievers . . . [The religious progressives] believed American Catholicism could not secure its faith nor fulfill its opportunities by proscription and withdrawal . . . it could validate its principles only by practicing them in the American scene.[42]

A similar conflict has arisen between the "mainline" and the "fundamentalist" Protestant denominations in America.

Much of Judaism, as of Christianity, has been naturally shaped by American conditions. In both cases, the stated rationale for the reformist majority has been that their purpose is not to weaken religious commitment but to strengthen it by adaptation to the needs of modern life. Moreover, if those Jews had simply been embarrassed or afraid, they could have more easily just abandoned their Jewish identity.

Whatever the causes, the question remains as to the effect of reform and integration on religious group solidarity. In remarking on the fact that the mainline Protestant churches—Methodists, Presbyterians, Congregationalists, Episcopalians—have lost between one fifth and one third of their membership since 1965, several Christian sociologists of religion have concluded that these denominations must return to traditional and particularistic religious themes and "provide compelling answers to the question, 'what's so special about Christianity?' "[43] That is the same imperative that Hertzberg and others pose for American Jews: a return to more particularistic and traditional practices and knowledge to determine "what's so special about Judaism." The more minimalist activities of the majority of American Jews, they say, do not serve that purpose.

But given the American pattern and the extent of Jewish integration, it is perhaps less startling to emphasize how many Jews have moved away from more traditional religious practices than to note how many have apparently clung to *some* religious involvement. Is their engagement in minimalist observances primarily an expression of their desire to maintain membership in the Jewish tribal community?

Religion and Tribalism—A Complex Relationship

After World War II, the second and third generation of East European Jews began to fully enter American society. But they were not yet at ease. Too much had too recently happened to them and their tribe, here and abroad. They dispersed to the suburbs, as befitted their new economic status, but the Jewish community qua community was still important to them. As they moved out, they formed new congregations and built synagogues and community centers at an unprecedented rate.

Will Herberg wrote at the time that the apparent Jewish renaissance was "a way of sociability or belonging rather than a way of orienting life to God."[44] As one promotional leaflet for a suburban synagogue read: "The community needs a place for our children and we adults need some place to carry on our social lives. What better place can there be than our synagogue?"[45]

Nathan Glazer put it well: "American Jews, if they believe in anything, believe in the instrumental efficacy of religion ... it keeps the Jewish people together. The conceptions that it is good in itself and that it embodies valuable and unique truths are foreign to the great majority of Jews in this country."[46] The classic statement of the instrumentalist view was pronounced by the French sociologist Emile Durkheim, himself a Jewish atheist, who wrote that "the idea of society is the soul of religion."[47] He universalized the belief that primitive groups used religious enthusiasm to build group solidarity.

The celebration of ritual is often just an expression of that solidarity, for defensive or communal reasons, rather than an acknowledgment of a durably and distinctively intrinsic value in religious Judaism. Even in the highly traditional Jewish society of the late Middle Ages, according to a historian of that period, Jacob Katz, "the internal cohesiveness of the Jewish community was undoubtedly nourished by the depth of the religious experience of the ever-recurring ritual ... [but] only where religion lives on its own independent resources—man facing God—is it unconsciously and paradoxically also transformed into an all-important social preservative."[48]

There is something simplistic and reductionist in this emphasis on a dichotomy between the communal and the religious, especially for Jews. Most people, otherwise engaged, never will have a scholarly knowledge of the "unique truths" in any religious tradition. Katz himself pointed out that in the dense system of Jewish education in medieval times, "thorough knowledge and preoccupation with the Talmud [was] acquired only by a minority."[49] Most of those Jews probably never had an overwhelming emotional religious experience. As Katz also noted, even the new and highly intoxicating Hasidism of the period appealed to a restricted audience "since ... [their] inherent hallmark—ecstasy—could be achieved only by an extremely limited group."[50]

But certainly the great majority of those Jews were religious by any sensible definition. In its course, the traditional educational system in old Europe, whose central purpose was to reach the scholars, also imbued the entire community with a basic and monolithic commitment to practicing Judaism. And, Katz observed, "In practice, the very circumstances which broadened the gap between the [Hasidic] leaders and the masses of ordinary Jews, also forged a link between them . . . Rapturous Hasidism . . . could be transmitted to a group of onlookers through a feeling of community."[51]

To an extent unknown in Christianity, the Jewish religion centers around the Jews *as a people.* The Covenant is between God and the nation. The references in the prayer book are almost entirely to the people. There is no way for Judaism to exist or continue as a religion without the communal entity. In the early part of the twentieth century, Mordecai Kaplan launched an influential movement, Reconstructionism, emphasizing the centrality of "peoplehood" for Judaism. He has been considered by some a religious minimalist because he deemphasized the chosen-people image that is tied to the focal religious concept of a literal covenant between God and the Jew: "No nation is chosen, or elected, or superior to any other, but every nation should discover its vocation or calling, as a source of religious experience, and as a medium of salvation to those who share its life."[52] Kaplan arrived at that relativist position partly because he felt it was more in accord with American democratic thought. Also, influenced by Durkheim, he did not see Jewish ritual primarily as a supernatural mandate but as an important mechanism for Jewish survival, as well as a source of personal spiritual fulfillment. In a real sense, he was emphasizing the tribal aspect of Judaism.

However, the very consciousness of being part of the Jewish community can itself carry some religious meaning because of the corporate nature of Judaism. For the religious scholar Arnold Eisen, chosenness is the metaphor on which collective identity partly depends: "Chosenness is such a useful rhetorical aid to the 'fabrication of identity' precisely because it seems to confer ultimate meaning . . . The individual is defined out of anonymity and into a unique fate through identification with the chosen people." To the extent that the minimally learned and observant merely cling to the "chosen" community, even they participate to some limited degree in that meaningful identity.[53]

While over half of American Jews say that the Jews do not primarily comprise a religious group, fewer than a fifth identify themselves as secular.[54] The majority typically do see that the rituals and community with which they are connecting have a long and distinguished history in which they take pride. And with some ambiguity, except for the ideologically secular, many of the less explicitly devout appreciate that the Jewish history to which they are attached is somehow religious and transcendental in nature.

The less demonstratively involved might be called "religious fellow-travelers," as long as the term is not used deprecatingly to suggest that they are not really religious at all. The phrase "folk religion" might well inform the concept, emphasizing religious expression primarily through rituals and symbols rather than through the explicit belief system which underlies the practices of "elite" religion. Folk religion accepts the organizational structure of the elite religion but is indifferent to the elite belief structure. As Charles Liebman describes folk religion, "Large numbers of people may affiliate with a particular religious institution, and even identify themselves as part of that religion, without accepting all aspects of its elitist formulation."[55] Folk religion is also often described as one that is distinct to a particular people.

Those religious fellow-travelers, by definition, typically affiliate with Jewish tribal institutions and traditions for defensive or communal rather than doctrinal reasons. But they do receive spiritual satisfaction from the sense that they are embraced by a higher, unique, and irreplaceable meaning which inheres in those ancient and dramatic Jewish traditions.

In that sense, religious Judaism is central to the tribal durability of the bulk of American Jewry. David Ben Gurion, the architect and first prime minister of Israel, was definitely not a traditional Jew, but he probably qualified as a religious fellow-traveler. He insisted on giving special privileges to the Orthodox in the new state, not just for political reasons but because he thought that the Jewish people had survived because of their religion, that the then founding secular majority of

Israelis owed their Jewish continuity, their very existence, to the believers.

Any attempt to measure the identity-state of American Jews, or guess at its future, must try to somehow take into account the complicated and somewhat impenetrable relationship of "tribal" to "religious" motivations.

Linkage Jews

Tribal cohesion has its roots, as we have seen, in three broad sources: the defensive need, the communal impulse itself, and the commitment to some distinctive group quality, notably, in the case of the Jews, a religious one. A neat typology of American Jews, therefore, would posit categories of Jews primarily driven by one of those motivations, or by none. Of course, no such neat classification is possible. The motivations of many or most individual Jews are inscrutably mixed. Defensiveness and affiliations with community are often related. Religious impulses, which themselves are highly varied, and involvements with the group are usually intermingled. The practice of certain religious rituals can also be linked to ties with community, or to religious commitment, or even to defensiveness.

Nevertheless, using the various surveys of the American Jewish population, we can identify and very roughly quantify some different tendencies. About half of American Jewish households report some formal Jewish affiliation; that is, they belong to a Jewish organization, or to a synagogue, or contribute to the Jewish community fund, according to the data of the 1990 National Jewish Population Study. Only a quarter indicate that they are neither organizationally affiliated nor ritually engaged.

Almost all Americans, including Jews, say they "believe in God." About one of ten Jews believes that "the Torah is the actual word of God," and another third feel that "the Torah is the inspired word of God but not everything should be taken literally." But fundamentalism is not the final measure of religiosity. While the majority of those who say they are Orthodox will choose the more fundamentalist answer on this question, many Orthodox Jews will not; and half of whose who give the more fundamentalist response are Reform or Conservative.

Behavioral observance thus becomes the most reliable, if approximate, way of identifying those who might be called the more devout. Different Jewish denominations mandate varying forms of behavioral observance. For example, Reform Jews generally do not feel that they have to keep a kosher home or kosher diet as part of their religious observance. But all denominations do optimally—and optimistically—call for weekly attendance at synagogue services, which might therefore serve as a behavioral measure of a more devotional tendency. As we have seen, 15 percent say they attend synagogue services at least a few times a month and qualify on this count. Among the Orthodox, 55 percent attend services at least three times a month, compared with 18 percent of Conservatives and 10 percent of Reform Jews. But in absolute numbers, many more of the Jews who attend at least three times a month are Conservative and Reform, since the Orthodox constitute well under 10 percent of all American Jews.

The popular media frequently mention a new "spiritual" mood among Americans, including Jews. Writing in 1993, Jack Wertheimer described "a passionate minority of Jews which has invested a lot of energy in creating and nurturing innovative programs that encourage religious renewal."[56] The Havurah movement, a fairly recent development of new, more intimate Jewish religious groupings, often associated with denominational institutions, is an example. But in their "spiritual" (or communal) yearning, some Jewish youth have also turned to Eastern religions. The Guru of a prominent Buddhist movement once came to the United States to try to find out why a majority of his members in this country were Jewish. The members of the Hari Krishna sect and the followers of the Reverend Sun Yung Moon are disproportionately of Jewish ancestry, although the total numbers are relatively small.

Not surprisingly, almost all those who might be considered the more devout, reflected in their regular attendance at religious services, are formally affiliated with the community and engage in some home religious ritual. Conversely, about half of those who attend only on special occasions or the High Holy Days have any organizational affiliation. But about three quarters of those who attend only on special occasions or High Holy Days, and about a third who never attend, say that they engage in some home religious ritual. Most of those who are less devout in terms of synagogue attendance, but organizationally affiliated, also report private ritual activity. Clearly, an incalculable but substantial number of the less devout and of those who are primarily communal in motivation are at least religious fellow-travelers.

While religiosity remains elusive, it is somewhat easier to identify those American Jews on the high edge of defensiveness. The defensive tendency is most clearly incorporated among that half of the Jewish population who, according to the 1990 NJPS, "strongly agree" that anti-Semitism is a serious problem in the United States today. (Another quarter of the respondents agree less vehemently with that proposition.) Most of those who give such a response know that the evidence and their personal experience are to the contrary, as we shall see, but their foreboding is weighty enough to express that strong defensive concern. Anxiety about Israel is the most active element in the concern about anti-Semitism in general. In a 1990 survey of affiliated Jews conducted by Raab, two out of ten said that anti-Semitism is growing in employment, and three out of ten said it is growing in political campaigns; but eight out of ten of them felt that there is an increase in anti-Semitism which is related to an upswing in "anti-Israel sentiments."[57]

A strongly perceived need for group defense has usually been enough to maintain tribal cohesion. But it is the weakest link in the durability of ancestry groups. When that concern wanes, the other cohesive activities become more vulnerable to American society's integrative qualities. The particular culture and values of the group becomes less important for its members, less capable of competing with the surrounding American culture and values.

When defensiveness is put aside, the momentum of the community itself, with its strong family traditions and other networks of association, can persist for some generations. But in the long run, it must decline in the absence of a quality strong enough to withstand the blandishments of the open society. Strong religious traditions and practice could help to preserve the group. But for most of its members, the community itself is often as much a creator of religious tradition as its heir.

In the search for linkage patterns among Jews that promise the most for the group's continuity, it would be worthwhile to try to distinguish between the tendency to adhere to the community for defensive reasons and to belong for other communal ones. To the extent that such distinctions can be made from the clues available to us, the dim outlines of four Jewish linkage sectors emerge, using configurations of defensiveness and affiliation.

There is a clearly *detached* sector: those who are neither affiliated nor tend to be defensive. A little more than a quarter of Jewish households do not belong to an organization or a synagogue, or contribute to a Federation, and do not strongly believe that anti-Semitism is a serious problem. Their self-identification as Jews tends primarily to be nostalgic.

More Jews observe home rituals than are formally affiliated. Half of those who have one or more organizational connections observe one or more home rituals, while only two of ten who observe one or more home rituals have some organizational connection. But a quarter of the Jewish households observe one or no home ritual and do not give the most defensive response, the same proportion which is unaffiliated and is least defensive. In sum, about a quarter of the Jewish population qualify as effectively "detached" by these proximate but practical standards.[58]

Using the same standards, another quarter, perhaps a little less, would clearly fall into a *minimally attached* sector: those who are defensively inclined but *not* connected, either organizationally or by way of any persistent family ritual observance. A most strongly attached sector, about a quarter of the population, is affiliated despite not being highly defensive. They are considered *most strongly attached* to their Jewish identity because fear of anti-Semitism is not a reason for their affiliation.

And, inevitably, there is the *mixed* sector, a little more than a quarter of the whole, who are both defensive and affiliated. This segment includes the more devout, who are somewhat more likely to be apprehensive about the status of the Jews than the rest of the population, probably because of their sense of separatism. Those, for example, who never attend synagogue services are much less likely than the more devout to agree that "in a crisis, Jews can only depend on other Jews." Within this mixed group are many who are affiliated primarily because they are defensive; they must be counted among the minimally attached.

In combination, these various indications, rough as they are, suggest what seems reasonable to the unsentimental observer of the American Jewish scene: only about half of the American Jews exhibit strong communal or devotional tendencies (or both). Another quarter are characterized by defensive tendencies. The remaining quarter tend to identify primarily in nostalgic rather than tribally cohesive modes. There is, of course, nothing fixed about these loose linkage sectors, and there is constant potential for osmotic movement among them. The foreboding impulse of American Jews, including a concern for Israel, will not disappear easily, even in the face of objectively improved circumstances, but it will decline somewhat if Israel experiences a prolonged period of peace with its neighbors. If circumstances worsen, the defensive sectors will swell, as they do whenever Israel seems seriously threatened. Depending on such circumstances, the protective cohesion of many American Jews could persist for generations.

But defensiveness is not a long-range prescription for tribal cohesion in option-rich America. There is no escaping the fact that the religious dimension of Jewishness is the key to continuity. This is obviously true for the relatively small minority who are personally devout, but it is also probably true for the much larger body of Jews who are primarily affiliated for communal reasons. If they yield their sense of the religious tradition and history attached to the Jewish community, they will eventually lose any sense of its particularity. In that case, experience strongly suggests that, given the possibility of fuller integrated achievement and absent the need for defensive reactions, other communal and familial involvements will not sustain commitment.

Intermarriage

Communal attachments in general, and even the traditions which are so significant for the religious fellow-travelers, are under assault by the burgeoning rate of intermarriage. The official figure given by the directors of the 1990 NJPS survey is that 57 percent of Jews married non-Jews in the five preceding years. If conversions of the non-Jewish partners are taken into account, the figure is reduced slightly to 52 percent. Other analysts, by manipulating the indicators of "who is a Jew," reduce that figure to "as little" as 40 percent. In either case, the rate is high and rising. The comparable intermarriage rate was 25 percent for those who wed in the decade between 1965 and 1974, and 8 percent for those who married before 1965.

Some have expressed the hope that the conversions to Judaism engendered by intermarriage would prevent any net loss. But only about one seventh of the intermarried has a spouse who has adopted Judaism. And, most important, only a small minority of their children receive any Jewish education. Seven percent of the children in the mixed families where the Jewish parent was religiously identified were enrolled in some formal Jewish education in 1990; 24 percent were expected to enroll. That compared with 62 percent who were enrolled or expected to enroll when both parents were Jewish and denominationally identified.[59] Just under a third of the children of mixed marriages are brought up as Jews (as compared with two thirds in entirely Jewish families). A similar proportion are not provided with a religious background, and the rest are raised in some other faith or in some amalgam of Judaism and other denominations.[60] The most shocking statistic of all from analysis of the NJPS data is reported by Barry Kosmin and Ariela Kaysar, who find "that living in a household composed entirely of Jews is a *minority* experience for the NJPS child population in the 1990s."[61]

These facts affect both the communal and devotional bases of tribal cohesion. Almost four out of ten entirely Jewish households, compared with almost nine out of ten mixed households, have no organizational connections.

Participation in family ritual observances also varies greatly between the two kinds of households. The mixed ones are twice as likely as entirely Jewish units to never attend synagogue services (42 percent as against 20 percent); and, by an even greater ratio, they are less disposed than entirely Jewish households to take part in such services at least three times monthly (7 percent as against 17 percent). Only a fifth of the fully Jewish households do not fast on Yom Kippur or observe Hanukkah or Passover in their homes, while about half of the mixed households ignore these occasions.[62]

These differences will not correct themselves. Mixed households are, of course, much less likely than entirely Jewish households to oppose intermarriage by their children (6 percent as against 23 percent, which is itself a significantly low threshold of resistance; 28 percent of mixed households support intermarriage, as compared with 19 percent of entirely Jewish households). According to the NJPS, only about 10 percent of mixed-marriage children marry Jews. The cycle is downward. There is some reason to give credence to the sour joke: "What do you call the grandchildren of intermarried Jews? Christians!"

Conclusion

According to Simon Rawidowicz, "He who studies Jewish history will readily discover that there was hardly a generation in the Diaspora period which did not consider itself the final link in Israel's chain."[63] Those lines should give pause to any prophet of the Jewish people's demise. Of course, history documents that some past Jewish communities *have* severely declined, but as Nathan Glazer hopefully cautions with respect to American Jewry, "There is no reason to believe there will not be further surprises in the future."[64]

Even in the absence of surprises, the American Jewish community obviously will not disappear. In that minimal sense, Jewish leaders need not despair about "continuity." While the majority of American Jews seem to be succumbing to the erosion of an integrative America, a minority—Orthodox, Conservative, and Reform—are actually intensifying their connections. The effect of the numbers apart, the evidence suggests that such a Jewish core will survive better than most other ethnic groups because of the religion-connected dimension of Jewish life.

But if the cycle of benevolent integration and intermarriage continues uninterrupted, then the cohesive American Jewish community can be expected to be reduced to a hard-core minimum in two generations. According to our linkage measurements, the loss could amount to at least half of the present population.

The more optimistic of Jewish leaders call for "outreach," hoping that the reculturation of minimally attached Jews might be in the realm of Glazer's "surprises." It is true that the substantial sector of the minimally attached will not disappear precipitately, given the intense activity of communal institutions and the probability that the large sector of primarily defensive Jews will melt away gradually under the most optimal circumstances. The factors that maintain this low-level tribal attachment among half of the American Jewish community must be explored, starting with the nature of the defensiveness which keeps such a large segment of Jews involved, even in America's open society.

~ 4 ~

The Riddle of the Defensive Jew

In 1985 about a third of those affiliated with the Jewish community in the San Francisco area said, in response to a questionnaire, that Jewish candidates could not be elected to Congress from San Francisco. Yet, three out of the four congressional representatives from that area—as well as the two state senators and the mayor of San Francisco—*were*, in fact, well-identified Jews at the time the poll was conducted. And they had been elected by a population that was about 95 percent non-Jewish.

In 1981 nine out of ten respondents in the same regional Jewish population said that they felt "comfortable" in America. But seven out of eight also believed that anti-Semitism is a serious problem in this country. Nationally, about eight out of ten affiliated Jews voiced serious concerns in 1990 about anti-Semitism, while the same overwhelming proportion replied that they felt "close" or "very close" to the American people.[1]

There are many such apparent contradictions among American Jews. To the extent that defensiveness is a strong basis of group cohesion, the solidarity of American Jewry would seem to be assured. Other immigrant groups have lost their cohesion as their perceived need for group defense disappeared. The riddle is why do so many American Jews cling to a defensive posture in the face of the high degree of economic and political acceptance they enjoy in the larger community?

Tevye, the character created by Sholom Aleichem, said that "fritters in a dream are not fritters but a dream." The bottomline "fritter" for so many Jews is being well liked. If they are not well liked, the good fortune which they seem to enjoy at any given time could turn out to be a dream and be reversible. Much of modern history has given life to that apprehension—and some apparent credibility to the words of a nineteenth-century Russian Zionist, Lev Pinsker, that the Jews are "the chosen people . . . for universal hatred . . . Judeophobia . . . is hereditary and . . . incurable."[2] Anti-Semitism is the term invented by an unfriendly nineteenth-century German journalist to describe Judeophobia—negative feelings about and attitudes toward Jews. Their own subjective perception of anti-Semitism on the part of non-Jews with whom they come in contact—that is, their perception of being disliked—is the measure which many Jews apply to the reality of their status and is the source of their uneasiness even when the society seems objectively beneficent.

Yet just as many Jews, because of their historical experience, overestimate the ominousness of modern American anti-Semitism, many non-Jews, because of their different background, underestimate it. Modern anti-Semitism is difficult to grasp just because it is not the genetic phenomenon Pinsker thought it to be. Nor is it simply psychological, cultural, historical, or political in nature. One way to approach the phenomenon is by examining three kinds of highly interactive variables. The first one is the *target factor*. This refers to the cultural reservoir of anti-Jewish attitudes that exists at any given time. The *trigger factor* is usually a precipitating event or condition which can swell that reservoir of negative attitudes and transform its passive force into action. The *constraint factor* describes the social or political conditions which, if strong enough, repress the acting-out of those attitudes and indeed reduce their prevalence. All three variables have operated, in conjunction with one another, in modern European and American history, and still do. In America, however, they function in ways that reflect some of the exceptional qualities of the society.

The Target Factor

The majority of Americans hold some store of anti-Semitic beliefs, the heritage of a centuries-old Western cultural tradition which newcomers from Europe shared before they arrived. It was endemic in the teachings of the various Christian denominations as well as in the folk memory.

When the English and Scotch-Irish first came to colonial America, they brought with them the famous "Ballad of Sir Hugh," or "The Jew's Daughter." That popular ballad dated back to the ritual murder accusation brought in 1255 against the Jews of Lincoln, England, when a Christian boy named Hugh was found dead. The ballad memorialized the Jewish woman who presumably killed Hugh after enticing him into her home. There were such lyrical lines as "The Jewess, she did me wrong," and "She's laid him on a dressing table and sticked him like a swine."

About two dozen versions of the "Ballad of Sir Hugh" were sung up and down the Atlantic coast of early America. The ancient reservoir of anti-Semitic attitudes traveled easily across the ocean with the aid of such popular ditties, along with Shakespeare's Shylock and similar literary images, not to mention pertinent sections of the New Testament. A 1937 American edition of *Roget's Thesaurus* of synonyms lists "Jew" under the following categories: cunning, lender, rich, extortioner, heretic.[3]

Only in the last half century have modern survey techniques attempted to uniformly measure the currency of such stereotypical and negative images of Jews among the American people. The extent of those negative beliefs in the 1930s and 1940s is startling, as is the apparent drop-off of those attitudes in recent decades.

The basic anti-Jewish stereotype throughout modern history has centered around the Shylock image. In four opinion surveys taken in 1938 and 1939, 42 to 49 percent of the American people said that Jewish businessmen are less honest than others in their occupation. Three comprehensive polls in more recent years repeated the same questions, with improving results. In 1964, 28 percent said that Jews are less honest than others; in 1981, 17 percent; in 1992, 16 percent.[4] The same dramatic decline in negative stereotyping has been found in response to questions about whether Jews are more willing than others to use "shady practices," or are more "shrewd and tricky."

In 1937, 46 percent of those interviewed said they would vote for a presidential candidate if he happened to be Jewish; in 1983, 90 percent said they would.[5] In 1940, 43 percent said that if they were employers, it would make a difference to them if the job applicant were Jewish; by 1962, only 6 percent gave that response. In 1940, 25 percent said they would prefer not to live next to a Jewish neighbor; by 1962, just 3 percent answered that way.[6]

Conversely, Americans are much more likely than they probably ever have been to express favorable attitudes about Jews. In the 1930s, for example, fewer than two out of ten Americans said they admired Jews because of their family loyalty. About 80 percent said in 1981 that they appreciated Jews for that reason. In 1986, 82 percent described their feelings toward Jews as "favorable and warm," close to the 85 and 91 percent—most of them Protestants and Catholics—who felt equally positive about Protestants and Catholics.[7] When samples of Americans were asked between 1988 and 1991 how they felt about Catholics, Protestants, and Jews as measured on a "temperature scale" from 0 to 100, Jews fared almost as well as the other groups.[8]

The decline in these negative images has been generational. The 1992 survey completed by Marttila and Kiley for the Anti-Defamation League (ADL) found that while one fifth of those under age 39 scored high on an anti-Semitic index consisting of eleven proposed stereotypes, two fifths of those 65 or over scored high. Large age-related differences have often been tied to educational attainment, and indeed a high score on the anti-Semitic index was registered by 17 percent of those who had graduated from college, compared with 33 percent who had only a high school education or less.[9] As a group, the younger generation has had much more formal education than the older. This cohort has also been exposed to a different historical and cultural environment.

Responses to questions about Jews vary depending on whether respondents are asked if Jews have a certain trait, or are asked if a number of groups, including Jews, have that quality. For example, the proportion voicing the belief that Jews have "too much power," which has been a central image of conspiracy theories, varies depending on the way it is presented. In 1945, 58 percent of Americans believed that "the Jews have too much power in the U.S." In the 1992 ADL survey, 30 percent of the respondents said that Jews had "too much power." But the 1992 poll also found that 48 percent of respondents thought "whites in general" had too much power, a view to which 41 percent of the white respondents themselves agreed.[10] In four Roper polls taken during the 1980s, when Americans were asked to designate which groups on a given list they thought had too much power, a small fraction, 7 or 8 percent, picked the Jews.[11] Respondents turned out to be less disturbed about the Jews than about most of the others.

Some people have argued that the radical drop in anti-Semitic responses to survey questions since the 1940s reflects only changes in respondents' willingness to express negative attitudes as a result of greater sophistication about which responses may be more acceptable than others. The underlying negative attitudes, it is alleged, have not changed radically. But we would argue that even a shift in expression is significant, because it indicates a substantial change in the culture of anti-Semitism. The historical evidence suggests, independent of the surveys, that the expression of anti-Semitic attitudes soared in the 1930s, then declined sharply in the 1950s, and has slowly fallen further since.

The cultural reservoir of anti-Semitism is variable, not constant. It can be reduced or refreshed by the extent to which anti-Semitism is publicly acted out and expressed. Upward variations do not result from a spontaneous overflow of negative attitudes but are typically triggered by spasms in social and economic circumstances.

The Trigger Factor

The United States, though in many ways exceptionally hospitable to an ethnically diverse population, has not escaped the xenophobia and racism—directed against Jews, blacks, other racial minorities, people of foreign birth, and some religious groups—that have plagued other countries. Definable changes in objective circumstances have been associated with turns in the prevalence of such bigotry both here and abroad.[12]

For example, perhaps contrary to intuition, history teaches that periods of prosperity have sometimes accelerated prejudice toward Jews. At times in the past when American Jews have achieved a level of education and income that would qualify them to enter the elite environments in society—to move into well-to-do neighborhoods, to visit prestigious and expensive resorts, to send their children to the best schools and universities, to join high-status clubs, and, in general, to become bona fide members of the American upper-middle classes—they have encountered resistance from many who have already secured these lofty social positions. This behavior was particularly evident in the United States in the late nineteenth and early twentieth centuries. In tandem with the influx of millions of Jews from Eastern Europe around the turn of the century, tens of thousands of German Jews attained economically privileged positions. Many of the high-status non-Jews, especially the newly rich, sought to keep Jews out of their milieux, or at least to hold their numbers to a minimum, by way of restrictive quotas in neighborhoods, resort areas, professions, and universities. In order to be perceived as elite, it is necessary to have other groups defined as non-elite.

In 1877 the leading resort hotel in Saratoga Springs established a new policy by refusing service to the Jewish banker Joseph Seligman. It was such a startling turn of events at the time that newspapers around the country expressed shock. Soon, however, the practice became commonplace.[13]

While affluence can be the trigger factor for anti-Semitism against successful Jews, the more frightening surges of hostility have been associated with prevalent hardship among the general populace. The citizens of Thomasville, Georgia, were called to a special meeting in the courtyard square on August 30, 1862. Union troops were only 50 miles away, and the embargo imposed by the federal navy had caused serious shortages in goods and consequent high prices. The residents of the town were suffering—and desperate for remedy or revenge.

The federal navy was beyond their reach, so Colonel J. W. Seward offered a different target to that assembly. His resolution, unanimously adopted, expelled all Jews for "doing great mischief to our people by their repeated acts of oppression and deception." It gave them ten days to leave, and barred Jews from ever living in Thomasville again. At the time, there were three Jewish families residing in the community that were engaged in commercial pursuits, plus a few traveling Jewish peddlers. They all quickly removed themselves from Thomasville.

Clearly an underlying layer of prejudice made it easy to scapegoat the Thomasville Jews as a group. But that prejudice largely lay dormant until crisis struck and Seward gave it voice. This, and General Grant's similar action in Tennessee, foreshadowed the way in which the trigger factor was to operate at points in American history to increase the expression of anti-Semitism.[14]

Perhaps owing to the relatively small number of Jews in America before the Civil War, there were few signs of any widely organized or disabling anti-Semitism. The historian John Higham notes that only one notable instance of anti-Semitic discrimination in the ante-bellum period has been so far reported, and it "is the kind of exception that helps to prove the rule." The incident involved Uriah P. Levy, a naval officer who "was repeatedly court-martialled for his scrappiness" and openly resented as a "dammed Jew."[15]

The mass deprivations and dislocations of the Civil War triggered more expressions of bigotry against Catholics than Jews. A number of books were published accusing the Catholics of assassinating Abraham Lincoln. Even the nativist organizations that arose after the Civil War, such as the American Protective Association, bigoted by definition and intent, overwhelmingly concentrated on attacking the Irish and Italian Catholic immigrants rather than the Jews.

On the other hand, some anti-Semitic currents did surface during this period. In the North, Jewish cotton speculators and traders were stigmatized as helping the South economically. The most noteworthy action against them was Ulysses S. Grant's order barring Jewish peddlers from the area under his command.[16] Abraham Lincoln promptly countermanded Grant's edict. The president did not object to penalizing individuals whose actions were aiding the enemy, which, as he told Grant, presumably "was the object of your order, but . . . it is . . . [the] terms [which] proscribed an entire religious class" that were objectionable.

Toward the end of the nineteenth century, the expression of anti-Semitism began to surge in America, against the background of an increasing Jewish population but always in connection with a particular large-scale social crisis.[17] The catalytic conditions over those decades included the rapid growth of the American economy, a new wealthy class and a mass proletariat, an urban build-up, massive immigration, and periodic economic dislocations. Depressions—notable setbacks in general prosperity—marked at least half of the years between 1870 and 1910 and reached a climax in the Great Depression of the 1930s.

Anti-Semitism in the late nineteenth century was directed against the growing affluence of the German Jews at a time when the Jews numbered about 250,000. As of 1889, 62 percent of Jews were bankers, brokers, wholesalers, retailers, collectors, and agents. Another 17 percent were professionals.[18] In the post-Civil War period, a number of Jews of German origin developed the leading banking houses of the country. They, together with New England scions of the Puritans, dominated investment banking.[19] Although they most often socialized and married among themselves, these extraordinarily successful Jews were opposed to the principle of social separatism in the general American society. Some were among the founding members of the high-status social clubs formed in many cities immediately before and after the Civil War. But as the number of affluent Jews grew, wealthy non-Jews began to look for ways to deny them social access.

Status strains endemic in a rapidly expanding and changing society upset people at different levels of the social structure. Those descended from the old wealthy of the pre-Civil War era found their claims to superior status threatened by the newly wealthy, some of whom were Jews. The non-Jewish nouveaux riches, in turn, discovered that wealth alone was not sufficient to earn them admission to high society, and they sought to differentiate themselves from the Jews to increase their own chances of acceptance. As John Higham describes the phenomenon: "At every level so many successful people clamored for admission to more prestigious circles that social climbing ceased to be a simple and modest expectation ... In order to protect recently acquired gains from later comers, social climbers had to strive constantly to sharpen the loose, indistinct lines of status. With a defensiveness born of insecurity, they grasped at distinctions that were more than pecuniary, through an elaborate formalization of etiquette, the compilation of social registers, the acquisition of aristocratic European culture, and the cult of genealogy."[20]

At the turn of the twentieth century, as the frontier closed, political power shifted from the agrarian areas, with their traditional Protestant and Western European populations, to the new immigrant-heavy cities. The old elite—beleaguered farmers and apprehensive "native" workers—became chronically concerned about displacement from wealth, jobs, and power.

The agrarian protest movements, including the Populist Party, developed theories that an international bankers' conspiracy was oppressing farmers through usurious mortgage interest and foreclosures. In 1896 the Populist Party platform proclaimed that "the influence of European moneychangers has been more potent in shaping legislation than the voice of the American people."[21] In the same year, the Democratic Party, entering into coalition with the Populist Party, repeated this complaint in its platform, arguing that the conspiracy led to "the enrichment of the money-lending class at home and abroad."[22]

Neither the Populist nor the Democratic party made any formal anti-Semitic statements, but particularly at the edges of the Populist party, individuals began to make a connection between the bankers' conspiracy and the Jews. The ancient reservoir of Shylockean stereotypes began to be stirred. A pivotal figure in that process was Tom Watson of Georgia, who ran for president on the remnant Populist ticket in 1904 and 1908. He attacked the Catholic hierarchy as "the deadliest menace to our liberties and our civilization," but he also concluded that "the Roman priests and the opulent Jews are allies."[23]

Watson was instrumental in the trumped-up conviction of Leo Frank, a Georgia Jew accused of murdering a young non-Jewish girl,

Mary Phagen, and in the mob lynching of Frank after his sentence was commuted. Watson had charged that Frank was supported by a "gigantic conspiracy of big money." No direct link has been established between Watson and the formation of the second Ku Klux Klan, but he had called for "another Ku Klux Klan." And the several dozen men who gathered on Stone Mountain near Atlanta on Thanksgiving eve, 1915, to form the new Ku Klux Klan were all members of the Knights of Mary Phagen, an organization which Tom Watson had created to help assure Leo Frank's execution.[24]

The KKK grew in spectacular fashion in response to the social dislocations occasioned by the end of World War I. At its height, in the early 1920s, the organization had a membership of three million, possibly many more, and demonstrated considerable political strength in a number of states, where its candidates won several local and state elections. The membership varied across the country, often rural and small-town in base but sometimes working class and urban. In Indianapolis in 1923 a Central Labor Union resolution condemning the Klan passed by only four votes, and a number of unions opposed to the resolution promptly resigned.

The varied KKK backlash against fast-moving shifts in political and economic power used religious, ethnic, and racial bigotry to provide visible targets and invisible conspiracies. One weekly Klan newsletter suggested these program targets to its paid organizers: "Catholic office holders in New England, Catholic power in the Middle West, Jewish predominance in the large cities, [the issue of] 'white supremacy' in the South, the I.W.W. in the Northwest, the 'yellow peril' in California, dislike of Mexicans in Arizona and Texas."[25] But by the late twenties, the movement had declined sharply and was of little consequence.

By the 1930s, as the Great Depression produced mass discontent, the forces of bigotry began to concentrate more singly on Jews as targets.[26] Immigration laws had cut off the specter of emerging non-WASP population groups. The rural fight against urban political and economic build-up had been lost, and with that loss the strength of the traditional Protestant impulse had faded. As the stark fact of the crippling depression of the 1930s took over, the unemployment rate rose from 3 percent in 1929 to 26 percent in 1933, about 5,000 banks failed, farms were foreclosed by the tens of thousands, and middle-class savings disappeared. Nativism gave way to fascism as the core of extremist protest.

The bigotry of the thirties was not directed against Jews because they were "culturally offensive" or had "forgotten their place"—the offenses attributed to African Americans and Southern Europeans by the mainstream society. Bigotry took the form of accusations that Jews were exercising some hidden power to crush the common man. Because of the ancient stereotype and because some of them were prominent bankers, the Jews fit that image in a way that African Americans could not. This did not remove blacks as targets of hostility in the decade before World War II, but the professional bigots now cast them as pawns of the Jews, who, it was said, were using the colored races to help destroy white society. Also helping to destroy the society for the benefit of the Jews were the communists and other radicals in whose ranks East European Jews were seen as prominent. Hitler's conspiracy theory, borrowed from the ages and featuring the Jews, neatly fit the needs of the extremist groups in America seeking to specialize in bigotry.

Henry Ford, in his fear that politically radical responses to America's problems would lead to national disorder, flirted with Hitler in the 1930s and was instrumental in circulating millions of copies of *The Protocols of the Elders of Zion,* a fraudulent czarist document purporting to describe a global Jewish conspiracy. In response to the Depression, a midwest Catholic priest, Father Charles Coughlin, developed a large fascist-like movement which, obviously breaking from the American anti-Catholic tradition in bigotry, established the Jews as the exclusive ethnic target. According to one 1938 poll, four out of ten Catholics and two out of ten Protestants approved of Coughlin.[27]

Dozens of other, smaller bigoted movements prospered in this era, including nativist successor organizations with such names as the Silver Shirts, the Black Legion, and the Defenders of the Christian Faith. Active anti-Semitism, which had increased in America since the turn of the century, reached its height in the 1930s in explicit political attacks and open discrimination by the population at large. Based on survey evidence alone, it could be argued that close to half of the non-Jewish population in America harbored strong negative feelings toward Jews during the 1930s.[28]

As the issue of America's aid to European opponents of the Nazis became more important in the political arena, significant figures such as Charles Lindbergh and other leaders of America First, the major noninterventionist organization, suggested that the Jews were attempting to push America into the war on behalf of their persecuted co-religionists in Germany. Jews did tend to be interventionist on that account. The events of the 1930s—the rise of Nazism in Europe and the growing expression of anti-Jewish sentiments in the United States—sharply increased Jewish defensiveness, which in turn contributed to a renewed sense of Jewish identification and group cohesion. Leading communal organizations such as the American Jewish Committee, which had developed early in the century largely to help beleaguered Jews abroad, now became known as "defense" agencies, with a dominant domestic agenda. The defensive temper among Jews was once more refurbished by the recognition that no matter how good the situation has appeared, there has always been some volatile pool of anti-Jewish attitudes which could be triggered when the circumstances were favorable.

The Constraint Factors

Many anti-Semitic demagogues emerged who were anxious to connect the mass disaffections of the 1930s with the ample reservoir of negative Jewish stereotypes, and to lead the United States down the cataclysmic European path toward annihilation of the Jews. They were not successful, in large part because of constraint factors in American society which inhibited anti-Semitic attitudes from being translated into oppressive behavior, even under conditions of extreme social stress.

The construction of a typology, while always more metaphoric than exact, can help to illustrate how such inhibitions or constraints might operate. At any given time, some segment of the population seems to hold anti-Semitic beliefs but, for one reason or another, is constrained from anti-Semitic behavior. A much smaller population sector is hard-core, generally defined as having an irreconcilable hatred of Jews high on their agenda, along with an unconstrained desire to act out that hatred. About 20 percent of Americans embrace anti-Semitic beliefs, according to the 1992 Anti-Defamation League poll, but that in itself does not qualify them as hard-core.

The ADL survey found that a somewhat higher percentage of African Americans than whites expressed anti-Semitic views. But Spike Lee, the African American filmmaker, made this comment in 1994 about the media discussion of black anti-Semitism: "They're blowing the whole black-Jewish thing up. There is no conspiracy among African Americans against Jewish people. I'm sorry, I mean the average black person doesn't know who's Jewish. It's just another white person."[29] By the same token, most whites who retain some pattern of negative stereotypes about Jews either do not have hostility toward the Jews as a conscious part of their personal agenda, or at the least, are constrained from acting out that hostility by more pressing considerations.

By contrast, the hostility of the hard-core is both urgent and unconstrained, produced out of some variegated combination of emotional dysfunction, extreme alienation, and involvement in a subculture of ideological bigotry. It is impossible to say with any certainty how large the sector of hard-core anti-Semitic activists is at any given time, but there are some clues. Evidence from the Anti-Defamation League and law enforcement agencies from the early 1990s place membership in American anti-Semitic organizations such as the Ku Klux Klan and various neo-Nazi groups at about 25,000, or one tenth of one percent of the population. As measured by the number of people willing to express rabid attitudes toward Jews when given an opportunity to do so by pollsters, the percentage of the population who currently qualify as hard-core anti-Semites comes to about 5 percent. In recent years, only some 3 to 6 percent have expressed unrelentingly hostile sentiments such as: they are less likely to vote for a candidate with Jewish organizational support; they would prefer to support a known anti-Semite; they have good reason to dislike Jews; or, flatly, they are anti-Jewish.[30]

Today, the percentage of hard-core anti-Semitic activists in the population is about as small as it has ever been. But the potential for bigotry cannot be measured by the number of unconstrained activists at any given time. There is always a more numerous and more dangerous population lurking in the wings, vulnerable to becoming more hard-core; it is made up of the *indifferent,* those who are neither committed to, nor opposed to, anti-Semitic behavior.

In 1964 a University of California survey asked a national sample of Americans whether they would vote for a congressional candidate because his platform included an anti-Semitic plank, against him on that account, or whether the anti-Semitic plank would make no difference to them one way or the other. About 5 percent said they would vote for the candidate (down from almost a quarter of the American public in 1945 who said they would vote for a congressional candidate because he was an anti-Semite).[31] A little more than half said in 1964 that they would vote against him because of his anti-Semitism. But about a third said that the position of the candidate *would not make any difference to them.* Altogether, 40 percent said it would not make any difference, or that they did not know how they would vote under such circumstances.[32] Those who said they were opposed to a candidate because of his anti-Semitism tended to hold almost as many anti-Jewish beliefs as those who said they were indifferent to such anti-Semitic political behavior.

In the 1992 ADL survey, a somewhat different question was asked, preventing an exact comparison, but the import was the same: "Would knowing that a candidate for President was anti-Semitic make you vote against him, or wouldn't it necessarily affect your vote?" This question represents a measure of the readiness of respondents to act in an anti-Semitic manner. Only 1 percent indicated that they were more likely to vote for a presidential candidate if he were anti-Semitic, and another 3 percent said they were not sure. A majority, 55 percent, reported that the candidate's anti-Semitism *would have no effect* on their vote.

The study also included an attitudinal scale to measure the classic negative beliefs about Jews which professional anti-Semites have used and continue to use as the basis of their propaganda: Jews are dishonest, greedy, treacherous, and disproportionately powerful. In the 1992 ADL survey, of those who registered as *highly* anti-Semitic on the belief scale, two thirds said they were indifferent to the anti-Semitism of the candidate. This response indicates that, even among those who do not like Jews, there were considerations other than anti-Semitism that would shape their vote. Almost half (46 percent) of the *least* anti-Semitic on the belief scale gave the same response, indicating that even though they did not particularly dislike Jews, there were other factors that might impel them to vote for an anti-Semitic candidate.

These findings illustrate the frequent disjunction between belief and behavior. Further, they indicate that today's cultural reservoir of anti-Semitism does not necessarily generate serious anti-Semitic behavior; situational triggers are decisive. But the evidence also suggests that a significant number of people are vulnerable to those triggers for reasons that have little to do with whether they like or dislike Jews. These are the indifferents, individuals who are deterred from acting out anti-Semitic beliefs by some constraint unrelated to Jews.

Father Charles Coughlin's anti-Semitic movement during the 1930s—one of the largest in American history—exemplified the volatility of the indifferent population. His program, enunciated in weekly radio talks and in the newspaper *Social Justice,* was mainly addressed to the economic discontents of the 1930s Depression. The anti-Semitic aspects of his policies became increasingly explicit and unmistakable in the late 1930s as he founded the Christian Front, excluded Jews from his "Social Justice Councils," supported Hitler, held Jews responsible for the war, and republished *The Protocols of the Elders of Zion.* Millions followed his radio programs and newspapers. Over a quarter of a national sample said they supported his views.

As late as spring 1940, when America was close to war against Coughlin's heroes, Hitler and Mussolini, two out of ten Americans still approved of what he said. But blatant anti-Semitic attitudes were not significantly stronger among Coughlin's supporters than among those who rejected him. Most of those who supported Coughlin, anti-

Semitism and all, were basically indifferent to the Jews, not avid anti-Semites.[33] It was not their attitudes about Jews but other considerations which determined their support.

According to this construct, at any given moment in history, in addition to those who are unconstrained in their bigotry and those whose constraints against bigotry are relatively deep-seated and internalized, there are the indifferents, whose restraint is conditional and who can be swayed easily one way or another by circumstances. These populations are not fixed but fluctuate over time, with changing circumstances. And it turns out that constraints against bigoted behavior not only are important in themselves but are of primary importance in reducing the reservoir of prejudice.

"Constraint" is, of course, an umbrella term covering a wide variety of phenomena. A natural kind, driven by practical considerations, was apparent in early America, as the fate of Benjamin Sheftall and his accompanying band of refugee Jews demonstrated. They had virtually sneaked into Georgia under orders of immediate deportation. The absentee English Board of Trustees for the new colony had licensed people to raise money for their venture. Members of the Bevis Marks synagogue in London accepted such licenses and raised some funds. These English Jews had a hidden agenda. Just as one of the purposes of the colony for the British was to settle some of the Protestants fleeing to England from the European mainland, the English Jews wanted to send some of their co-religionist refugees from the mainland.

So, in January of 1733, when the *William and Sarah* set sail, 43 Jews "happened" to be aboard, more than half of the passenger complement. It was the third or fourth ship to leave for Georgia, and the largest single group of Jews to emigrate to the colonies. After seven months of difficult travel, including battering storms and at least two passenger deaths, the *William and Sarah* landed in Savannah.

The English Board of Trustees had not intended that outcome at all. When it was discovered that the ship had sailed with Jews aboard, the Trustees withdrew the fund-raising licenses from the London Jews, who courteously and discreetly apologized. The board then ordered the Georgia Governor James Edward Oglethorpe to expel the Jews. One trustee, Thomas Coram, warned that Georgia would "soon become a Jewish colony," and that Christian settlers in Georgia would "fall off and desert it as leaves from a tree in Autumn." Despite his colorful warning and the urgent instructions of the Board of Trustees, who also felt that the neighborhood was tipping, no effort was made by Oglethorpe or his Christian settlers to deport the Jews.

The level of anti-Jewish sentiment was at a relatively high point among Englishmen at the time. Neither Oglethorpe nor his other settlers had suddenly been cleansed of their anti-Semitic attitudes by setting foot in America. A few years later, when Benjamin Sheftall's son Mordechai and the Savannah Jewish community tried to buy ground for a Jewish cemetery, a number of residents opposed the idea, saying in effect, "There goes the neighborhood." They successfully argued that Christians would not "choose to buy or rent a house whose windows looked into a burial ground of any kind, particularly one belonging to a people who might be presumed, from prejudice of education, to have imbibed principles repugnant to those of our most holy religion."[34] Mordechai Sheftall finally donated a five-acre tract he owned elsewhere.

With those kinds of beliefs prevailing, why did not Oglethorpe and the other settlers respond more heartily to the request of the English Board of Trustees that they expel the interloping Jews? They were constrained from doing so by the fact that they had bigger fish to fry. They needed manpower; Oglethorpe had already initiated efforts to get some from the Caribbean. They required the talent of the Jews, including the services of the doctor who came with them. They preferred to use their own energies for more urgent purposes than exporting Jews. In other words, their traditional prejudices were outweighed by their other, more immediate needs. This "rule of countervailing needs" inhibited bigotry in Europe on some occasions, as when heads of state required the experience of Jewish financiers. But early America's unique conditions made that behaviorally restrained mode much more prevalent here. The effect of countervailing needs as a hedge against bigotry was built into the American marketplace imperative from the beginning.

The practical political institutions that have developed in America have applied their own rule of countervailing pressures. In the United States, third parties, whether radical or not, racist or not, have been limited by the fact that the country is effectively a winner-take-all system. Third-party presidential votes are wasted, and consequently many sympathizers with extremist politics usually wind up voting for the lesser evil of the two major parties.[35] And constraining extremism within the major parties is their need to unite a coalition of disparate elements behind their national or statewide nominees.

The formidable Ku Klux Klan of the 1920s, like the Progressives and Socialists, came apart for several reasons, but it was not insignificant that the core of their agenda was coopted by one of the major political parties. The Republican Party adopted the concerns about immigration trumpeted by the KKK, leading to the successful effort of 1924 to pass restrictive immigration laws. The party did so without the Klan's kind of comprehensive bigotry, which would have alienated the GOP's more moderate elements and some of its potential constituencies. Meanwhile, the KKK was robbed of a primary political agenda and purpose.

Another constraining factor has been the unprecedented social integration of ethnic groups in America. Immediately after the expulsion of all Jews from Thomasville, Georgia, a similar meeting was held in nearby Macon to complain of prices and scarcity resulting from the blockade. But the leaders of that session carefully explained that they were not charging local Jewish merchants with responsibility for the problem. Macon was larger than Thomasville and had long had a more substantial Jewish community. A whole company of volunteers in the Confederate army had been nicknamed "the Macon Jewish company." Not just the size but the integration of the Jews had some constraining effect in Macon, as it had in Savannah, where the Thomasville Jews fled. The Jewish community which Benjamin Sheftall and his companions had established in Savannah over a century earlier had become intertwined in the public life of that general community.

Proximity itself does not necessarily create such a beneficent effect. In certain circumstances, "getting to know you" may cause more rather than less intergroup conflict. Effective integration requires at least three things: (1) equal-status contact in the marketplace, (2) levels of common achievement and common culture partly reflective of common education, and (3) a degree of interdependence on the job or in the neighborhood. America has provided a singularly high level of such integrative components for the descendants of Jews and most other immigrant groups. Such integration not only tends to blur the classic stereotypes but describes the kinds of social networks among coworkers, neighbors, citizens in common cause, and students which further inhibit support for active anti-Semitism. At the same time, of course, this social integration increases intermarriage and assimilation.

So far, "constraint" may sound like a negative term, implying the need to constantly curb the kind of genetic human bent toward anti-Semitism that Lev Pinsker mistakenly announced over a century ago. Certainly people can be found whose steadfast refusal to engage in anti-Semitism derives from a strongly internalized moral imperative. However, objective conditions of the kind described above have often been influential in shaping such a moral imperative. And those objective American factors have been symbiotically intertwined with the explicit and positive national values relating to freedom, equality, and pluralism.

Many of those values have themselves been expressed in terms of constraint. In the resolution introducing the Bill of Rights, Congress referred to these amendments as "restrictive clauses." Although based on the kinds of positive values included in such documents as the Declaration of Independence and the Constitution's preamble, the amendments themselves prescribe freedoms "from" rather than freedoms "for." At first, they only spelled out "freedom from" the federal government. Much later, state and local governments were included.

The Bill of Rights is one of the most important sources of the values that make up the American national character. It has also helped turn the United States into the most litigious nation in the world, a characteristic already noted by Tocqueville in the 1830s. Americans learned to hire lawyers to petition the courts to protect them by restraining the actions of their governments and their fellow citizens. Ultimately, the Bill of Rights fostered institutions like the American Civil Liberties

Union, the Anti-Defamation League, and the National Association for the Advancement of Colored People, which have used the law to protect against the invasion of individual and group rights. Comparable organizations do not exist or are much smaller in other countries lacking constitutional protections.

From the 1950s on, with the further impact of new constituencies pressing on the political process, legislatures have adopted statutes prohibiting certain private parties from capriciously interfering with equality of opportunity. Thus, private employers, homeowners, landlords, and operators of public accommodations are restricted from discriminating against individuals because of their membership in religious, racial, ethnic, and other covered groups.

A common axiom for those who opposed such laws was that "you can't legislate morality." But of course societies do legislate morality. Their restrictions, both formal and informal, create conditions that shape behavior and establish standards of conduct, both of which affect attitudes.

The fact that the more highly educated tend to be markedly less prejudiced as measured by attitudinal scales has bearing on the internalization of constraints against bigotry. Two distinguished researchers, Gertrude Selznick and Stephen Steinberg, concluded that "the uneducated are cognitively and morally unenlightened because they have never been indoctrinated into the enlightened values of the larger society and in this sense are alienated from it ... The official culture contains the ideal norms that characterize our society in its public and secular spheres."[36] Children are typically socialized by the attitudes implicit in the behavior of their society. Without formal pronouncements, generations of southern children accepted the implications of institutionalized behavior toward blacks, such as their exclusion from all-white restaurants and restrooms. These patterns of behavior became explicit norms when southern states passed legislation to enforce them, and the ideology of racism was officially expounded by figures of authority. The forceful civil rights movement in the decades following World War II not only reversed many of these de facto patterns, thereby influencing attitudes, but also enunciated ideal norms that buttressed the changes, thereby becoming official constraints on racism.

It is true that the better educated are more likely to be well placed and have more of a stake in opposing lawlessness and extremism. Further, the better educated are more likely to understand what politically correct answers are expected of them when responding to surveys, although that understanding itself indicates a constraining change in the public culture of bigotry. Yet it would be a mistake, as Selznick and Steinberg suggest, to discount the socialization of young people in society's "ideal norms" to which they are exposed in the schools.

Recent Years: Changing Conditions

Beginning in the late 1940s, the tide of anti-Semitism seemed to reverse rapidly; the level of opposition to prejudice rose swiftly. Apart from the positive results signaled by attitudinal surveys, this conclusion is sustained by evidences of omission, such as the absence of any anti-Jewish focus in two extremist political movements whose general ideology resembled those associated with anti-Semitism in previous decades.

In 1950, as the Korean war was starting, U.S. Senator Joseph McCarthy announced at a meeting of a women's Republican club in Wheeling, West Virginia, that "I have here in my hand a list of two hundred and five that were known to the Secretary of State as being members of the Communist Party and who nevertheless are still working and shaping the policy of the State Department."[37] Without ever revealing his list, whose numbers constantly changed, McCarthy typically invoked "a great conspiracy . . . high in this Government . . . a conspiracy on a scale so immense as to dwarf any previous such venture in the history of man."[38]

McCarthy faded in 1953–1954 after he took on the Republican establishment—especially after he charged the U.S. Army with being soft on communism by allowing an army dentist to be promoted as part of a communist plot to infiltrate the armed services. Before he collapsed, however, McCarthy wielded considerable political power, intimidating politicians, intellectuals, universities, and the media. At one point in 1953, about half of the American people told pollsters they supported his beliefs. Americans were worried about the declining U.S. position in the world, especially after the Soviet Union built an atomic bomb—indeed, with the apparent help of some spies in America, a few of them notably Jewish. The country's inability to defeat China and North Korea added to their sense of foreboding. McCarthy appealed to populist, anti-establishment feelings through his attack on an Eastern elite which he said was soft on communism.[39]

McCarthy's political crusade, complete with conspiracy theory, was just the kind of phenomenon that in the 1920s and 1930s had been linked to anti-Semitism. His support base closely resembled that of Father Coughlin, but Jews were not among his targets. In fact, some of McCarthy's own principal aides were Jewish. Although large segments of the public had become particularly sensitive to the dangers of communist infiltration in elite governmental and educational institutions, relatively few tied actual communist activities, such as the Party or Soviet spy apparatus, to Jews. Opinion polls found very few respondents who said Jews constituted an important segment of Communist Party membership, or even identified as Jewish those with Jewish names who were accused of spying, such as the Rosenbergs, Greenglass, or Coplan.

Like McCarthy's anticommunist campaign in the 1950s, George Wallace's anti-integration movement in the 1960s also resembled prior campaigns that had attacked Jews. A segregationist governor from Alabama, Wallace was able to touch a nerve in those Americans who were concerned about the civil rights revolution and the rapid rise of black power. When a federal court ordered the University of Alabama to admit two black students for the first time, Governor Wallace personally stood at the university entrance to confront the federalized National Guard which was escorting the black students. Of course, he stepped aside after a short statement, but his image had been established as the leader of the fight for white supremacy.

In the populist mode, he, like McCarthy, also identified his opponents—those who pressed for black integration and power—with the

Eastern establishment and the intellectual elite. And, like Coughlin, he supported economic programs that appealed to the less privileged working-class and rural population. The South's most militant black leader, Julian Bond, once remarked that Wallace "confuses me because he's liberal on a great many questions." In the official platform of his American Independent Party, Wallace called for universal health coverage, a substantial increase in social security, a job-training program, stronger collective bargaining rights for organized labor, and other progressive initiatives. When Wallace ran for president as the party's candidate in 1968, the early pre-election surveys showed that four out of ten white Americans viewed him favorably.

McCarthy was notably careless of due process in his accusations; and, later, Wallace spoke of the need for a "police state" to guarantee law and order. Both openly criticized constitutional protections of minorities and argued, in good populist fashion, that majorities should have their way, regardless of what the law or the Constitution had to say. Many in the American Jewish community expressed great concern about both men because they so resembled the kind of demagogic political extremists who had targeted the Jews a few years before.

The fact was that neither McCarthy nor Wallace ever invoked anti-Semitism in their programs or their rhetoric—even though Jews figured prominently among the people who opposed their views, and opinion polls indicated that few Jews supported them. During the 1950s and 1960s, there were the usual splinter anti-Semitic groups, presumably involving the ever-present hard-core bigots. But the conditions that sustained McCarthy and Wallace did not produce any major anti-Semitic organizations or manifestations. Random cases of anti-Jewish vandalism, usually juvenile in origin, were reported, but there was no major anti-Semitic movement in the field and no important anti-Jewish manifestations, as had occurred in the 1920s and 1930s.

The answer to this conundrum is probably not to be found in the fact that America had just won a popular war against Hitler. While the war was on, opinion polls showed little or no decline in the massive level of anti-Jewish feeling that had grown up during the Depression.

One Jewish agency that had been involved during the war in a mass-propaganda campaign to lower the expression of anti-Semitism by linking it to Nazism, found that the targeted audience, though anti-Nazi, retained their relatively high level of expressed anti-Semitism.

Why did anti-Semitism decline so much while populist, anti-communist, and racist campaigns made such headway? The economy, frequently cited as the trigger for movements of bigotry, was one of unparalleled prosperity during the postwar period, and not just for the rich. In 1940 three out of ten Americans were in white-collar jobs; by 1970 the proportion was five out of ten. During those years, the most menial kinds of laboring jobs dropped from 21 percent to 7 percent.[40] For most, it seemed like a permanent sleighride upward; America was the only economic superpower in the world.

A disastrous economy, however, is not the only goad to bigotry, as we have seen. There are other possible mass disaffections, fears, and concerns about status deprivation around which dangerous movements can be built. By the same token, a good economy does not just represent the absence of a trigger factor. It also creates a broad population which has a strong stake in an orderly society and which is therefore constrained from extremist action.

As the work of Selznick and Steinberg suggests, a major factor in the decline of prejudice in recent years has been the increased educational level of Americans. In 1940, for those aged 25 to 29, the average number of years of school completed was ten for whites and seven for blacks and others. In 1970 it was thirteen for whites and twelve for blacks and others. In 1940 four out of ten who had entered the fifth grade graduated from high school. In 1970 eight out of ten did. In 1940 two out of ten who had entered the fifth grade went on to college. In 1970 the figure was five out of ten.[41]

In addition to education, another culturally constraining force was the rapidly increasing social integration of Jews in postwar residential and occupational spheres. This was preceded by mass involvement of Jewish youth with their non-Jewish peers in the military and government during World War II.

For all of these reasons, the marked decline in anti-Jewish hostility in the 1950s and 1960s did not provide much grist for the mill of Jewish defensiveness, at least not on the domestic scene. Then, in the late 1960s and into the 1970s, Jewish apprehension on the home front began to escalate as America was shaken by a massive surge of civil disorders related to the Vietnam War and other social ills. Fear of violence gripped the country. Students trashed universities, fought with the police, and followed the teachings of academics like Herbert Marcuse, who called for the tearing down of the government without suggesting credible alternatives. Underground groups sprang up, like the Weathermen and the Symbionese Liberation Army, whose political strategy included bombing buildings and kidnapping notables. Race riots spilled out of the depressed racial ghettoes.

The political disorder of the 1970s seemed to dissipate, but in its wake came a heightened public consciousness of declining standards of civility and social conduct. The media featured, and continues to emphasize, increases in violent crime, racial tension, and drug abuse. The media may exaggerate the extent to which these pathological phenomena are more pervasive than in the past, but there has been enough evidence of a growth in lawlessness and loss of constraint to create apprehension. Crime has risen to the top of most surveys about issues that worry the public. In this atmosphere, anti-Semitism has not pervaded the mainstream society as it did in the 1920s and 30s, but Jews have been faced with more acting-out by the fringe anti-Semitic groups in the 1980s and 1990s than in the 1950s and early 1960s.

Small racist and anti-Semitic groups, such as the Order and the Aryan Nations, which had always existed, have recently become more overt and violent. In 1984 Alan Berg, a Jew who attacked white supremacists on his radio program in Denver, was murdered by two leaders of the Order. Anti-Semitic vandalism also seems to be on the rise, partly as a result of better reporting methods. In 1993 the Anti-Defamation League reported 788 cases of vandalism and 1,079 cases of harassment, threat, or assault against Jewish individuals or institutions. Together, they represent the highest total of incidents in the fifteen-year history of these reports. Among those episodes were 31 crimes described as "serious," including three of attempted or accomplished arson, three of attempted or accomplished bombing, and 25 cemetery desecrations.

Many of these acts were committed by local juvenile gangs, some of them called "skinheads" in reference to their hairstyle. In Dallas, they called themselves Confederate Hammer Skins, and in Harrisburg, Pennsylvania, Up Starts. In 1993 the Anti-Defamation League estimated that there were 3,300 to 3,500 of such gang members around the country, with arsenals of knives, bats, chains, and steel-toed boots as well as firearms. According to the Anti-Defamation League, fewer of their criminal acts were directed against Jews than against African Americans, Hispanics, or homosexuals.[42]

Groups such as the Order and the Aryan Nations have remained small, when they did not disappear altogether, and for the most part must be considered part of the unconstrainable sector of hard-core anti-Semites. The official establishment uniformly abhors them, and the law enforcement agencies hunt them down whenever they engage in violent activity. The man who planned Berg's murder was himself killed while resisting federal agents. Others from these groups have been convicted and given long prison sentences for various offenses. Finally, the political influence of such groups has been limited, for the same reason that American diversity caused the political influence of the second KKK to fade. In the near future, about half of the American population will consist of people belonging to ethnic groups that these hard-core organizations would oppress and expel.

Blacks and Jews

From the 1970s to the 1990s, the level of anti-Semitic attitudes in this country did not increase, but the unrepressed activities of those who were already anti-Semitic, or willing to use anti-Semitism, became more public and more violent. Not surprisingly, this growing climate of lawlessness caught the attention of defensive Jews. Contributing more to Jewish insecurity, however, was the rise of anti-Semitic expression in quarters of the African American community.

Hey, Jew boy, with that yarmulke on your head
You pale-faced Jew boy—I wish you were dead;
I can see you Jew boy—no, you can't hide,
I got a scoop on you-yeh-you gonna die.[43]

In 1968 that poem, allegedly written by a fifteen-year-old black girl, was read and praised on a New York City radio station by a black teacher in the public school system. Addressed to the Jewish president of the teachers' union, it was one episode in a bitter confrontation between African American and Jewish school teachers and administrators. The blacks wanted an acceleration of promotions and power in the school system.

A month later, in January 1969, an exhibition on Harlem opened at the Metropolitan Museum of Art, and the preface to the official bulletin read in part: "Behind every hurdle that the Afro-American has yet to jump stands the Jew who has already cleared it . . . The lack of competition in this area allows the already exploited black to be further exploited by the Jews . . . Our contempt for the Jews makes us feel more completely American in sharing a national prejudice."[44]

That language was not uncommon in some black activist circles. American Jews were shocked because it suddenly seemed that after a couple of sanitized decades, mainstream anti-Semitism had come out of the closet.[45] The upset was all the greater because the organized black and Jewish communities had been close companions in the civil rights campaign and other causes.

Leonard Jeffries, a tenured professor at the City College of New York and chairman of its Black Studies Department, became a center of controversy in the 1990s with his constant public references to Jewish conspiracies against blacks. He accused Jews of having controlled the colonial slave trade (an obvious absurdity) and claimed the existence of a "conspiracy, planned and plotted and programmed out of Hollywood [by] people called Greenberg and Trigliani . . . Russian Jewry [who] had a particular control over the movies, and their financial partners, the Mafia, put together a financial system of destruction of Black people. It was by design, it was calculated."[46]

Even more disturbing to Jews has been Louis Farrakhan, the head of the Nation of Islam, sometimes known as the Black Muslims. This nationalist American religion (which is not accepted by the major branches of the mainstream Islamic religion) is built on the rejection of Christianity as an acceptable religion for African Americans because of its history as the religion of slaves. Farrakhan has developed a substantial African American following because of his espousal of positive self-help programs, but his rhetoric features fiery antiwhite sentiments, attacking such figures as the Pope but concentrating on the Jews. He has accused Jews of controlling the media and financial institutions that oppress African Americans. An editorial in his newspaper, *The Final Call,* stated that "evidence revealed incontrovertible realities of vile plots being hatched against Black people by clandestine organizations dominated by Jewish interests, including the South Africa Apartheid system, which was helped to be formed by Jewish doctors."[47]

In 1993 Khalid Abdul Muhammad, Farrakhan's "national assistant" in the Nation of Islam, speaking to Kean College students in New Jersey, brought matters to a new head. Repeating some of Farrakhan's anti-Semitic charges and adding a few rhetorical flourishes of his own, he accused the "hook-nosed, bagel-eating, lox-eating Jews . . . from the synagogue of Satan" of having monopolized the slave trade, raping black women and "sucking our blood in the black community."[48]

It seems to be all there once more: the demonology, the conspiracy theories, the false and prejudiced images, and—most crucially—the connection of anti-Semitism to a benign message that appeals to the distressed. Farrakhan inserts his anti-Semitism in a message which demands economic acceptance and self-sufficiency for blacks, a program that appeals to the needs of those who are essentially indifferent to the uses of anti-Semitism one way or another.

The Nation of Islam has mounted some highly publicized programs against crime and drugs, which 40 percent of a representative black sample surveyed by Yankelovich in 1994 chose as the main problems facing the country.[49] On the basis of these social messages, Farrakhan draws large black audiences, often markedly middle class and young, as he speaks in cities and on campuses around the country.

It was particularly shocking to Jews that some leading African American leaders and politicians either have refused to criticize the Black Muslim or have praised him. Before the Kean College affair, the moderate and nationally distinguished black leader Andrew Young, at one time the U.S. Ambassador to the United Nations, voiced disagreement with Farrakhan's anti-Semitism but said that he agreed with nine tenths of what Farrakhan said. He "is a legitimate player in the mainstream of black ideas," said Young, adding that Farrakhan's ideas should be viewed as "simply mechanisms for survival for people who have been locked out of the economy." That sentiment has been expressed again and again by some black leaders.[50]

The U.S. Senate did vote 97 to 0 to condemn Khalid Abdul Muhammad's unvarnished attacks on Jews in his Kean College speech. The Congressional Black Caucus, which had just entered into a pact with the Nation of Islam, and Jesse Jackson, who had formerly used Nation of Islam members as bodyguards, called on Farrakhan to take some action against Khalid. Farrakhan demoted his assistant and chastised him for his style, but affirmed the "truths" that Khalid had spoken. Among the "truths" Farrakhan then specifically affirmed was that 75 percent of the black slaves in the Old South had been owned by Jews, although a more accurate figure, according to an African American scholar, was closer to three tenths of one percent.[51] Nevertheless, the NAACP said that it was "satisfied" by Farrakhan's response to Khalid.

Several explanations have been put forward for the reluctance of some mainstream African American leaders to wholly renounce Farrakhan, at the same time that they have dissociated themselves from his anti-Semitism. Black leaders are reluctant to undermine the constructive social message and programs (working hard, helping oneself, fighting crime and drugs) that Farrakhan propounds. Black politicians, of course, take into account the size of his constituency. By way of explaining their silence, moderate black leaders have noted that highly placed white bigots are not vigorously denounced by those moderate white leaders who denounce African American bigotry. An example cited is Senator Hollings of South Carolina, who was generally excoriated—but not excommunicated—by white leaders when he referred to African diplomats in 1993 as "cannibals."

It has also been suggested that African Americans have a deep psychological grievance against Jews deriving from two sources: first, from the fact that blacks have not been able to advance in the way that the once disadvantaged Jews have done; and second, from their resentment of the emphasis by Jews on the extent to which they have suffered from bigotry. Some blacks point out that the Holocaust receives much attention, while the massive loss of African lives during the long passage of slaves to America and during their subsequent slavery is largely ignored. In short, exposing African Americans to *Schindler's List* has not necessarily been the way to make friends; it can be counterproductive because it presses many of them into a defensive mode.

Jews have had tragic experiences with political figures who, like Farrakhan, tie bigotry to constructive social messages. Due to those experiences, most Jews have come to believe that a public figure whose platform is, say, 90 percent constructive and only 10 percent bigoted must be 100 percent disowned. Largely because of the fulminations of such demagogues and the apparent reluctance of mainstream black leaders to totally disown them, recent polls reveal that Jews consider African Americans more anti-Semitic than other groups.[52]

Some survey evidence suggests that they are partially right in that perception. In 1992, 49 percent of blacks, compared with 23 percent of whites, registered in the "most" anti-Semitic category on a standard index. The percentage of blacks scoring as highly prejudiced against Jews dropped from 58 percent for those with no college to 39 percent for those who were college graduates, but the comparative decrease among the total population was a deeper 33 to 17 percent.[53]

The meaning of this evidence can be exaggerated. In the 1992 survey, 41 percent of blacks, as contrasted with 29 percent of whites, accepted the statement that Jews have too much power in America; but 83 percent of blacks agreed that whites in general have too much power. In the 1994 Yankelovich poll cited earlier, 80 percent of the African American respondents said that whites have too much power, and 28 percent felt that Jews have too much power, about the same proportion who believed that Catholics have too much power. Slightly more blacks than whites said they would vote against a presidential candidate who was anti-Semitic (almost all the rest, in both cases, were indifferent).[54]

If placed in context, the black population as a whole is not that much more significantly anti-Semitic than it is antiwhite. There have been few violent confrontations between blacks and Jews; the notable exception has been in the continuing tinderbox of Crown Heights, Brooklyn, where Hasidic Jews and blacks largely from Jamaica live in contiguous but segregated neighborhoods. It was there, in 1991, after a Jew killed a black youth in an automobile accident, that another Jew was slain by black youths. However, across the country, the physical confrontations between African Americans and Jews have been fewer than those between blacks and Asians and fewer even than between blacks and Arabs, some of whom now own stores in African American neighborhoods, just as Jews once did. Blacks and Jews are currently more likely to meet and interact in universities than in any other setting; and there, militant and often separatist ideologies secure support among African American students. Liberal Jewish students, who have traditionally sought to ally themselves with black campus groups, open themselves to rejection by the many African American militants who do not want to mingle with whites, liberal or not, Jewish or not.

Thus, in terms of both survey measurements and most patterns of behavior, the Jews would not seem to be the special target for the anger of the African American population as a whole. In naming blacks as one of the country's most threatening anti-Semitic groups, American Jews may be partly exhibiting a "lover-scorned" reaction. But more important, their defensiveness ignores the under-influential status of the black population, which is, for obvious reasons, the least likely American group to become an integral part of any large Nazi-like movement.

Nevertheless, the blatant anti-Semitism of some black intellectuals and leaders such as Jeffries and Farrakhan—and the failure of some mainstream African American leaders to thoroughly repudiate them— understandably pricks the Jewish sense of foreboding. Too familiar is the classic scapegoating syndrome, wrapped around a benign social message that is attractive to a disadvantaged and embittered—in this case, black—population. Concomitantly, so many in that population feel such little future investment in American society that countervailing restraint is weak or absent among them.

Furthermore, survey evidence aside, it is difficult for Jews to be certain that the anti-Semitic fulminations of such leaders as Farrakhan will not work, that eventually they may reach the consciousness of alienated African Americans. In the past, Jews became the surrogate symbol of oppressive social forces for white groups such as the Russian peasantry; in the future, among blacks, Jews could become a surrogate symbol for the evil white population. That classic use of anti-Semitism by deprived peoples—which was described as "the socialism of fools" by leftist intellectuals in czarist Russia and imperial Germany—is not so much a widespread reality among African Americans as it is a possibility that cannot be dismissed.[55]

Another more dangerous possible consequence of black anti-Semitism is that it may spread and be accepted or used by white sympathizers of the civil rights struggle, especially liberals and leftists. As among the university student members of the Narodnik ("Go to the People") movement in czarist Russia, affluent advocates of greater equality for the lower strata may feel that the more well-to-do Jews do not need protection, while the impoverished and uneducated, even if wrong in their anti-Semitism, require external support. Feelings such as these led wealthy Russian leftists, including a number of Jews, to defend or even engage in anti-Semitic attacks on the "rich Jews." There is in fact a direct link between anti-Semitism in czarist Russia and in the United States today: the distribution by the black anti-Semites of the czarist forgery, The Protocols of the Elders of Zion.

While the attacks of Farrakhan and others on the Jews are limited to African American academics and black-oriented media, whites can and do hear and read about them. Coming from a depressed group, these attacks may someday help legitimate anti-Semitism among segments of the white community. Thus far, there is little evidence that this is occurring, but the possibility should not be ignored. Nor to be dismissed is Farrakhan's role as a harbinger of separatism in American life, a subject to be discussed in Chapter 7. For these reasons, Farrakhan is seen by so many Jews as scary in portent, even if not yet currently dangerous.

Defensive Jews: A Sense of Foreboding

"Portent" is the key to the riddle posed earlier: How can defensive Jews believe that anti-Semitism is so serious in an America which makes them feel at home? As comfortable as they feel today, Jews retain a sense of foreboding about what can happen tomorrow.

In one 1981 regional study, the majority of Jews surveyed felt that "the neo-Nazi movement in America is today a major threat to the Jews." Only a small proportion of those agreed strongly that the anti-Semitic acts taking place in the country were being committed by organized groups. One out of ten who thought the neo-Nazis were a major threat gave as their primary reason that the neo-Nazis were actually becoming stronger in this country. But most felt that under certain circumstances such a group *could* become stronger.[56] In a 1990 survey, six of ten affiliated Jews said that anti-Semitism was growing in America. But only two or three out of ten thought anti-Semitism was increasing in those employment, governmental, or political spheres that fundamentally define serious anti-Semitism.[57] Even the belief that anti-Semitism was gaining in those spheres bore no relation to any objective evidence.

In one sense, this prevalent foreboding among Jews is an ingrained habit developed over the centuries, almost an intuitive fear of being too complacent about the future. As noted earlier, the scholar Simon Rawidowicz has written an essay called "Israel, the Ever-Dying People" which deals precisely with this Diaspora-old concern of Jewish generations with their fate.[58]

This intuitive reluctance to abandon foreboding is partly based on the hard evidence of history and partly on the constant refreshment of that history in tribal ritual and education. The story of Jewish defensiveness literally begins with the book of Exodus in the Bible, which records discrimination against Jews in Egypt. The Passover seder, repeated every year especially for the benefit of the children in attendance, reiterates this tale of persecution and escape. The story of Purim, another religious holiday heavily involving children, is about the persecution of the Jews in ancient Persia. Hanukkah—the holiday which occurs in seasonal tandem with Christmas, and during which children receive gifts for eight days—is again a commemoration of the Jews fighting powerful Gentile rulers who seek their destruction (this time Greeks and Romans). The first century of the Christian era is marked by the destruction of the temple and Jerusalem and the Bar Kochba revolt (involving the killing of tens of thousands of Jews by the Romans in the second century A.D.).

Medieval Jewish history is not commemorated, for the most part, by holidays. However, Jews learn that the Middle Ages were highlighted by discrimination, torture, and murder by Christian governments and mobs. The story of Spanish Jewry from the ninth century on includes great magnificence and success, but it ends with persecution and expulsion in 1492. The more recent history of European Jewry was marked by repeated episodes of severe persecution, particularly in Eastern Europe and czarist Russia.

The most important event that affects contemporary Jewry is, of course, the Holocaust. Most of the adult Jews now living were alive when millions of their fellows were murdered by the Nazis. To appreciate Jews' ever-present sense of foreboding today, one must remember that pre-Hitler Germany was regarded by Jews and non-Jews alike as the acme of culture, in which German Jews played a major role. Hence, the argument is made that American Jews are living in a fool's paradise if they believe that what happened in Germany could never happen here. Some Jews, no matter what their position at a given moment, still feel that the paradise in which they are living in America may come to an end, as it did for affluent Jews in Germany.

It is not just a preoccupation with the malignant past but a recognition of the reversibility of benign history which sears the consciousness of many Jews. The fact that the reservoir of anti-Semitic attitudes is at its lowest point in the Diaspora experience has symptomatic significance, but—as we have seen—it is a mutable fact, depending on the future state of trigger factors and, especially, on the strength of constraints. Even constitutional restrictions are not necessarily forever. They were made possible by particular conditions and can conceivably be eroded by contrary situations.

It is not paranoid—and may even be healthy—for a majority of Jews to harp on the possibility that anti-Semitism could conceivably become a serious problem in America's future. This is not yet the time for American Jewry to completely shuck off its sense of foreboding. Two out of ten Americans still profess some package of anti-Semitic beliefs. Jews have reason to believe that critical masses of people in America as well as in Europe—those essentially indifferent to the uses of anti-Semitism—are capable of "going along" with bigotry in order to "get along." The American experiment is not over, and a sense of general license seems to be growing in the land. Fear of crime and violence appears to be on the increase. A strong sense of communal foreboding, rather than the weight of current personal experience, produces defensive Jews and explains a sizable part of Jewish tribal cohesion.

A vignette of that somewhat tenuous connection was provided by a Jewish author, who in 1993 reported the effect that an anti-Semitic episode in Hardwick, Vermont, had on her. Anti-Semitism in Hardwick, she says, "has made me a Jew. This fall, I attended Yom Kippur services—my first time ever—at the nearest synagogue, 30 miles away. There, listening to prayers in a language I don't understand to a God I don't believe in, I felt at home in Vermont."[59]

All that foreboding is misplaced if it is based on some belief in an eternal malevolence toward Jews, or in the inevitability of enmity kicking in when triggered by adverse events. Less simplistic hopes—and fears—inhere in certain exceptional qualities of the American society, and these comprise a unique if still experimental body of constraints. Evidence even strongly suggests that there is a longevity rule: the longer and stronger the constraints, the better the prognosis. If anti-Semitic behavior is subdued long enough over generations, if the integration of Jews becomes thorough enough, and if the reservoir of anti-Semitic attitudes consequently recedes far enough, then anti-Semitism could atrophy.

Some cynics might reply with the old Yiddish saw that "if my grandmother had wheels, she'd be a Cadillac." But to recognize that the end of Judeophobia as a cultural phenomenon is at least within the realm of possibility is to understand the nature of anti-Semitism. American society has drawn the outlines of that possibility—just as it has suggested that such a possibility carries with it hazards to group solidarity and identity.

America today remains the unprecedentedly safe and hospitable environment for Jews that it has been, particularly since the end of World War II. Perhaps most indicative of the widespread acceptance of Jews in contemporary America is the appointment by President Clinton of Jews to fill his first vacancies on the Supreme Court. Ruth Bader Ginsburg and Stephen Breyer are both identified Jews. Bill Clinton is as sensitive to public opinion and to the factors that may affect his chances for re-election as any person to occupy the White House. Presumably, he considered the possibility that these appointments might impact negatively on significant sections of the electorate and decided they would not. His estimations appear to have been accurate as indicated by the remarkable absence of any media coverage of Breyer's religious background. It was a non-event that Clinton appointed two Jews. This was not true of their earliest co-religionist predecessors on the Court—Brandeis, Cardozo, and Frankfurter.

The unique structure of constraints in America remains strong. To the extent those conditions persevere, the sense of foreboding will certainly lighten. And as a consequence, the large sector of American Jews who are primarily "defensive" in their group identity will tend to melt away, to leave the community.[60]

That prophecy is largely based on what is happening within American society itself. A significant factor is missing, however: the new state of Israel. Israel has been a potent factor in maintaining the defensive American Jew; but it has also been a strong if complex factor in shaping American Jewish identity and solidarity on other grounds.

~ 5 ~

Israel, the X-Factor

Most American Jews say that "if Israel were destroyed, I would feel as if I had suffered one of the greatest personal tragedies of my life."[1] But such feelings of bereavement differ considerably in nature and intensity. Israel has a variety of possible meanings for American Jews: a religious prophecy that has been fulfilled; a homeland to which Diaspora Jews can return; a political refuge for persecuted Jews. Israel, as a source of inspiration and culture, has clearly enriched American Jewish identity and revitalized American Jewish life.

But Israel has another set of possible meanings, with political and personal implications that are, to many American Jews, more immediate and tangible: it is a familial land inhabited by relatives who must be protected against deadly enmity; it is a cause that could conceivably place a strain on relations between Jews and other Americans; it is a country whose vulnerability to attack reminds American Jews of their own vestigial sense of insecurity.

The American Jewish community has not been anxious to explore this diversity in the meaning of Israel for Jews. The subject is seen as delicate. Certain institutional and community-making needs—expressed in such slogans as "We Are One"—cause Jewish leaders to abhor these variations. The emergence of the state of Israel has not only affected the nature of American Jewish identity but has presented a radical test of American exceptionalism's capacity to tolerate ethnic activism in support of a foreign state— something it has been willing to do to a lesser degree for others, such as the Irish and Greeks.

Israel has become the X-factor in American Jewish existence, shaping tribal aspects of Jewish life in fundamental ways which have often been sentimentalized and caricatured, but not often fully fathomed, either by American or Israeli Jews.

Jewish Attitudes Before the State: The Benevolent Mode

Mordechai Manuel Noah, dressed in a Richard III costume, led a procession to St. Paul's Episcopal Church in Buffalo, New York, on September 15, 1825. Amid the ceremonial firing of cannon, he proclaimed, with these words, the re-establishment of a Jewish state on a wooded island in the Niagara River: "I revive, renew and re-establish the government of the Jewish nation under the auspices and protection of the Constitution and laws of the United States." At his side was Chief Red Jacket; Noah included Native Americans among those invited to take refuge in the new Jewish state, saying that the Indians were "in all probability, descendants of the lost ten tribes of Israel."

The Jewish island-state did not work out, but Noah was not a crank. A descendant of Dr. Samuel Nuñez, who had come to Savannah with Benjamin Sheftall, he was perhaps the most distinguished observant Jew on the American public scene during the years between the establishment of the Republic and the Civil War. He was variously prominent as a journalist, politician, author, and Jewish communal leader.

Despite his dramatic gesture in Buffalo, Noah shared the biblical aspiration for Jews to someday be restored to their homeland in Palestine. He made a prophetic speech in 1844 about the potential role America could play in the establishment of a Jewish state. "Where, I ask, can we commence this great work of regeneration with a better prospect of success than in a free country and a liberal government? Where can we plead the cause of independence for the children of Israel with greater confidence than in the cradle of American liberty? . . . The Jews are in a most favorable position to repossess themselves of the promised land, and organize a free and liberal government."[2]

Noah's speech referred to the international politics of the time and suggested that the political "restoration" of the Jews in Palestine would benefit the interests of America and the Christian West. A century later the United States was the first country to recognize the state of Israel, and soon thereafter became the new state's main ally and protector. Noah also twitted Christian evangelists for trying to convert Jews in America when they knew very well that the orthodox evangelical Christian goal was to convert Jews *after* they returned to the promised land.

Noah's words reflected the fact that a return to Jerusalem was a standard article of faith among early American Jews. But his speech, perhaps the most politically sophisticated on the subject to that date, presaged a durable theme for the future: while the American people should help establish Palestine as a homeland for the beleaguered Jews of the world, and while American Jews should stimulate that help, they had no need themselves to go to Palestine.

On its face this was a benevolent philanthropic theme, one of *noblesse oblige,* whether it had to do with political or financial help. In 1830 some American Jews formed an organization to help support Jews in Palestine. In 1854 one of America's most prominent Jewish citizens, Judah Touro—for whom a Liberty ship was named during World War II—left a modest portion of his estate ($60,000) "to ameliorate the condition of our unfortunate Jewish brethern [sic] in the Holy Land, and to secure to them the inestimable privilege of worshiping the Almighty according to our Religion, without molestation."[3] Touro's gesture was one of obligation; like Noah, he did not aspire to personal repatriation. Touro proudly noted in the opening paragraph of his will that it was written in the seventy-eighth year "of the Independence of the United States of America."

In fact, while early American Jews typically acknowledged a particular religious debt to the Jews of Palestine, they made philanthropic contributions and took benevolent political action on behalf of beleaguered Jews everywhere, not just Palestine. In 1840, when Syrian Jews were imprisoned and tortured on charges that they had killed Christians and drawn their blood for use in unleavened bread, American Jews gathered in protest. The purpose of the meeting was to urge the intervention of the American government, and the appeal was addressed to the "liberal and enlightened views in relation to matters of faith, which have distinguished our Government from its very inception."[4]

This pattern was repeated every time oppression of Jews abroad was reported. In 1870 American Jews asked Congress to intervene to stop the Rumanian pogroms. After the Kishinev pogrom in Russia in 1903, not only were protests held by fifty American Jewish communities, but a magnificent sum at that time—over a million dollars—was collected for the relief of the victims.

Relief for indigent Palestinian Jews remained a constant cause, but Noah's vision of some "repossession" of the promised land grew dimmer as American Jewish immigrants from Germany reformed their religion and established their at-homeness in America. Isaac Mayer Wise, a German rabbi who arrived in 1846, epitomized the sentiment that Palestine was fine for those Jews who had nowhere else to go but that it had no special meaning for American Jews. Wise, who became one of the dominant rabbinical figures in the last half of the nineteenth century, was noted for speaking plainly. "The idea of the Jews returning to Palestine is no part of our creed . . . This country is our Palestine, this city our Jerusalem, this house of God our Temple. American and European Jews would not immigrate to Palestine, not even if the Messiah himself, riding upon that identical ass upon which Abraham and Moses rode, would come to invite them."[5]

In 1869 a conclave of rabbis explicitly renounced the idea of a homeland in Palestine. When the Reform rabbis adopted the Pittsburgh Platform of 1885, they formally took the position that "we consider ourselves no longer a nation, but a religious community, and therefore expect neither a return to Palestine . . . nor the restoration of any of the laws concerning the Jewish state."[6]

As late as 1897, with the first Zionist Congress approaching in Basel, Rabbi Wise, then president of the Central Conference of American Rabbis, had further opportunity to comment on "the utopian idea of a Jewish state." "We are perfectly satisfied with our political and social position. It can make no difference to us in what form our fellow citizens worship God, or what particular spot of the earth's surface we occupy. We want freedom, equality, justice and equity to reign and govern the community in which we live. This we possess in such a fullness that no state whatever could improve on it. That new messianic movement over the ocean does not concern us at all."[7]

Such a trenchant anti-Zionist attitude was not held unanimously, even among Reform leaders. Some were not so sanguine that the American Jewish future was assured. In 1899 one professor at Reform's Hebrew Union College questioned "the roseate view taken of the future by those who enjoy at this moment comparative ease."[8] He pointed out that "our statesmen could not hitherto foretell the outbreak of anti-Semitism in Germany, the Dreyfus case and the anti-Jewish riots in France." An outbreak of anti-Semitism in France following a series of bank failures during the 1880s had culminated in the conviction of army captain Alfred Dreyfus for treason, a charge which was later officially repudiated. The conviction, however, was accompanied by anti-Semitic demonstrations in the streets. There had also been a wave of public anti-Semitism in Germany in the early 1890s, drawing its support largely from impoverished rural districts.

Sitting at the trial of Dreyfus was a Viennese news correspondent, Theodore Herzl, who then became convinced that charges of disloyalty against the Jews would disappear only when they had their own land. Herzl organized the First Zionist World Conference in 1897. A sector of the Eastern European immigrants to America brought with them an interest in Herzlean Zionism, which called for the in-gathering of all the world's Jews to a new political state in Palestine. But Zionism became a movement of some respectable consequence in America only after the involvement of Louis Brandeis, by then a wealthy influential Boston lawyer. Brandeis brought the benevolent American temper to the movement in this country. One Jewish leader later wrote that the Zionism of Brandeis and his followers "was almost entirely philanthropic in nature. It was no more than a desire to 'help others.' They did not feel that they needed Zionism for themselves in any way."[9]

The European and American visions of Zionism came to direct clash at the 1921 Zionist convention in Cleveland. As leader of the opposition to the Brandeis point of view, Chaim Weizmann, the German-born Englishman who was to become the first president of the state of Israel, said to the Americans, "I do not agree with the philosophy of your Zionism. We are different, absolutely different. There is no bridge between Washington and Pinsk."[10] European Zionism won out as the official ideology, but that did not affect the characteristic bent of most American Jews on the subject.

It was only when European Jews were drastically threatened in the 1930s that American Reform rabbis formally accepted the principle of political Zionism, holding that in "the rehabilitation of Palestine, the land hallowed by memories and hopes, we behold the promise of renewed life for many of our brethren. We affirm the obligation of all Jewry to aid in its upbuilding as a Jewish homeland . . . a haven of refuge for the oppressed."[11] But this sentiment was still in the benevolent mode. American Jews were to help create the "homeland" for the European refugees, not for themselves.

Jewish Attitudes After the State

Since the creation of the state of Israel, the affinity of American Jews for Israel has been expressed on a dramatic and even heroic scale, both financially and politically. Much of that expression has continued in the philanthropic mode. The sense of at-homeness in America for almost all American Jews grew even stronger during the same period. Yet it is clear that Jewish support for Israel has represented something more than making a contribution to the local charity.

Following World War I, Palestine became a British mandate, although England carved an Arab kingdom, Jordan, out of the largest part of that territory in 1922 and established its independence in 1946. In 1947 the United Nations General Assembly voted to partition the remaining Palestinian territory into two states, one Jewish and one Arab. The Zionist authorities in Palestine accepted the partition and declared Israel's statehood on May 14, 1948. Rejecting the United Nations action, six Arab states—Egypt, Syria, Jordan, Saudi Arabia, Lebanon, and Iraq—sent armies to invade the new state the next day, on May 15, but were quickly repelled by Israeli forces. Owing to land seizures by Israel, Jordan, and Egypt during the hostilities, an Arab state was not established in Palestine.

The Jews of Baltimore, polled by the American Jewish Committee in 1948, were almost unanimous in their enthusiasm for the new state of Israel. Most of them, however, saw it primarily as giving "displaced persons a chance to live and rehabilitate themselves." One interviewee explained that such displaced Jews "should have a little place to call their own."[12] The majority did not see Israel as central to their own personal Jewish identity.

Most American Jews viewed the state as firmly in place and, because the War of Independence against the Arabs had been fought successfully by a ragtag Jewish force, tended to dismiss the hostility of what they stereotypically perceived as an incompetent Arab world. The rest of the Western world, having just smashed Hitler, seemed rather well disposed toward Israel as a refuge for Jewish survivors. Some funds were needed to get Israel going, but otherwise Israel's existence and future were taken for granted by most American Jews, who, along with everyone else, were fully engaged in "making it" in a benign postwar America.

American Jewry was jolted out of this complacency by the 1967 Six-Day War against Egypt, Syria, and Jordan. Israel was vulnerable after all. It could be threatened by an increasingly formidable Arab world. From all over America came reports of a dramatic transformation of the Jewish community.

San Francisco had been at the center of an anti-Zionist movement known as the Council for Judaism. One of its staunch supporters, a leading merchant, said after the Six-Day War that it had "touched a nerve I didn't realize I had." He became a strong supporter of the state of Israel. The Council for Judaism faded away.

San Francisco was also national headquarters for the body of counter-cultural youth known as the "flower children" who flocked to the Haight-Ashbury section of the city in 1967. Among them were a large number of Jewish youth who, like many of their peers, had made a point of cutting their emotional ties to families and traditions. On the morning after the war broke out, its results still undetermined, a delegation of Jewish flower children made their way to the downtown offices of a Jewish agency that previously they had considered part of the despised "establishment." They wanted to use the mimeograph machine to print a leaflet in support of Israel to be distributed in the Haight-Ashbury district. These youth also had discovered "nerves" they never knew they had.

All those suddenly discovered feelings had nothing to do with Zionist ideology. A relatively small sector of American Jewry clung to the secular Zionist tradition of their East European immigrant ancestors. There was a segment of religious Zionists, although some Orthodox groups rejected the political concept of Zionism. For the most part, American Jews were not proper ideological Zionists of any kind, but pro-Israel out of newly discovered tribal defensive concerns for the Jewish state.

That still essentially benevolent attitude was initially intensified at the time of the 1967 war by a surge of fear for the survival of the new state, refuge for the remnant of Hitler's victims. But it coincided with the Holocaust's belated emergence into world consciousness. The term "Holocaust" had not been in evidence before the 1960s; the public mind had seemed unable, unwilling to grapple with the ineffable horror of the death camps. Suddenly, a searing literature of the Holocaust began to appear. The Six-Day War raised in American Jewish minds the fear of another Holocaust, this time for Israelis.

Certainly some element of guilt was mixed with the fear. Part of it may have reflected a sense that American Jews had not done enough to prevent the horror. Revived were memories of America's denying entry to many Jewish refugees before the war, and refusing to bomb the railways to the death camps during the conflict. The culpability of American Jews was often exaggerated—American Jews had been more powerless than careless—but some sense of guilt prevailed, even if it was only guilt at having comfortably survived.

Impelled by fear or guilt, a defensive circling of wagons was perceived as necessary for the protection of the remnant of the European Jews in Israel. A tribal context was scarcely surprising since so many of those murdered by Hitler were literally related in some way to many American Jews. But it would be foolish to believe that the concern of American Jews about Israel's fate is not also directly related to a sense of foreboding about themselves. The removal of Israel from the landscape would again signal a prevalent indifference to the fate of Jews in general, and this fear explains a large part of the defensiveness of American Jews relative to Israel.

The American Government and Israel

The defensiveness of American Jews about Israel has been profoundly heightened by the recognition, especially after 1967, that Israel's survival substantially depends on the support of the American government and public.

In early America, non-Jews in positions of political influence had expressed some passing interest in the idea of a Jewish nation, mainly drawing on America's biblical tradition. John Adams said in 1818 that "I really wish the Jews again in Judea, an independent nation."[13] Various Christian evangelists took up the cause, notably William Eugene Blackstone, whose book, *Jesus Is Coming,* sold over a million copies. In 1891, five years before the modern Zionist movement was established, Blackstone acquired the signatures of over 400 prominent Americans, including John D. Rockefeller, J. Pierpont Morgan, and the chief justice of the Supreme Court, on a letter to President Benjamin Harrison, asking his support for a Jewish Palestine. But none of these recurring and essentially Christian sentiments resulted in any political action, primarily because American Jewry was not yet on board. The American consul in Jerusalem responded to the Blackstone petition that "1. Palestine is not ready for the Jews. 2. The Jews are not ready for Palestine."[14]

The question of a Jewish state only began to attain serious political stature in 1917, when President Woodrow Wilson was asked by American Jews and others to support the British Balfour Declaration, which called for a Jewish national home in Palestine. England's foreign secretary, Arthur J. Balfour, had promulgated this declaration partly at the petition of Chaim Weizmann, who, as a German-Jewish chemist, had performed important wartime research. More importantly, however, the Declaration represented a move to ensure Palestine for Britain in the event of the collapse of the Ottoman Empire. The British also hoped that American Jews would influence the American government to support England in the war. Wilson struck the standard religious note when he said to a Jewish leader, "To think that I the son of the manse should be able to restore the Holy Land to its people."[15]

Once the creation of a Jewish state was placed on the serious political agenda, countervailing issues of American national interest kicked in. Wilson approved the Balfour Declaration, but did so secretly. There was opposition within his administration, based heavily on the desire not to alienate Turkey, even though Turkey was on the German side in the war.

The issue of a Jewish state emerged even more seriously toward the end of World War II, when the plight of European Jewry attracted international attention. Franklin Roosevelt's thinking on the subject was dominated by practical foreign policy considerations. Prominent among them was the desire not to alienate oil-rich Arab nations. Nor did he and his advisors wish to antagonize the British, who by this time opposed an increased Jewish presence in Palestine for the same Arab-related reasons. Roosevelt handled these political pressures in his typically labyrinthine manner. He authorized a statement by Jewish leaders that America would support a Jewish homeland, at the same time that he made sure that Congress did not pass a resolution supporting the objective. He made a campaign promise to work for a Jewish nation while simultaneously reassuring Arab leaders that he would stand by their concerns. David Niles, a special assistant to the president and a supporter of Jewish nationhood, said afterward that "there are serious doubts in my mind that Israel would have come into being if Roosevelt had lived."[16]

President Harry Truman was not an avid supporter of a Jewish state before that country actually came into existence in 1948. Most of the major figures in his State and Defense departments were opposed to its establishment. Their considerations were based on perceptions of national interest, mainly centering around Arab oil and concomitantly countering Soviet interest in that area. Those two national interests were to continue to heavily influence American foreign policy on the Middle East. As the Cold War congealed, President Dwight Eisenhower said of the Middle East that "there is no more strategically important area in the world," and he made his position explicit that Israel was not to be favored by the United States. The only reason for American military assistance was "for the common purpose of opposing communism."[17]

For some time after the flush of the 1948 War of Independence, American Jewry's defensive spirit with respect to Israel was not in broad evidence. To most American Jews, establishing a formal American–Israeli defense arrangement and securing American arms sales to Israel did not seem urgent. Even after Eisenhower forced the Israelis—along with the French and British—to withdraw from their successful military incursion into the Suez in 1956, it was Israel's military success against Egypt, rather than the diplomatic withdrawal, which seemed to impress most American Jews; the twice badly defeated Arabs were still not regarded as a threat.

But the third Arab attack on Israel in the Six-Day War of 1967, even though it was quickly and totally repelled, frightened American Jewry. The war did not just convince American Jews that there was a threat to Israel from Arab forces; it also highlighted Israel's dependence on the United States. The Jewish state was fast becoming a client of the United States. Since the effective British departure from the scene in 1956, the American government had been interested in establishing a regional collective security system in the area, akin to NATO in Europe, to offset Soviet adventurism in the Middle East. The State Department had assumed such an alliance would have to be based on friendly Arab regimes. The American foreign policy establishment had seen Israel as an impediment to such an arrangement. Yet Egypt, the largest Arab presence in the area, shifted away from the West after Gamel Abdel Nasser seized power and negotiated a Soviet arms deal in 1955. After the 1958 revolution in Iraq, the new leadership there ended collaboration with the West and turned to the Soviet Union. After a 1966 coup in Syria, the new regime strengthened its ties with, and eventually became the client of, the Soviet Union. There were mounting Russian arms deliveries to those three countries especially.

The signal failure of the Arab states in the Six-Day War then further convinced the American administration that Israel was a stable and reliable ally that the United States could ill afford to lose. American annual military aid to Israel rose from about 44 million dollars in 1963 to almost a billion in 1968, and subsequently escalated to a standard 2 billion.

Although Israel never receded as a prime focus of American support, subsequent state departments and administrations did not relinquish their interest in establishing friendly relations with Arab countries. That desire has led to some highly publicized tensions between the United States and Israel, not only around such issues as an American sale of advanced air equipment to Saudi Arabia but also, chronically, around ways to resolve the Israeli–Palestinian conflict. At the end of the Six-Day War, Israel had taken control of the West Bank, an area mainly peopled by Palestinian Arabs and formerly under the control of Jordan. A Palestinian Arab movement, organized around the goal of self-determination, called for this area between Israel and Jordan to become an independent Palestinian state. Some Israelis wanted to annex the West Bank, which, as Judea and Samaria, had been an essential part of the ancient Jewish kingdom. But the majority of Israelis were primarily concerned that relinquishing this area to the Arabs for a Palestinian homeland would cut Israel in two without guaranteeing a credible peace with the Palestinian Arabs, some of whom, in 1964, had organized the Palestine Liberation Organization with the expressed intention of destroying the state of Israel. Although, to say the least, the neighboring Arab states had not historically demonstrated interest in Palestinian self-determination, the issue became attractive to them after 1967. They then put the problem near the top of the agenda in negotiations with the United States, for which Palestinian self-determination did not always have the same practical import as it did for Israel.

The recognition by American Jews that Israel's security largely depended on the United States was strengthened by the massive and critical American arms lift to Israel when the Egyptian and Syrian armies, later joined by forces from nine other Arab nations, attacked with initial success in 1973. American Jews were strongly reminded of their own increased responsibility to prevent a Holocaust in the Middle East, not just as philanthropic private donors but as citizens of America. They were shaken by tensions that emerged between Israel and America, whose perceived national interests did not always coincide. Although President Nixon made the decision to send an emergency arms lift to Israel in 1973, earlier in his administration his secretary of state, Henry Kissinger, had proposed a plan for the West Bank that would have called for more severe concessions by Israel than its government thought prudent. The U.S. State Department, which offered its plan in order to let the Arab world know that America would not automatically reject its case, called Israel's attitude "evasive" and "negative." American Jewish organizations were troubled.

For the same purpose, President Ford announced a "reassessment" of American Middle East policy, which came to nothing. The Carter administration's overtures to the Palestinian Liberation Organization, a stated enemy of Israel, were especially disturbing to Israelis and to American Jews. Even President Reagan, considered to be a close friend of Israel, expressed some differences with the Jewish state, such as his insistence that certain sophisticated aircraft be sold to Saudi Arabia. Such periodic tensions never seriously undercut America's commitment to Israel's security, but they often left American Jews wondering how deep that commitment was.

Furthermore, in a kind of "foreboding" mode, the majority of American Jews were chronically concerned about the possible volatility of American public support for Israel. It declined precipitously during the Lebanese war of 1982, when, after eliminating some terrorist PLO forces in southern Lebanon, the Israeli armies proceeded to the outskirts of Beirut. President Reagan publicly protested this move, and American public support for Israel dropped 15 points, to 32 percent.

The defensive anxiety about American public opinion on Israel contained both elements of exaggeration and reality. The American public has always been relatively favorable to the Israelis and to the idea of a Jewish state. The biblical tradition was operative for some, but beyond that most Americans have felt culturally closer to Israelis than to Arabs. By a five to one ratio, Americans have said that Israelis are "more like Americans" than are Arabs.[18] It is not just that Israel is a more Western political state than those of the Arabs, but that the Israeli people are more Western. And that image has been strongly polished by favorable perceptions of Jews in this country. Israel, in a sense, is seen as an extension of American Jewry, that is, of a major force in our own society.

Between 1947 and 1949, before national interests in Middle East oil and in halting the spread of communism in that region of the world became articulated factors, six surveys showed a median of 33 percent of Americans favoring the Israelis, compared with 12 percent for the Arabs. Between 1969 and November 1973, after America's strategic interest in the Middle East had been proclaimed, another six polls showed a median of 45 percent of Americans supporting the Israelis, and 6 percent backing the Arabs. This kind of overwhelming public favor for Israel has persisted in almost all of 63 surveys asking that specific question since 1967.[19] In 1992, for example, a poll found that 51 percent of Americans said they favored Israel, while 17 percent were for the Arab nations.[20]

These statistics, however, do not imply an uncritical and constant level of support for Israel. The favorable margin has fallen when Israel and the American government have clashed, diluting the public perception that Israel was strategically important for America. In November 1947, when the United States approved the United Nations' plan for partition of Palestine to establish a Jewish state, 65 percent of the American people said they backed the proposal. Six months later, in April 1948, after the United States' delegation to the United Nations reversed their opinion and voiced opposition to the plan, popular support dropped to 24 percent.[21] When Israel was faulted by some administration officials in 1978 for an apparent breakdown in America-sponsored talks between Israel and Egypt, only 33 percent of the American public said they favored Israel, the second lowest such figure since the Six-Day War in 1967. And, as we have seen, when the

American government protested the 1982 massacre of Palestinians in the camps of Sabra and Shatilla by Lebanese forces that had been co-operating with the occupying Israeli forces, the backing of the American people for the Israelis over the Arab nations fell to 32 percent. A few months later, when the American government softened its position, the national surveys sprang back to their normal finding of overwhelming support for Israel.[22]

These pro-Israel attitudes do not measure the strength of the commitment, that is, the depth of the American public's willingness to back serious action on behalf of Israel. In eighteen surveys since 1967, a majority of Americans has consistently opposed sending American troops to war in the Middle East, even if the Arab nations should invade Israel.[23] Americans have been much more willing to send arms to help England, West Germany, and Mexico repel invasion than to help Israel.[24] Americans appear to like Israel and Israelis, certainly much more than they admire Arabs as a group. They undoubtedly feel that Israelis are "more like Americans" than are Mexicans. But, for reasons related to their sense of the national interest, Americans do not think it is as important to guarantee Israeli security as that of Mexico.

So, while America has clearly had a strongly favorable bias toward Israel, many American Jews are understandably nervous about how far America may go to save an imperiled Israel. On this issue, as we have seen, American public opinion can be heavily shaped by prevailing government opinion, which has on occasion been volatile, depending on perceptions of national interest.

In general, there can be no reasonable complaint about America's support of Israel. In 1994, as in past years, more American foreign financial aid went to Israel than to any other nation, a disparity that is overwhelming if calculated in per capita terms. Yet four out of ten American Jews surveyed in 1990 agreed with the statement that "few non-Jews" would come to the aid of Israel "when it comes to the crunch." And even after the peace negotiations between the Jewish state and its neighbors began in 1993, the proportion of American Jews who felt this way actually increased to five out of ten.[25]

Some of the concerns about Israel merge with insecurities about

Jewish status in America. Seven out of ten affiliated Jews believe that anti-Semitism in America is somehow tied to attitudes about Israel. More specifically, six out of ten agreed in 1993 that "the criticism of Israel that we hear derives mainly from anti-Semitism."[26] The belief of many American Jews that anti-Semitism motivates negative reactions to Israel is partly a Holocaust-related fear about what might happen to the Jewish population in Israel. Many strongly believe that the hardline Arab nations and Palestinians are bent on wiping out Israel and Israelis, an objective that many of Israel's enemies have voiced at one time or another. Immediately after the dramatic initiation of the peace process in 1993, 66 percent of American Jews surveyed felt that Israel's situation was "better" than it had been, only 5 percent believed that it was "worse." But almost half still agree that the goal of the Arabs is "the destruction of Israel," and only a third believe that the Palestine Liberation Organization will honor its agreements. This anxiety has led some Jews to look suspiciously at what they perceive as unfair media criticism of Israel, even though many American Jews have been publicly critical of Israeli foreign policy under the Likud and Labor administrations (the "doves" of Shamir and the "hawks" of Rabin).

The most cogent concern of Jewish Americans, however, tends to be less about anti-Semitism fostering anti-Israel feeling than about anti-Israel feeling causing anti-Semitism in America. A dozen surveys conducted since 1964 have demonstrated that anywhere from a quarter to a third of Americans believe that American Jews are more loyal to Israel than to America.[27] In 1991 and 1992 close to four out of ten Americans felt that if "there were a fundamental conflict between the national interest of Israel and that of the United States," most American Jews would probably back Israel. In both years, 37 percent said that American pro-Israel lobby groups have "too much influence" in shaping U.S. policy toward the Middle East. Not surprisingly, there is a strong relationship between negative answers on these two questions and a propensity to give anti-Semitic responses to questions that measure attitudes. However, many who score low on anti-Semitic attitudes also believe that the Jews' prime loyalty is to Israel.[28]

As long as the American government and public remain strongly supportive of Israel, these statistics are nothing more than interesting numbers in a survey; there has been no significant backlash against Jewish activity on behalf of Israel. The perceived possibility of a changing temper toward Israel, and the associated specter of the charge of "dual loyalty," however, has been a steady cause of uneasiness in the minds of many American Jews.

The charge of dual loyalty has been, after all, a classic item of anti-Semitic belief. Long before Israel ever existed, one of the chief articles of modern anti-Semitic feeling has been that the Jews would not be loyal to the nation which hosted them, a belief voiced by the Egyptian pharaoh Ramses II before the Exodus and by Josef Stalin after World War II. Stalin complained that Jews were "rootless cosmopolitans" who could not be trusted. One of the arguments in Edouard Drumont's book *La France Juive,* published in 1886, was that the allegiance of the Jews was only to themselves, that they would be perpetual aliens in France. Jewish treason was the point of the climactic Dreyfus affair a few years later in 1895. And the *Protocols of the Elders of Zion,* the concoction by czarist police which has remained a staple of propaganda for American as well as world anti-Semites, is focused around the Jewish international conspiracy and the inability of Jews to be loyal to any nation.

In that tradition, the Ku Klux Klan Wizard Hiram Wesley Evans said in 1923 that for Jews, "patriotism as the Anglo-Saxon feels it is impossible." The term "dual loyalty" or "divided loyalty" flourished in the jingoistic and nativist environments just before and after World War I and was one of the themes of the campaign to restrict immigration. Its use, however, has not been limited to the Jews. Theodore Roosevelt denounced divided loyalty as "moral treason" and attacked Americans of German descent who called themselves German Americans. Woodrow Wilson publicly repudiated the "hyphenate vote," particularly as it applied to Irish Americans.

American Jews, in fact, have not been notably subject to such attacks, except by the professional anti-Semites, who modernized their "international conspiracy" approach by associating Jews with communism.

However, even during the conspiracy-minded anti-Communist campaign of Joseph McCarthy after World War II, neither he nor other mainstream anticommunists singled out the Jews.

After American Jews began to engage in vigorous advocacy on behalf of the new state of Israel, they became sensitive to public attitudes deprecating their loyalty. The level of that uneasiness has been demonstrably raised by the occasional statements of some public figures. As recently as 1992 President George Bush complained bitterly that "thousands" of pro-Israel lobbyists, obviously mobilized by American Jewish organizations, had descended on Washington to oppose his position on certain loan guarantees for Israel. Jews saw this as a dual-loyalty reference, and the president eventually made an apology.

The prominent television and print journalist Patrick Buchanan, a former aide to Presidents Nixon and Reagan and later a candidate for the Republican nomination for president, created a furor among Jews in 1990 when, in opposing military action against Iraq, he said: "There are only two groups that are beating the drums for war in the Middle East—the Israeli defense industry and its amen corner in the United States . . . [war would result in Americans] humping up that bloody road to Baghdad . . . kids with names like McAllister, Murphy, Gonzales and Leroy Brown."[29]

Allusions to divided loyalty came from the political left as well as the political right. The novelist Gore Vidal, in a left-wing publication, referred to the Israelis as "a predatory people . . . busy stealing other people's land in the name of an alien theocracy," and accused some leading American Jewish supporters of Israel of being an "Israeli Fifth Column . . . [who] stay on among us, in order to make propaganda and raise money for Israel."[30]

There has been no perceptible backlash among the American public as a result of these occasional comments, but they have been noted by Jews. The foreboding of American Jews about Israel's national security is clearly related to their own insecurity about their status in America. The two phenomena feed each other.

Beyond Defensiveness: The Affinity for Israel

Whether impelled by a Holocaust-related fear for Israel's security, a defensive concern about Jewish status in America, or passionate feelings about Israel's intrinsic meaning for Jews and Judaism, profound institutional consequences for American Jewry have followed from the emergence of the state of Israel. The amount of money raised by the central Jewish community apparatus quadrupled between 1945 and 1948, to about 200 million dollars annually. The total dropped in ensuing years, although it picked up a bit at the time of the Sinai war of 1956. Falling again after that conflict, fundraising exploded after the 1967 Six-Day War, from about 136 million to 317 million. It is now well over a half billion dollars per year.

At least half of that money has been sent to Israel, more in "emergency" years. The fundraising enterprise has become a booming business. Combined fundraising agencies, the Federations, which were designed to solicit support for most Jewish agencies and causes, rapidly grew in stature, staff, and volunteer involvement after 1967. Although the chief source of this communal growth has been concern for Israel, the domestic Jewish educational and welfare agencies supported by the Federations benefitted greatly in the process. Most contributions to Jewish causes remain in the United States, and authorities on the subject estimate that non-Jewish institutions and groups receive even more from individual Jewish contributions than do Jewish causes, whether domestic or foreign.

In recent years, some American Jews and Israelis have suggested that Israel's growing economy is no longer dependent on American Jewish funds, and that collections can be allowed to decline. Counterconcerns have been expressed that, Israel's needs aside, any relaxation of fundraising would weaken a prime—perhaps *the* prime—source of communal ties among American Jews. One campaign chairman for State of Israel Bonds said that "the money we raise is nice. But the full support we give to Israel is what ties us together more." Not just fundraising but increasing political advocacy on behalf of Israel after the

1967 war also led to the creation of new Jewish institutions. Jews remain tied together in common enterprises around concern for Israel's survival and prosperity.

Still, the state of Israel is not the core of a new American Jewish identity for most American Jews. As the Jews of Baltimore and others had testified in 1948, they do not need Israel "for themselves in any way." Philanthropic defensiveness does not constitute that special quality which assures tribal durability.

After 1967 Israel did seem to gain a substantive meaning among American Jews that it did not possess before, a meaning associated with an emergent root-seeking mood in America generally. Many young Americans seemed to be seeking community during the 1960s, even to the point that the deracinated formed non-ethnic communes of their own.

Self-definition movements have waxed among the young throughout American history and have often been associated with growing affluence and education. Such a movement was evident in the early 1920s but was then interrupted by the Depression and the war. In the seminal Free Speech upheaval in 1964 in Berkeley, Mario Savio's keynote—"dismantle the machines"—expressed the revolt against anonymity and anomie, and reverberated throughout the nation's campuses. This was followed by the ethnic-is-beautiful motif initially promoted by the intense black activism that followed earlier civil rights successes. During one period in the late 1960s, many black students, in high schools as well as colleges, demanded the teaching of Swahili. They sometimes won their battle, but few then wanted to study Swahili. What they sought was a symbolic political victory through the official recognition of their African roots.

Much of that development turned out to be politically catalytic for those ethnic groups still deeply disadvantaged. The Black- Brown-Yellow-Is-Beautiful slogans of the time largely served important communalizing functions linked to the defensive politics of equality, although using the language of root-seeking. Other young Americans without such defensive political needs, but with an equally strong urge to find personal meaning, engaged in their own search for ethnic roots.

Many Jews were part of this movement, and the place turned to in search of roots was Israel.

In keeping with the temper of the sixties, Jews, like African Americans, looked for group behaviors of which they could be proud, and they found those admirable qualities in Israelis. The new profile of Israeli Jews was far removed from the ghetto-victim stereotype of the past. American Jews were proud of what the Israelis were doing, not just in defending themselves but in building a new country in the desert. It was this miraculous place, "the land," so full of identifiable Jewish history, which tens and tens of thousands of marveling American Jews began to visit.

They still did not move to Israel in more than trickling numbers, however, much to the dismay of most Israelis. In fact, Israelis emigrating to the United States, *yordim*, have far outnumbered American Jews moving to Israel. Instead, American Jewish life embodies a kind of "cultural Zionism," which recognizes Israel as a spiritual center, inspiring rather than assembling the Jews of the world. Some early Reform Zionists had formally called for just this sort of attitude, even drawing on the writing of Ahad Ha-am (Asher Ginzberg), who broke with Theodore Herzl's primary emphasis on a political refuge for persecuted Jews. Ahad Ha-am did not reject the need for such a refuge— he spent the last years of his life in Palestine—but he thought the main mission of Zionism was to make of Palestine "a center of [Jewish] learning and knowledge, of language and literature."[31]

One American follower of Ahad Ha-am wrote in 1907 that "the endeavor to bring about a Jewish renaissance in Palestine will, in turn, breathe a spirit into the dry bones of western Judaism, and it shall live."[32] Indeed, after 1967 it did seem that American Jewry was launched into some de facto version of that prophecy. A new kind of subculture began to pervade the American Jewish community, featuring Hebrew words, Israeli artifacts, and Middle Eastern food. Confirmation classes traveled to Israel as the climax to their Jewish education. Israeli writers, artists, and scholars were feted in America. The Jewish community seemed to be moving beyond the tribal obligations of defensiveness, to a more positive affinity based on spiritual and cultural similitude, to a common Jewish identity. "We are one," proclaimed the American Jewish Federations in raising funds for Israel. The overwhelming majority of American Jews tell pollsters that "caring about Israel is a very important part of my being Jewish."[33]

Still, there is a nagging question as to whether the relationship between Israel and American Jews—the vaunted unity and expression of "caring"—has really moved seriously or durably beyond the obligations of familial philanthropy or defense. There are signs that the common cultural and spiritual identity has in fact been eroding rather than growing for most Jews. The emotional attachment of many young American Jews to Israel seems to be thinning. Steven Cohen's national surveys of American Jews uses an index of "high," "moderate," or "low" attachment to Israel, based on responses to a number of questions. In 1989, only 34 percent of the Jews under forty registered as high on that scale, compared with 59 percent of those sixty and over.[34] Age aside, in a 1990 survey of Jews formally affiliated with nine middle-sized American Jewish communities, about 40 percent said they felt close to the Israeli people; about 80 percent felt closeness to American Jewry; and 75 percent reported feelings of closeness to the American people.[35]

These disparities in expressed affinity could be expected, given variations in experience, generated by differences in both age and place. In the 1990 National Jewish Population Study, four out of ten interviewees aged eighteen to thirty-nine proclaimed that they had no emotional attachment to Israel, as compared with one of ten aged sixty and over. To begin with, these two age cohorts had different experiential relationships with Israel's two watershed events: the birth of the state in 1948, and the nerve-touching Six-Day War of 1967. The youngest members of the older group were eighteen years old when Israel was born, and in their late thirties when the 1967 war broke out. The oldest of the younger cohort were born after Israel was founded, and were sixteen years old at the time of the 1967 war. The great emotional swells that come from living through historic events cannot quite be replaced by lectures in the classroom or synagogue.

More than that, Israel has been changing. When Israel was created, most Israelis were Ashkenazim, their roots in Europe. Over time, as a result of waves of immigration and differential birth rates, the majority of Israelis have become Sephardic and Oriental, of North African and West Asian origin. The Ashkenazi population of Israel, largely from Russia, Western Europe, and America in recent origin, is familiar—indeed, familial—to American Jews. Many saw Israel as a mirror of the European culture of their grandparents, minus Yiddish. The great majority of the Israeli Sephardim are not descended from those who came to America in the eighteenth and nineteenth centuries but rather are descended from Jews who for centuries had lived in Arab countries, plus Turkey, Bulgaria, Greece, and others. These new Israelis follow their own forms of traditional religious observance and are generally less educated and less touched by modernity than European Jews. The Ashkenazi population of Israel is Eurocentric, as are American Jews. In the 1980s about six out of ten of American Jews said they felt closer to Ashkenazi Jews than to Sephardic Jews, and only two out of ten replied they did not. The rest were unsure.[36]

The Israeli army, which almost all young people enter, was structured to provide a kind of universal educational experience, in addition to military training. In the 1960s, when the Sephardim were being brought en masse to Israel by its government, the army educational programs included some tell-tale Ashkenazi biases, such as introducing the inductees to European classical music. But the Sephardim inevitably made their own strong mark on Israeli culture, eventually playing a major role in electing the more nationalist Likud party to power in 1977.

Other aspects of daily life experience are sharply different for Israeli and American Jews. Compared with Israelis, the Americans live compartmentalized Jewish lives. The national history that Israeli children learn in the mainstream schools is Jewish history—the two are synonymous—and the land of that history lies recognizably around them. Biblical nameplaces are familiar sites in which they live or hike or picnic. But most of the American Jewish children who study Jewish history do so outside of their regular schools and in the context of learning foreign history. In Israel, all Jewish Holy Days, including the weekly Sabbath, are national holidays, even for the large number of Israeli Jews who consider themselves secular and eschew regular synagogue attendance. Daily Israeli newspapers and most Israeli periodicals cannot be read by the overwhelming majority of American Jews, relatively few of whom are fluent in modern Hebrew.

Is it any surprise that a cultural distance between Israeli and American Jews continues to grow? One Israeli recently put it this way. "In 1948 we Israelis and American Jews were brothers and sisters; our children are naturally only cousins."

Levels of Connection to Israel

We have no quantitative way to surgically disentangle defensive, benevolent feelings about Israel from a more substantive tribal affinity. In the early 1990s, when Israel was experiencing a wave of Palestinian terrorism known as the Intifada and Iraqi missiles were being fired into the country, Steven Cohen found that American Jewish attachment to Israel went up—especially for the younger Jews. About 47 percent of those under forty scored "high" in 1991, compared with 34 percent in 1989.[37] The cohesive tribalism inspired by defensive concerns as well as the more substantive communal or religious affinities are clearly intertwined and mutually nourishing.

When the *Los Angeles Times* asked a national sample of Jews in 1988 which of three qualities was most important to their Jewish identity, over five out of every ten American Jews in the sample, a majority, chose "equality," two said Israel, and two said "religion."[38] Similarly, when communally affiliated Jews were asked in another survey in 1990 about the issues that are "most important" in their evaluation of political candidates, two out of ten said Israel, while four named "social justice."[39] In various surveys over the years, two to three out of ten have indicated that they feel "very close" to Israel, while the same proportion have consistently reported that they feel "distant" from Israel. Half of the American Jewish population have usually chosen more moderate terms.[40] In the 1990 National Jewish Population Study, 10 percent reported being "extremely" attached to Israel, 20 percent said "very" attached, but 46 percent said they were "somewhat" attached, while 24 percent reported no attachment at all. In 1994 when the Israel Policy Forum reinterviewed a subset of respondents in the NJPS, only 30 percent responded affirmatively to the query, "Do you consider yourself a Zionist?" while 63 percent answered negatively.

About one third of American Jewish adults report having visited Israel. Such visits are sometimes used as an index of interest in Israel. But the Israeli Government Tourist Office found in 1981 that almost as many American Jews had been to Italy as to Israel. Since most Jews can presumably afford to travel to Israel on more than one occasion in their lives, it is worth noting that fewer than two out of ten American Jews have been there more than once.[41]

Those indicators of attachment suggest that emotional and cultural affinity to Israel is relatively high for about two to three out of ten American Jews. Interest in Israel is peripheral at best for a similar proportion at the other end of the scale. For half of American Jewry, Israel is not at the center of their Jewish identity, but they do not consider themselves "distant" from Israel. The large majority would consider it a personal tragedy if Israel were to disappear.

On the face of it, Israel's emergence has radically communalized American Jews, certainly for reasons of defensiveness and shared enterprise. Some observers, such as Charles Liebman, a leading Israeli political scientist of American origin, have deemphasized the importance of these motivations for affinity with Israel. On the basis of his survey of the attitudes of American religious and secular leaders toward the state of Israel, Liebman concluded that with the exception of Orthodox rabbis, Israel is only a small part of the self-identity of the American Jew. He suggested that Israel "is not a spiritual, cultural, or ideological center for American Jews."[42] Liebman's conclusion fairly well describes the "soft" American Jewish middle—"soft" not in political support of Israel but in personal affinity. His evaluation also emphasizes the eventual vulnerability to de-communalization of "the soft middle" under the benevolent assault of America's integrative force. But we believe he underestimates the intrinsic impact of Israel on the less traditional, less ideological Jews—an impact which, intermarriage apart, will continue to slow (but not halt) the dissolution of the Jewish community.

The evidence indicates a positive relationship between feelings for Israel and religious observance. While only a quarter of those American Jews who say they are not attached to Israel practice two of the three most observed rituals that take place in the home, about half of those somewhat attached to Israel, and about three quarters of those who are very or extremely attached, report observing these rituals.[43] The causative dimensions of this relationship are, of course, not clear. The more observant Jews have religious feelings for Israel to begin with, although its existence as a state may further activate those feelings for many of them. But just as the process of communalization often has its own effect on intensifying Jewish identity, so can it deepen affinity for Israel.

Furthermore, increasing affinity for Israel can enhance core religious feelings. In pointing out the importance of Israel even to the most non-Zionist of Diaspora Jews, Ben Halpern cites this acknowledgment by Jacob B. Agus, as a theorist "anxious to declare the Zionist movement defunct": "In any synthesis of national sentiments with religious values it is the latter which must be raised to the supreme level of importance . . . But when subordinated to higher considerations Jewish nationalism may continue to be a powerful creative force, serving the ends of Jewish religion as it did in the past by bringing to the aid of piety additional motivation, and by supplying foci of sentimental loyalty within the Jewish community."[44] After all, even for those who have been described as religious fellow-travelers, Jewish tribal history is inseparable from the cherished, magical, time-laden, religiously central image of Jerusalem, of Israel.

Conclusion

Nevertheless, the major impulses that have communalized most Jews around Israel have not stemmed from Zionist ideology or religious conviction but from tribal charity and defensiveness. The defensive posture of American Jews is sustained in part by anxiety about potential anti-Semitism in America and even more by concern about the security of Israel. The two reinforce each other and have frequently merged.

As long as Israel is perceived to be embattled, it will be an important factor binding the "soft middle" to the formal Jewish community, as it has been in the past. But that perception has been steadily diminishing, as has Israel's dependence on American Jewish charity. Funds raised by American Jews make an increasingly insignificant contribution to the growing Israeli economy. The amount extended to Israel by the American government has been very much larger than the sum of Jewish donations. But even these American government funds will become less significant, especially if Israel's defense needs decline.

With the demise of the Soviet Union—the major patron of Syria and hardline Palestinian Arabs—and after the convulsions of the Gulf War which divided the Arab world, the possibility for a successful peace process between Israel and some of its Arab neighbors has increased substantially. The 1993–95 negotiations among Israel, the Palestinians, and Jordan have put the peace process on a more solid track and augur the end of armed hostilities. The outbreak of a real peace will obviously reduce the part of American Jewish defensiveness that relates to Israel.

If the benevolent and defensive stance on behalf of Israel should languish for lack of a perceived and present need, and if nothing countervailing occurs, many of those in the soft middle will gradually slip into the ranks of those who are, at best, peripherally concerned about Israel. The Israel connection as a factor sustaining American Jewish identity will lose much of its force.

One aspect of Jewish political identity that does not seem to be losing force, however, is the tradition of liberalism within the community. Regardless of their socioeconomic status, most American Jews have tended to identify with the social democratic ideals of their parents or grandparents, albeit somewhat diluted. In the next chapter, we document and explain the sources of this phenomenon.

~ 6 ~

Still on the Left

A national gathering of political consultants was convened in early 1990 in San Francisco on the subject of improving campaign techniques. Among such major workshops as "Media Buying" and "Opposition Research" was one on "Raising Money in the Jewish Community." No other ethnic or religious group was so targeted.

While American Jews on average have become relatively affluent, they represent a very small portion of American wealth, and many of them, of course, are poor. The special interest of fundraisers reflects the fact that Jews contribute a much higher proportion of their income to political campaigns than non-Jews at comparable economic levels. Although figures are hard to come by, it is estimated that Jews—less than 3 percent of the population—contribute from a quarter to a third of all funds collected by major political campaigns.[1] That is just one expression of the extraordinary political involvement of American Jews, who also vote and join activist organizations at a much higher rate than any other group.

Jews were able to participate politically as voters, political leaders, and elected officials from the earliest days of the republic, despite the existence of laws to the contrary. Yet from the beginning their pattern of participation has differed from that of other Americans of similar socioeconomic status. They have consistently been on the liberal side with respect to issues and voting behavior. Both their disproportionate level of involvement and their opposition to conservative politics, as we shall see, have been in large part a defensive response, distinct from the effects of their religious values.

This commitment to liberalism creates a dilemma for the affluent Israel-attached Jewish community. On the domestic front, liberalism in modern times has called for substantial government intervention in the national economy, in the form of policies whose intention is to redistribute income. In terms of foreign policy, liberalism has entailed support for Third World peoples, including the Palestinians. A vocal minority of Jews, disproportionately Orthodox, has suggested that the typical liberal-left stance of the American Jewish population is a strategic mistake.

In this chapter we will ask why American Jews have remained consistently more liberal than their fellow citizens of similar socioeconomic status, and we will try to determine if recent trends are changing these historical patterns of political behavior in the Jewish community.

Political Involvement

After the First Continental Congress had called for a boycott of England in 1775, a British ship sailed into the port of Savannah and advertised ten hogsheads of "melasses" for sale. The local safety committee told the ship's captain that, because of the revolutionary boycott, he would have to return to Jamaica with his cargo. The unhappy captain reported to British authorities that when he went before the committee, he "saw sitting in the chair one Mordechai Sheftall of Savannah [and] Minis of Savannah, both of which persons profess the Jewish religion."[2]

The chairman of the safety committee for two years, Mordechai Sheftall was the son of Benjamin Sheftall, who had been smuggled to Savannah in 1733 with the complicity of a London synagogue committee. In that same year, Francis Salvador, the grandson of a member of that London synagogue committee, had emigrated to South Carolina, where he became a prominent landholder and a member of both the First and Second Provisional Congresses between 1773 and 1776, as well as a state legislator. Salvador was killed and scalped by pro-

British Cherokees in a Revolutionary battle, and is memorialized on a bronze marker in a Charleston city park with these words: "An Englishman, he cast his lot with America. True to his ancient faith, he gave his life for new hopes of human liberty and understanding."[3]

Mordechai Sheftall and Francis Salvador exemplify the deep involvement that American Jews have had in their country's government since the inception of the nation, a level of activity which was then impossible in Europe. The relatively small number of Jews present before the Civil War were encouraged to play a full role in the society. But at the same time, American Jews often hesitated to mix in partisan politics, because of an inherent dilemma they faced. They knew that activism would eventually mean calling the attention of political parties to the special issues that affected them as Jews; as citizens, they wanted to avoid the appearance of being a special-interest group that was not thoroughly American.

During a debate on their political role within the larger Jewish community in the 1850s, Rabbi Leeser wrote, "With politics . . . Jews have little concern, except to vote for those whom they individually may deem most fitting to administer the offices created for the public good. To do this, they require no national organization, nor to be told by their leaders how to proceed. In the Synagogue and congregational meetings, we want Jews; in public matters only American citizens."[4]

His point of view was not uncontested. Robert Lyon, editor of the first Anglo-Jewish weekly in New York, wrote in 1851 that "like all other denominations, they [should] cooperate so as to promote the general influence of that class of citizens called Jews."[5] Indeed, as early as 1859 an editor of the Portland *Oregonian* was blaming Jews for his failure to win a seat on the state legislature, saying that "they have leagued together . . . to control the ballot box . . . by a secret combination."[6]

This controversy over the proper political stance of Jews continued to varying degrees within the community until after World War II. But in spite of these concerns, Jews could not restrain their passion for politics, one which would magnify after World War I. They have seldom hesitated to raise a public clamor on behalf of beleaguered Jews abroad or about threats to Jewish status at home, as when Congress stipulated that each chaplain in the Union army "must be a regularly ordained minister of some Christian denomination"; American Jews— Abraham Lincoln and the Constitution on their side—vigorously and successfully petitioned for reversal.

While European Jews were still mired in ancient discriminations, many American Jews (most of whom were of British and German descent) were able to reach high places in the American military and political systems, including Congress. During the first quarter of the nineteenth century, Jews were elected governor of Georgia and mayor in Richmond and in Charleston; they were in the first classes in both West Point and Annapolis.[7] Mordecai Noah served at different times between 1813 and 1841 as U.S. Consul to Tunis, High Sheriff of New York, Surveyor of the Port of New York, Associate Judge of the New York Court of Sessions, and editor of six different New York news-papers. He also headed a number of Jewish communal organizations.[8] Two more Jews who, unlike Noah, were unaffiliated with any Jewish organization, David Yulee of Florida and Judah P. Benjamin of Louisiana, were elected to the U.S. Senate, the former in 1844 and the latter in 1854. Benjamin is better known as Confederate secretary of the treasury and Jefferson Davis's closest advisor during the Civil War.[9] There were at least four Jewish generals in the Union Army, and in 1860 the commander of the Mediterranean Fleet was Uriah Levy, who, as we have seen, was a graduate of the first class at the Naval Academy and was involved in the Jewish community.[10]

In the West as well as the East, Jews rose swiftly to public prominence. Elkan Heydenfeldt became chief justice of the California Supreme Court in 1852. One historian noted that "the first [Jew] did not show up in Portland, Oregon, until the 1850s, but by 1880, two had served as mayors, and the city council regularly held meetings in the store of Rosenblatt and Blaumer."[11] Jewish merchants, especially in the smaller cities, were well known and influential. They were frequently voted into local and state legislative office.

August Belmont, a highly assimilated Jewish banker who had once represented the Rothschilds, served as chairman of the Democratic

National Committee from 1860 to 1872. Oscar Straus, another eminent financier, made substantial contributions to political candidates and was the first Jew to serve in a presidential cabinet, as secretary of commerce. When Theodore Roosevelt offered Straus the job, he said he did so because of his high estimate of Straus, but also because "I want to show Russia and some other countries what we think of the Jews in this country."[12]

The East European Jews who immigrated at the turn of the twentieth century increased Jewish political involvement. Largely poor, more activist and radical than their predecessors, lacking high-level connections, and concentrated in a critical mass in the big cities, many of these immigrants jumped with open zest into the political arena, often as socialists, which they had been in Europe. However, it was President Franklin Roosevelt who began to move Jews in greater numbers onto the national scene. He not only built a larger political apparatus than any previous administration, but he looked for bright young minds to help him break new ground. He gave specific instructions for recruitment in New York, where generations of Jews had begun to spill into the legal and academic professions. "Dig me up fifteen or twenty youthful Abraham Lincolns from Manhattan and the Bronx to choose from," he told one of his aides. "They must know what life in a tenement means. They must have no social ambition."[13] Many of these younger Jews did join the Roosevelt administration, along with such highly influential notables as Felix Frankfurter, Henry Morgenthau Jr., Samuel Rosenbaum, and Benjamin Cohen.

In the years following World War II, the political activism of American Jews began to be reflected in the number of Jews elected to public office and in a Jewish community fully and openly organized for political action. By the end of the 1994 elections, there were 43 Jews in the U.S. Congress (ten of whom were in the Senate), making up about 8 percent of the Congress, a proportion almost four times higher than that of Jews in the population. This disproportion was a mark not just of the intense interest of Jews in politics but of the educational achievements that allowed them to pursue that interest, and of the decline of active anti-Semitism in the general population that elected them.

Jews' involvement in the political sphere has not been limited to their election to public office. Another measure of their status—and of the exceptional nature of American society—has been provided by governmental efforts on behalf of beleaguered Jewish co-religionists abroad. These have often been taken in the name of principles of American religious equality, and have demonstrated the responsiveness of the American government to politically active constituencies. Concern for the welfare of Jews in other parts of the world has been characteristic of Western Jewry since Roman times. What is particularly notable about the phenomenon in the past two centuries, especially in America, is the extent to which American Jews have been able to garner support from the larger political system, with its Christian majority. In 1840, for example, at the request of American Jews, the United States protested the persecution of Jews in Turkish-controlled Syria. The secretary of state charged the American minister to Turkey to do what he could to mitigate the oppression. His letter noted that the United States places "upon the same footing the worshipers of God, of every faith and form, acknowledging no distinction between the Mahomedan, the Jew and the Christian."[14]

The American government also frequently sought to intervene on behalf of the Jews of Rumania, demanding that both native and visiting American Jews be accorded equality before the law. Secretary of State Evarts wrote in 1879 to the American minister dealing with Romania, "As you are aware, this government has ever felt a deep interest in the welfare of the Hebrew race in foreign countries, and has viewed with abhorrence the wrongs to which they have at various periods been subjected by followers of other creeds in the East."[15]

In the period between the Civil War and World War I, protests against anti-Jewish policies and pogroms in czarist Russia were voiced frequently, especially from 1903 to 1906, when over three hundred pogroms occurred during those tumultuous revolutionary times. Many government protests stemmed from an 1832 commercial treaty between the United States and Russia which provided that local laws would apply to nationals of each power in the other country. However, when these provisions were used by the Russians to validate restrictions on American Jews, every administration from Garfield in 1881 on as well as every Congress complained about American Jews not having equal rights. Resolutions were passed by Congress calling for the abrogation of the treaty. In 1908 the platforms of both major parties denounced it, and it was canceled in 1911.[16]

The willingness of the American government to intervene on behalf of Jews abroad has not been unlimited, however. When American Jews applauded President Theodore Roosevelt in 1902 for responding to their request to protest against the Romanian government's treatment of Jews, Secretary of State Hay commented privately and with some amusement, "The Hebrews—poor dears—all over the country think we are bully." Hay's wry comment suggested the calculus of politics to which American Jews have been subject in democratic America. President Roosevelt's protest to Romania had cost him nothing—and drew little attention from Romania—while gaining him a measure of political support and possibly a measure of moral satisfaction.

A different result had ensued much earlier, in 1858, when American Jews rallied just as vigorously to protest the kidnapping and forced conversion to Catholicism of an Italian Jewish youngster, Edgardo Mortara, an action which the Vatican refused to reverse. But in this case the State Department did not respond to American Jewish pressure or to many supportive editorials in the public press. The failure may have reflected the weakness of President James Buchanan, but more importantly, Jewish pressure was countered by Catholic efforts, and the incumbent Democratic politicians apparently did not want to alienate a large group of supporters.[17]

In the years following World War II, the long debate about whether the organized Jewish community should maintain a low or high profile in the political arena ended. In the 1980s *Newsweek* magazine described one frankly Jewish lobby supporting Israel, the American Israel Public Affairs Committee, as having a "lock on Congress," while the *New York Times* headlined that this "pro-Israel group exerts quiet might as it rallies supporters in Congress."[18]

In fact, the political arena surrounding Israel offers a good test of Jewish political power, since this is the place where Jews have attempted to exert the most influence. Their strength turns out to be something short of *Newsweek*'s simple "lock on Congress." Generally speaking, the Jewish community has been able to influence American policy on Israel only to the extent that it has not made a substantial difference to what is otherwise strongly perceived as America's best foreign policy interests.

In his detailed study of American government actions on Israel, Steven Spiegel concludes that "the pro-Israel lobby . . . [does] not have a determined impact on U.S. Mideast Policy." At best, "friends of Israel have created a positive atmosphere toward Israel on Capitol Hill. [But] the fact remains that pro-Israeli statements by congressmen have not prevented disputes between every administration and the Israelis . . . When the pattern of decision-making within the executive branch is studied, it becomes clear that individual decisions are ordinarily made for reasons unrelated to domestic politics."[19]

Nevertheless, the marginal power of the Jewish groups has sometimes been determinative, especially with respect to congressional decisions on foreign aid. By voting more, contributing more, joining more, attending more, and writing more, the Jewish community has generally helped to shape the perception of America's national interest in the Middle East. The politicians have listened. The domestic political game played around the activity of the United States in the Middle East has had only one major player, the organized Jewish community. Although the pro-Arab forces gained strength in the wake of the 1973 oil price increases, they remained much weaker in political resources, particularly in terms of public opinion. Support for Israel, therefore, has not been a partisan political issue between the major parties. Even less controversial and uncontested since the 1950s have been the various domestic issues directly related to the first-class citizenship of Jews in this country, around which the Jewish community has been openly and vigorously organized.

The political influence of the Jews is linked to a number of factors, including heavy financial contributions, their disproportionate presence in opinion-making professions (such as journalism and academia), extraordinary levels of activism and voting, an extensive organization network, and, last but not least, sizable blocs of Jewish voters in key states.

In evaluating these power resources, it is useful to distinguish among expert power, reward power, and coercive power. The Jews, of course, have no direct coercive power. Their expert power, sometimes underestimated, comprises a disproportionate number of individual activists as well as agencies that provide advice, ideas, and volunteer manpower to candidates and officials. The reward power stems from political contributions and voting patterns.

The power of the organized Jewish community, to which approximately half of American Jews belong in one form or another, is enhanced beyond its numerical weight by its not being unified in a hierarchical structure. It consists of dozens of major national organizations and thousands of local associations whose ties with one another are voluntary and often tenuous. Together with the less involved majority of the Jewish populace at large, they form, particularly with respect to liberal and Israel-related issues, the kind of mediating political associations Tocqueville described as furnishing "the public assent which a number of individuals give to certain doctrines."

The Community and Its Political Values

The political flowering of American Jews, both as individuals and as an organized community, after World War II was never haphazard. An "agenda," a set of political dispositions, has characterized American Jewry throughout those years, independent of the socioeconomic position of the individuals who constitute the Jewish group.

It has long been noted that modern voters tend to move from Democratic to Republican ranks as they become more affluent, a presumed function of "pocketbook" voting. This trend has not happened among Jews. They have remained Democrats even when they have become well-to-do. Two different dimensions may be invoked to explain that unusual behavior: an internal set of tribal and religious values that emphasize "social liberalism," and a special defensive need.

Social liberalism, as the term is used today, denotes social compassion, an interest in the welfare of the disadvantaged; politically, it has come to mean the active intervention of the government on behalf of those values. Right after World War II, a poll of different religious groups' attitudes toward public policies guaranteeing economic security for the underprivileged found a strong correlation between each denomination's support of government guarantees of economic security and that group's own relative lack of economic security—except among the Jews, who were the most affluent and, in seeming conflict with their own self-interest, the most liberal. Thus, 51 percent of the Baptists were manual workers, and 51 percent supported guaranteed economic security. About 55 percent of Catholics worked with their hands, and 58 percent of Catholics endorsed such guarantees. The other Christian denominations followed the same pattern. Among the Jews, however, 56 percent backed government guarantees of economic security—more than among any other religious groups—although a significantly smaller proportion, 27 percent, were blue-collar workers, less than in any other one.[20]

That pattern has persisted. In CBS's 1984 election exit poll, for example, 60 percent of Jews said that government spending on the poor should be increased, as against 40 percent of the general population, although Jews reported a much higher income level than that of the general population and stood to gain the least from such programs, and to pay the most for them in higher taxes. Jews remain more consistently to the left on economic, political, and social issues than any other ethnoreligious group in the country. The only other one that approaches their level of liberalism is the African Americans. But while blacks are liberal on social welfare issues, they are not particularly liberal on government intervention to protect women's rights or the environment. Of all tribal groups surveyed, Jews are the most supportive of activist policies on behalf of the less fortunate, including maintenance or expansion of welfare programs, reliance on the state as an employer of last resort for the unemployed, wage and price controls in inflationary periods, and government regulations to remedy assorted ills for which business or other large organizations are held responsible. And overwhelmingly, they have taken the liberally correct position on such issues as abortion, gun control, and nuclear freeze proposals.[21]

In spite of their relative affluence, Steven Cohen reports that, as of

1988, "more Jews than whites or blacks endorse raising taxes as a way of cutting budget deficits" and oppose reductions in domestic spending.[22] Similarly, the results of the 1992 elections, as reported in many opinion and exit polls, confirm the generalizations that while Jews earn more than any ethnoreligious group for whom data exist (including Episcopalians), they are more liberal to left in their opinions than other white groups, and they vote like Hispanics. In November 1992, according to most exit polls, over 80 percent of Jews supported Clinton. Republican presidential voting among them has declined steadily since 1980, when Ronald Reagan, a staunch supporter of Israel, secured just above one third of their ballots. George Bush in 1992 was backed by only 10 percent. The only identifiable subset that is disproportionately conservative and Republican is the Orthodox, particularly the more fundamentalist and less affluent among them. But a majority of the Orthodox voted for Bill Clinton.[23]

Actually, the Jewish vote for Democratic and other liberal-party nominees has, since early in the twentieth century, gone up and down in the same directions as the vote of the general electorate, but it has always been much higher for Democratic and leftist third-party candidates than the general electorate.

Jews are also much more likely than non-Jews to support organizations that call on the government to guarantee noninterference by others with individuals' civil rights and privacy. Organizations such as the National Association for the Advancement of Colored People (NAACP), Planned Parenthood, the National Organization for Women (NOW), and the American Civil Liberties Union (ACLU) have all been able to count on active support from the Jewish community in this half-century.

As the nature of the groups makes plain, the term "liberal" carries two kinds of political meaning in current usage. The first, as we have seen, entails generosity or compassion (as in "a liberal contribution"), which today's liberals take to mean government intervention in the form of social welfare programs for the less fortunate. The second entails freedom, as in individual freedom from government intrusion and popular bigotry.

Jews have a stake in both meanings of liberalism. Long before America or the modern world, Jewish communitarian values were shaped by a tribal sense of responsibility for their co-religionists. These communitarian values, dating at least from medieval Europe, have been extended by contemporary Jews to the social welfare responsibilities of the society at large. And in most polls taken in recent years, twice as many Jews on the average describe themselves as liberals rather than conservatives, and about twice as many Jews call themselves liberals as do Americans generally. In May 1994 a survey conducted for the Israeli Policy Forum found that the pattern continues—55 percent placed themselves on the liberal side, compared with 27 percent on the conservative.

There has often been a tension among Jews between the two concepts of liberalism. Coming from a rich history of communitarian values, American Jews, as we have seen, favor government involvement on social welfare matters having to do with economic security, and they also support state intervention in favor of civil rights, gun control, and regulation of the environment. But also coming from a long history of individual initiative in the face of great political oppression, they oppose government interference that would itself abridge civil rights, such as antiabortion legislation and economic and educational quotas. Quotas in particular come into conflict with the value Jews place on the operation of a meritocratic marketplace above the level of the severely socioeconomically disadvantaged.

Religious and Cultural Values

Jewish religious values are often invoked to explain this liberal bent in both of its meanings. Lawrence H. Fuchs points to "non-asceticism"—an abiding concern with the quality of earthly life—as a value that particularly characterizes Jewish religious belief and presses Jews toward social compassion.[24] Another factor commonly cited is the religious principle of *tzedekah,* the obligation of the fortunate to help individuals and communities in difficulty.[25]

It is not easy to isolate the factors of tribal history from religion. While *tzedekah* is indeed a religious principle, the emphasis on *tzedekah* was strengthened among European Jews during the Middle Ages when it was literally a condition for survival, given that some communities were periodically experiencing severe persecution, while others were doing well. Conscience and norms obligated the prosperous, as individuals and groups, to give to the less fortunate.

Survey research indicates that secular intellectual achievement is linked to holding liberal values. (Those with postgraduate education are the most liberal and Democratic.) And among Jews, the religious emphasis on learning has been transmuted into a stress on secularized education. Shortly after World War I, in discussing "the intellectual pre-eminence of the Jews," Thorstein Veblen commented that not only do they contribute a "disproportionate number of leaders of modern science and scholarship," but they "count particularly among the vanguard, the pioneers, the uneasy guild of pathfinders and iconoclasts, in science, scholarship, and institutional change and growth."[26] Creative intellectuality, as Veblen and many others have recognized, includes an emphasis on innovation, on newness, and on rejection of the old, of the traditional.[27]

Creativity in the humanities and sciences is also linked to universalism in that the value of knowledge to the intellectual is independent of the background of its exponents. Secularized Jews, in their desire to be treated like others and to become part of the larger society, support a universalistic ethic, which emphasizes equal treatment for groups and individuals. Intellectuality and universalism predispose American Jews to liberalism. Thus Charles Liebman notes: "The basic [Western] Jewish commitment . . . is to Enlightenment, the optimistic faith that the application of human intellect can create a constantly progressing universal cosmopolitan society. Internationalism, libertarianism, and welfarism are consequences of this basic commitment."[28] These values predominate in the liberal arts in leading academic institutions, the very places where the large majority of American Jewish youth spend four to six years on the threshold of their adult lives.

Jewish tribal values, religious and cultural in source, are certainly compatible with, and can be seen as contributory to, liberalism, but their ability to determine Jewish political ideology is frequently exaggerated. The fact that the Orthodox and more devout tend to be significantly less liberal than other Jews reminds us that references to religious factors can be selective, and often follow rather than precede tribal social positions partly shaped by other, more secular considerations. Indeed, citation of the biblical prophets to support the centrality of political liberalism in Jewish life has often been emphasized by the more secular Jews—such as nonobserving socialists—as a means of moving *away* from religion and religious particularism.[29]

Moreover, the strongest emphasis on social liberalism in the Jewish community emerged only recently, about a century ago, aligned initially with the Protestant social gospel movement. It was then strengthened immeasurably by the arrival of many poor, radical, often nonobserving East European immigrants.

Defensive Needs

However significant the role of intrinsic tribal values, the defensive impulse has also played a major, sometimes dominant, role in the modern liberal political disposition of the Jews. Even the leftist political values imported from Eastern Europe were linked directly to a history of oppression, which in the minds of many Jews originated much more to the political right than to the left.

Helped by the Catholic vote, in 1848 an Orthodox rabbi, Dob Berush B. Isaac Meisels, was elected to represent Cracow in the provisional Austrian parliament, and took his seat to the left of the house. In European parliaments it had already become the tradition of the more liberal parties to sit on the left, following a pattern established during the French Revolution. The chairman of the Austrian body showed some surprise at seeing an Orthodox rabbi sitting on his left, to which the rabbi commented, "Juden haben keine Recht" (Jews have no Right), a *double entendre* which expressed the defensive element often present in Jewish political inclinations.

Most American Jews still have a visceral feeling that they belong in the company of political liberals. They were released from the medieval ghettos by "the liberals." They were joined in the fight against Nazism by "the liberals." Anti-Semitism, religious intolerance, and immigration restrictions, in their memory, have been associated with "the conservatives." And Steven Cohen has found in polls taken in the mid- and late eighties that Jews are more likely to say, by a four to one ratio, that a higher proportion of conservatives than of liberals are anti-Semitic, even though the actual evidence from opinion polls among American liberals and conservatives does not validate this European-born stereotype.[30]

Nor is support for leftism just a matter of reacting to anti-Semitism. Some part of Jewish liberalism has been a familiar attempt to accommodate to the American ethos, but it has reflected a recognition of the extent to which the ideology of the society, Americanism, has been good for the Jews. As we have seen, that awareness came early. When Benjamin Nones, a Revolutionary War hero, explained why he supported the Jeffersonian Republicans rather than the Federalists, he said, "I am a Jew, and if for no other reason, I am a Republican . . . In the early history of the Jews are contained the earliest warnings against kingly government . . . In the monarchies of Europe we are hunted from society . . . Among the nations of Europe, we are inhabitants everywhere but citizens nowhere unless in Republics . . . How then can a Jew be but a Republican?"[31]

In fact, throughout European history, monarchs and other strong authorities had occasionally been the "constraints" which saved Jews from anti-Semitic mobs. Nevertheless, the natural constitutional restraints developed in America were infinitely more reliable and durable sources of protection; and, in the minds of Jews, these constitutional guarantees were identified with liberalism.

When Benjamin Nones made his statement, the economic self-interest of the Jews would seem to have lain with the Federalists and their bias toward the commercial class to which most Jews belonged. But the Federalists also displayed an anti-immigrant and antidemocratic prejudice. They were responsible for the Alien and Sedition Acts of 1798, which prolonged naturalization periods, strengthened the government's ability to deport, and criminalized "malicious" antigovernment criticism. There were some prominent Federalist Jews, but most Jews, like Benjamin Nones, supported the Jeffersonians.[32]

That may be an early example of Jews' political behavior running counter to their economic interests. But it was less a matter of Jews voting against their own self-interest than of their defining self-interest beyond the pocketbook. The qualities inherent in a free and achievement-oriented America were most important for the well-being of Jews. While political liberty and civic equality are moral values in themselves, worthy of altruistic support, for Jews they are also matters of defensive priority. Throughout American history, lofty political values and Jewish defensive needs have often seemed to converge. That entanglement of motivations has frequently complicated the story of American Jewish political behavior.

Civil Rights and the Jewish Political Agenda

The American Jewish community became highly organized in fostering a comprehensive public affairs agenda only after World War II, as a result of the Nazi experience. With a more sophisticated appreciation of America's unique environment for Jews, as well as with a budding sense of empowerment, some Jewish organizations came together in 1944 in a loose confederation now called the National Jewish Community Relations Agency. Comprising thirteen national agencies and over a hundred local councils, that confederation had and still has the explicit purpose of

> protecting and enhancing conditions conducive to the creative continuity and well-being of the Jewish community. Such conditions can be achieved only within a social framework committed to democratic pluralism; freedom of religion, thought, expression and association; the wall of separation between church and state; equal rights, justice and opportunity; and, a climate in which differences among groups are accepted and respected, and in which each is free to cultivate its own distinctive values while participating fully in the general life of the society. History has bred in Jews the deep conviction that such conditions which accord

with ethical and religious values derived from Judaism and Jewish tradition afford Jews and all others the best opportunity to enjoy secure
and meaningful lives.[33]

That is a fair statement by the organized Jewish community of its
domestic public affairs agenda and mixed motivational basis.

For a number of years after the formation of this confederation, civil
rights, centering around the disadvantage of blacks, became its major
domestic preoccupation. Some of the recent tensions between African
Americans and Jews have focused on whether Jews have given up their
liberal position on civil rights, or, alternately, whether blacks have
failed to appreciate liberal Jewish contributions to civil rights. Both
propositions are flawed. Contrary to the charges of some blacks, American Jews remain markedly more liberal on civil rights issues than any
other white group. This has been documented in poll after poll. Yet,
contrary to the claims of some Jews, Jewish liberalism on civil rights
has never been altogether altruistic. Jewish involvement with civil
rights for blacks is a fine example of the entanglement of tribal political
values with defensive needs, and precedes the sophisticated under-
standings of today's organized Jewish community.

A paradigm of that entanglement might be found in a double
lynching which took place in Franklin, Tennessee, in 1868. A young
Russian Jew, S. A. Bierfield, who ran a drygoods store there, employed
a black clerk and had a heavily black clientele. Although he was known
as a radical Republican and brought his own values to the situation,
Bierfield, in catering to black customers, was also following a sensible
business practice. One historian has written of the Jewish businessmen
in the South during that Reconstruction period: "Sticking to their business and treating the freedman as an important businessman, not eschewing to call him, 'Mister,' they [the Jews] secured ... a great
amount of the Negro's trade."[34] Outraged by the extent to which the
alien Jew was fraternizing with the blacks, and the temerity of the
blacks in joining in, a masked band of the local Ku Klux Klan broke
into the store on the night of August 15, while Bierfield, his black clerk,
and a black visitor—who escaped—were eating watermelon. The mob

started to hang Bierfield; when he tried to flee, they shot and killed him, and then murdered his black clerk, Lawrence Bowman.

American Jews have had a sense of shared fate with blacks, in terms of both their own history of oppression and of common enemies in this country. The financier Jacob Schiff, for example, spoke up on many occasions for black rights, frequently attended black meetings at the Henry Street settlement in New York City, and protested to President Wilson about the segregation of black employees in government departments.[35] Jews have been the main white supporters of the civil rights and racial equality causes—in terms of both participation in and funding of organizations such as the NAACP from their inception at the beginning of the century down to the present. This involvement has not been just a strategy formulated by the organized Jewish community. The social liberalism of Jews, reinforced by defensive needs, resulted in empathy toward oppressed African Americans that affected Jews as individuals as well as organizationally.

The record of American Jews was emphasized in a speech in midsummer of 1994 by a major African American leader, Hugh Price, the president and chief executive officer of the National Urban League. He noted that Jews are "long-standing allies [of blacks] . . . Many whites of good will have accompanied us on our long journey for racial, social and economic justice. None has matched the Jewish community as long-distance runners in the civil rights movement."[36]

On occasion, however, the perceived defensive needs of Jews have conflicted with their liberal sense of shared fate with blacks. Southern Jewish congregations embraced the anti-Union, proslavery cause during the Civil War. Some southern Jewish communities pointedly opposed the civil rights demonstrations of the 1950s in which so many northern Jews participated. They may have been influenced by the fact that in one year, from November 1957 to October 1958, eight southern Jewish synagogues were bombed. Southern Jews tried to repress publicity about the fate of two Jewish youths, Michael Schwerner and Andrew Goodman, who were murdered along with their black companion while on a civil rights mission in Mississippi in 1964.

Hiring and college admissions quotas—an extension of the general principle of affirmative action which Jews initially supported—have created a more recent tension between blacks and Jews. In New York City during the 1960s, the demand was voiced that Jewish school teachers in African American districts be fired and replaced by blacks and that, in general, preference for government jobs be given to blacks. The highly publicized and prolonged 1968 New York teachers' strike was viewed as a black–Jewish struggle.[37] The imposition of quotas, although not usually proving directly disadvantageous to Jews in any serious way, has raised Jewish defensive concerns because prior to World War II quotas were associated with limits on the entry of Jews into universities, professions, and opportunities generally. Their reemergence as an entitlement for blacks and other disadvantaged groups may be seen as changing the nature of an achievement-oriented America, as placing group rights ahead of individual rights.[38]

Black political candidates in such cities as Los Angeles, Philadelphia, Chicago, and New York have in past years typically received a much higher proportion of votes from Jews than from any other definable white group other than academics. That pattern was partially broken in the 1993 mayoralty election in New York City, when the exit polls showed that Rudolf Giuliani, a Republican, received 68 percent of the Jewish vote in his defeat of David Dinkins, the displaced black mayor of the city, an increase of 5 percent over 1989 Republican support.[39] This followed the confrontation between Jews and blacks in Crown Heights, during which, in the opinion of many observers, Mayor Dinkins had not been forceful in providing protection for Jews. Jews supporting Giuliani also expressed their concerns about crime in the city. Because of such factors, the sense of shared fate with blacks seems to have been blunted somewhat among the Jewish population at large.

Despite these local setbacks, across the country Jews continue, as Hugh Price stressed, to be among the principal supporters—certainly the prime white backers—of civil rights and pro-black liberalism. The 32 percent of Jews who voted for Dinkins in 1993 should be compared with the 12 percent of white Catholics and 17 percent of white Protestants who backed the re-election of the black mayor. But in terms of anticipating the political future of American Jews, the sharp division among them in the New York City mayoral race might well portend a change. On the Upper West Side, composed largely of religiously liberal, or secular, younger and more assimilated Jews, Dinkins received 62 percent of the Jewish vote, a little higher than he had secured in the previous election. Elsewhere in Manhattan, in districts whose Jews were generally older or more religiously observant, Giuliani received 81 percent of the vote, somewhat higher than four years earlier.

Israel and the Jewish Political Agenda

For the reasons outlined in Chapter 5, the American government's support for Israel has been the top public affairs item on the American Jewish agenda since 1967. Although it certainly has the positive tribal attributes that led American Jews to act politically on behalf of endangered co-religionists in both czarist and Soviet Russia, American Jewry's political behavior with respect to Israel must also be seen in a defensive context.

Indeed, the vaunted liberalism of American Jews—or, more accurately, their status in some liberal-left circles—has been under some apparent strain with respect to their support of Israel. Although most Jews have found it difficult to acknowledge the fact, every administration—with the one exception of Ronald Reagan, the most philo-Semitic of presidents—and the overwhelming majority of Americans have believed since 1967 that Israel should exchange most of the territory it occupies on the West Bank and Gaza for a peace treaty incorporating security guarantees. Aside from the foreign policy interest in thereby reducing Middle East tension, that position conforms to the liberal principle of national self-determination in which most Americans believe.

Actually, the majority of American Jews also agree with that position. Nine months before Arafat said publicly in December 1988 that he would recognize Israel and reject the use of terrorism, both the *Los Angeles Times*' and Steven Cohen's surveys indicated that during the time that the Israeli government, led by Itzack Shamir, opposed the idea of giving up territory for peace, and before a new cabinet under Itzack Rabin actually entered into an agreement with the Palestine Liberation Organization in 1993, most American Jews favored the exchange of land for peace. Cohen found in 1983 that 67 percent agreed with the statement: "If the PLO recognizes Israel and renounces terrorism, Israel should be willing to talk with the PLO," while only 16 percent disagreed. By a plurality, 42 to 33 percent, they favored "territorial compromise . . . in return for credible guarantees of peace."[40]

However, while two thirds of affiliated Jews in nine midsized Jewish communities around the country also agreed in 1990 that "Israel should trade some land in the territories in exchange for credible guarantees of peace," the same Jews split (47 percent each way) on whether "Palestinians can ever be trusted to keep a security agreement with Israel."[41] That fairly expresses the constant dilemma in which so many American Jews feel caught. They favor land for peace as a principle, but they are not at all sure that it will work, and they fear any experimental arrangement that will put Israel at Holocaust risk. Jews expressed that same ambivalence in an American Jewish Committee poll after the preliminary agreement of 1993. Nine out of ten supported the agreement, and a similar proportion felt that Israel's situation was "better" as a result. But only half rejected the idea that "the PLO is determined to destroy Israel." In 1994, when queried by the Israeli Policy Forum, 78 percent of a national sample of Jews said they support the "agreement with the PLO that gives Palestinians autonomy in Gaza and Jericho" (58 percent supported the agreement "strongly"). Only 9 percent voiced any opposition. Yet when asked whether different words describe their feelings about the recent Gaza–Jericho peace agreement, they revealed a considerable degree of apprehension. While 84 percent said they were "hopeful," a comparable 85 percent were "cautious."

Whenever heightened terrorism seems to reflect an irreconcilable Arab hostility toward Israel, American Jewish attitudes harden, further adulterating their belief that the land-for-peace formula will succeed. In any case, nine out of ten Jews have consistently backed American support of Israel, whether they believe in land for peace or not, whether they are critical of some Israeli policies or not, and whether they are personally much interested in the Jewish state or not.[42]

This steadfast concern of the Jews created a tension between them and some of the more liberal left. Following the Six-Day War, Israel, seen as a powerful state linked to imperialist America, became anathema to major sections of the international left. As a result, many people active in the peace movements in the United States and elsewhere became openly anti-Israeli and pro-Palestinian. This phenomenon put a serious strain on the loyalties of various Jewish leftists, who felt both Jewish and radical. They were faced with the choice of giving up their attachments to Israel or dropping their ties to the left. At this juncture a significant and visible number of Jewish radicals deserted the radical left.

Most Jews were less disturbed by the opinions expressed by the radicals than by attitudes in some mainstream liberal circles which seemed careless of the fragile security of Israel. Jesse Jackson's espousal of the Palestinian position, and his influence in the Democratic Party on behalf of that cause, created more Jewish animosity than the anti-Semitic remarks he would make and apologize for from time to time. Other black intellectuals, out of a Third World ideology, have also been prominent in the Palestinian cause.

Jews behave similarly in the country most comparable to the United States.[43] As in America and other Western countries, Canadian Jews contributed heavily to the communist and early socialist movements. After World War II, in a three-party situation, Jews have given disproportionate support to the socialist party, the CCF/NDP, compared with the other two, and have heavily preferred the center-left Liberals rather than the Conservatives by a substantial margin. In trying to account for this outcome, the Canadian political scientist Jean Laponce suggests that "in democratic countries of immigration such as Canada and the United States, center-left parties became particularly attractive to the groups and communities that are not at the cultural core, that are not part of the dominant historical stream of the society—groups that may have been persecuted or harassed or subject to discrimination (Jews in Canada, Protestants and Jews in France)."[44] In almost all Western countries prior to the last two decades, Jews had given labor and socialist parties disproportionate support.

These patterns no longer hold true in most of Europe.[45] Symbolic of the change to conservatism there is the fact that Margaret Thatcher represented the most heavily Jewish constituency in Britain, Finchley. The majority of Jews who once voted Labour shifted to the Conservatives. Some have explained these changes as derivative of British Jews having achieved a high level of acceptance and affluence in recent decades. But then why are American Jews different? Why do they remain on the left?

There is no simple answer to this question, but in large measure the shifts, particularly in Australia and Britain but in much of Europe as well, can be traced to the fact that the socialist left, especially its youth affiliates and intellectuals, turned openly and vigorously to support the Palestinian Liberation Organization in the seventies and eighties. Efforts were made within Europe to push Jewish supporters of Israel out of socialist organizations, and even to deny them, as "Zionist racists," free speech on university campuses.

The European conservatives, on the other hand, whose historic record was likely to have included anti-Semitism and opposition to Zionism, have in recent decades become friendly to the Jewish state and have made overtures to their Jewish electorates.[46] In effect, Jews outside of North America and to some degree France have been rejected by the left and courted by the right, an inversion of traditional relationships.

In North America, except among the now tiny Marxist and militant black movements, the dominant left forces have not behaved in the same way. Although many American left-liberals share the same predispositions as their European ideological soulmates, as polls of the delegates to the 1984 and 1988 Democratic national conventions revealed, Jews are too important to—and integrated into—the liberal and Democratic forces in America for them to risk alienating their support by turning against Israel. From 1972 through the collapse of the Soviet Union and beyond, Democratic Party leaders who in general have opposed military spending and American involvement abroad have continued to back military and other forms of aid to Israel.

Hence, American Jews, unlike their European brethren, have not been pressed to choose between their commitment to Israel and their traditional ties to the left. They have been able to remain liberals and Democrats. European developments raise questions about the duration of such a relationship, but it was strengthened again by the election of a moderate and Israel-leaning Clinton administration, which has included many Jews in its major appointments.

The strain between the liberalism of Jews and their avid support of Israel can also be seen in the discrepancy between their militant stance vis-à-vis Israel's defense and their dovishness in other foreign arenas. Although clearly not pacifist, Jews are remarkably antimilitarist, a position linked to their left-wing sympathies. For example, various polls have consistently found that a much larger proportion of Jews than non-Jews have said that the United States should reduce military spending. Israel, however, complicates Jewish foreign affairs liberalism. In the 1984 National Survey of American Jews, the respondents approved by a 64 to 24 percent ratio the statement that "in order to be a reliable military supporter of Israel, the U.S should maintain a strong military capacity." But the same respondents also agreed by a 59 to 27 percent ratio with the opinion that "to help reduce deficits and relieve world tension, U.S. military spending should be cut."

Even on the military front, American Jews have not viewed their insistent support of Israel as illiberal. While many are pained by the conflict between Palestinian Arab and Israeli aspirations, they consider nothing more *liberal* than preventing the destruction of democratic Israel and a possible holocaust of Israelis. However militant their stance might be when faced with a particular threat to Israeli security, the main framework of American Jews' political support of Israel is defensive in nature.

Voting Behavior

Domestically, Jewish political behavior in America has been heavily shaped by a special type of non-economic self-interest: support for democracy and pluralism, the optimum conditions for Jewish continuity.

Jews are not immune to considerations flowing from their socioeconomic status, but unlike the political behavior of most other white Americans, theirs is dominated by considerations that override pocketbook concerns. The considerable evidence gathered through research on voting behavior points in this direction. All of the postwar studies indicate that Jews of high socioeconomic status are somewhat more likely to support Democratic candidates than those with low status. They are clearly much more disposed in this direction than affluent non-Jews.

As Benjamin Nones attested in the late eighteenth century, a liberalism dominated by its reference to freedom (that is, by defensive considerations) is one to which Jews have responded from 1800 to 1994. The record suggests that Jews in early America largely were staunch Democrats, backing Jefferson, Jackson, and Van Buren as the more open and antinativist party. Electoral research also indicates that the subsequent Jewish immigrants from Germany became Republicans because it was the antislavery party. On the whole, they backed the radical or progressive wing of the GOP. They were pressed to reject the Democrats at the turn of the century because its major leader, William Jennings Bryan, was considered to be an anti-Semite.[47]

The tensions between Jews and other immigrant groups that developed in the poor, crowded tenement districts of the major northern cities presaged some of the more serious working-class-based anti-Semitic movements of the 1930s. These conditions helped to keep many Jews loyal to the then large progressive faction among Republicans, led by Theodore Roosevelt, Robert La Follette, and Hiram Johnson, before World War I.[48] The Republican appeal to Jews on the presidential level seemingly ended in 1912, when the conservative GOP Presidential incumbent, William Howard Taft, faced three left-of-center rivals with attractions to different segments of American Jewry: former President Theodore Roosevelt, who had strong links to the community, running as a Progressive; Woodrow Wilson, as a liberal Democrat; and Eugene Debs, as the Socialist Party nominee. From then on, Democratic candidates, or a combination of Democratic and left third-party nominees, secured clear majorities among Jews.

Many East European Jews came to America as socialists, an orientation they first adopted in reaction to the anti-Semitic regimes from which they were forced to flee, as well as the low economic position of most of them. Barred from being members of conservative parties, they supported left-wing movements.[49] In America, the major Yiddish newspaper, the *Daily Forward,* became the most widely circulated socialist and Jewish newspaper in the nation. The predominantly Jewish unions in the garment and other industries—joined in the United Hebrew Trades—backed the Socialist Party.[50] The only two congressmen that party elected before World War I, Meyer London from the East Side of New York and Victor Berger from Milwaukee, were Jewish.

Zionism, an alternative secular political strand available to Jews, was much weaker than socialism in this country, with only 12,000 members in 1914; and in any case, it included a socialist wing. The Socialists constituted the second largest party in many Jewish districts in New York until the New Deal. They subsequently voted for Franklin D. Roosevelt, often on a third, American Labor, party line. As the foremost student of the subject, Arthur Liebman notes, "American Jewry has provided socialist organizations and movements with a disproportionate number—at times approaching or surpassing a majority—of their leaders, activists, supporters."[51] Similar statements can be made about the supporters of subsequent other left third parties, including the La Follette Progressive Party in 1924, the communist dominated Progressive Party in 1948, and the John Anderson Independent candidacy in 1980.[52]

The radical bent of so many poverty-stricken East European Jews reflected conventional individual self-interest related to their economic position as well as group self-interest directed against the perceived forces of anti-Semitism. Their more affluent brethren of German descent retained their Lincoln-born Republican attachments until the 1930s, but, as earlier, they backed the liberal or progressive Republicans who were a significant force in the party. The one important genuinely conservative segment among Jews came from the Orthodox minority. Their journalists emphasized the complementarity of conservatism in religious matters and in politics. But the circulation of the socialist *Daily Forward* was far greater than their newspapers.[53]

In the era of gathering darkness marked by the rise of Nazism in Germany, by serious anti-Semitism in America, and by the Depression, Franklin Roosevelt strongly appealed to the Jews. His pro-trade union and welfare state policies and direct links with major Jewish socialist and labor leaders like David Dubinsky and Sidney Hillman, as well as his strong opposition to Nazi Germany and endorsement of aid to the Allies, unified the vast majority of Jews in the New Deal Democratic camp. Even the old socialists moved over to vote Democratic.[54]

The politics of the immediate postwar period, for Jews, was centered first around the plight of the Holocaust survivors and then around support for the creation of the state of Israel and its struggles with its Arab neighbors. Again, the Democrats and the left backed the Jewish cause. Harry Truman supported a special quota for displaced persons entering the country and then gave immediate recognition to the new Jewish state and aided it in international forums. Three quarters of the Jews voted for him in 1948, while another 15 percent opted for the leftist third party candidate, Henry Wallace.[55] Truman's Republican successor, Dwight Eisenhower, however, who had a strong appeal to Jews as the leader of the Allied military effort, was able to secure close to two fifths of their votes in 1952. His turning against Israel in the 1956 Sinai war, while the Democrats voiced support, helped to refurbish the Jewish attachment to Democratic and liberal politics.

In the 1960s Jews gave over 80 percent of their votes to John Kennedy, Lyndon Johnson, and Hubert Humphrey. In 1972 George McGovern—a left liberal perceived by many Jews as an isolationist who, if elected president, would weaken American support for Israel—was still able to secure close to two thirds of the Jewish presidential vote. This was noted as a setback for the Democratic Party, since Hubert Humphrey had won over four fifths of the Jewish ballots in a three-party race in 1968. But the almost two thirds who voted for

McGovern were more than the support he obtained from any other white group. In 1976 Jews again led among whites in overwhelmingly backing Jimmy Carter against Gerald Ford, with three quarters of the vote.

In 1980 Ronald Reagan, who had been a strong public supporter of Israel from 1948 on, secured a higher than usual GOP vote among Jews, 35 or more percent. Jimmy Carter, who in office had shown himself to be a less than enthusiastic supporter of Israel's foreign policies, received under 50 percent of the vote among Jews. One sixth of Jewish voters opted for the liberal independent candidate John Anderson, which was three times his vote among the entire electorate. But four years later, when the Democrats nominated Walter Mondale, a consistently strong supporter of the Jewish state and a disciple of Israel's strongest political ally, Hubert Humphrey, Reagan's vote among Jews actually declined to 30 percent. Except for blacks, whose vote distribution did not change, Jews were the only group to shift against Reagan when he was gaining among all others.[56]

The results of the 1988 elections, as indicated in many opinion polls, confirmed again that while Jews on average earn more than any other American ethnoreligious group, they were still more liberal or left in their opinions than all other white groups. In November 1988 over 70 percent of Jews backed Dukakis. Jewish support for Republican presidential candidates had declined slightly but steadily since 1980. Well over 80 percent backed Democrats for Congress. As in the past, the only identifiable subset that voted conservative and Republican was composed of the Orthodox (who constitute less than 10 percent of Jewish voters), particularly the more extreme and less affluent among them.[57] George Bush actually received over 85 percent of the vote in areas in Brooklyn and elsewhere inhabited by Hasidic sects.

In 1992 the exit polls indicated that almost eight of ten Jews voted for Bill Clinton in a three-candidate race, as against a little more than four out of ten Americans in general. Only one out of ten Jews backed George Bush, a third of the Jewish vote he had received in 1988.[58] The idiosyncratic absence of a pocketbook factor for Jewish voters was again evident. In a Voter Research poll conducted by the national television networks, 24 percent of all Americans who said they were financially "better off" after the Republican years in office and 61 percent who said they were "worse off" voted for Clinton. That gap was much smaller among Jews in an American Jewish Congress exit poll, in which 78 percent who said they were "better off" and 90 percent who said they were "worse off" cast their ballots for Clinton.[59] And in 1994, when interviewed by the Israel Policy Forum, 60 percent of a national sample of Jews said they were Democrats or leaned toward the Democrats; only 19 percent gave the same response for the Republicans.

While Jews have voted for Democratic Party and other left-party presidential candidates about 25 percent more often since 1920 than has the general population, for most of those presidential years Jews have followed the upward or downward trend of the larger voting public.[60] In 1932, for example, the Jewish vote for Franklin D. Roosevelt increased by 10 percentage points over that received by Al Smith four years earlier. The total Democratic presidential vote increased 16 points. In most presidential elections, the changes in partisan support by Jews have been similar to that of the electorate as a whole. In other words, in most cases Jews were partly responding to the same stimuli as the rest of the population, although their Democratic and left vote was always significantly higher.

In six presidential races, moreover, Jewish voters varied more sharply, sometimes by 25 to 35 percent. This was the case in 1940 and 1944, when Roosevelt took on the Nazis; again in 1948, when Truman's support of Israel was decisive; in 1960, when Nixon, tarred by the extremist brush in his California campaigns, opposed Kennedy; in 1984, when Reagan ran against a "traditional" Democrat and Humphrey's friend, Walter Mondale; and in 1992, when Jewish support for the GOP was undermined by severely critical anti-Israeli remarks made by President Bush and Secretary of State Baker and by the visible presence of the religious right at the Republican convention.

Have Jews Shifted to the Right?

In the 1960s, some Jewish commentators began to predict an eventual shift to the Republican Party or to argue strongly that the American Jewish population *should* turn conservative in the modern world, as a matter of altered self-interest.[61] That debate has turned around several kinds of issues.

The first issue is upward mobility. In spite of the record presented here, some suggest that a sizable number of economically successful Jews are close to becoming conservatized because of their viewpoints on the domestic agenda. The argument is not that Jews will turn away in any large numbers from a liberal bias toward support for the underdog, but that more of them are ready, along with many other Americans, to accept the social philosophy of "fiscal responsibility" and to turn away from New Deal liberalism, which they perceive as having produced welfare dependency. Indeed, at the same time that Jews continue to indicate support of welfare programs, in recent years they also tell pollsters that balancing the budget is more important than greater social spending.[62] In that, they reflect the schizoid state of many American liberals.[63]

A more fundamental argument favoring a right turn among Jews emphasizes that the populism inherent in modern liberal politics is dangerous for Jews. The concern here is with the need for constraints. Jews have always had an understandable fear of radicalized mobs, with images of French revolutionary *sans-culottes* plundering Jewish homes and Bolshevik-led peasants conducting pogroms in the Ukraine. The sociologist Werner Cohn notes a comparable reaction before the Civil War among American Jews who opposed slavery. Some feared that the Christian-linked fanatical abolitionist movement appealed "directly to plebeian malcontents" who might turn on the Jews after their Christian enthusiasms helped to liberate the slaves.[64] Ironically, the emergence of well-publicized anti-Semitic activities among segments of the African American population during the 1990s have revived these concerns. And, as we have seen, the constraints on them within the black community are weak.

Conservative advocates see a somewhat related danger for Jews in an end-of-the-century American "liberal" society that is too permissive. That permissiveness is thought to be evident in the burgeoning breakdown of law and order, of family structure, of moral and cultural standards in general. Some critics, such as Irving Kristol, blame "liberalism," which they equate with secularism, and suggest that Jews are endangered both from within and without by such developments.[65] They also feel that the Democratic Party is particularly responsive to a liberalism that encourages license.

The tendency of some circles in the American liberal left to be critical of Israel led some Jewish observers in the 1970s to argue that the Republicans would be more durable supporters of the Jewish state than their partisan opponents, much like European conservatives. A number of prominent conservatives, including Ronald Reagan and various Christian fundamentalist ministers, strongly backed Israel, viewing the alliance with the Jewish state as part of the larger struggle against communist expansion and the rise of radical anti-Western Third World leaders. They also opposed the isolationist and antimilitarist positions typically found among some Democrats. Even though most of those Democrats supported Israel, conservative Jews argued that a generically anti-interventionist stance would eventually threaten America's support of that state.

The Persistence of the Democratic Party Allegiance

Despite these prophecies and caveats, the evidence we have seen simply does not sustain the thesis that Jews as a group are becoming more conservative. American Jews continue to present an anomaly— they are the wealthiest ethnoreligious group in the country by far, and yet the most liberal in attitudes and behavior.

In recent years leftist intellectuals have cited the appearance among their stratum of a predominantly Jewish group of neoconservatives as evidence of Jewish behavior generally. This evidence is very weak as an indicator of increased Jewish conservatism, for a number of reasons. First, the number who have been labeled as neoconservative is a tiny proportion of the total group of Jewish intellectuals. Jews are still to be found in disproportionate numbers among those associated with various left-wing journals and causes. Studies of Jewish elites, including intellectuals, academics, and media personnel, indicate they are more liberal than non-Jewish elites in their voting behavior, self-identified ideological position, and responses to questions. Jews in this stratum regularly vote for Democratic presidential candidates by margins of more than four to one.[66] Close to one third (31 percent) of these Jews agree that "the U.S. should move toward socialism."[67] In any case, the majority of those originally described as neoconservatives are still Democrats and have never backed Ronald Reagan or George Bush.[68]

What those labeled neoconservatives have had in common has been a deep suspicion of the Soviet Union (before Gorbachev and Yeltsin), advocacy of hardline foreign military programs, and a passionate concern for Israel's security. But many of them still retain an identification with social welfare policies and support for trade unions. Almost all had reacted strongly against the New Left movement of the 1960s and early 1970s. Identifying with democracy as an end in itself and strongly attached to the values of scholarship, they argued that the attacks by the New Left on the ideals of the university and the democratic political system were not only unwarranted but played into the hands of anti-democratic extremists, both on the left and the right. More recently, they are united in opposition to the pressures for "political correctness," for adherence to liberal positions on affirmative action and multiculturalism, within the intellectual community.

Most of the Democratic neoconservatives now reject the term because it has also been widely applied in Europe and Canada in recent years to mean Reagan-Friedman classically liberal laissez-faire free-market economic programs, as distinct from (for these countries) traditional Tory communitarian *noblesse oblige* economic policies.[69] Most of those labeled as neoconservatives in America identify much more with the *New Republic* than with *Commentary*. They would prefer to be known as "neo-liberals." This label, however, has been taken over by others who have been somewhat more fiscally conservative on domestic policies but much more dovish on foreign issues. Morton

Kondracke, past executive officer of the *New Republic*, solved the dilemma by referring to himself as a "Neo-Lib-Neo-Con."

In addition, world events, particularly the dissolution of the Soviet Union, have robbed these intellectuals of much of their distinctive ideological platform. Soviet adventurism in the Middle East is obviously no longer to be feared. Support of Israel by the United States must now be defended on considerations other than American security. Indeed there is some confusion over which party is now most isolationist in temper. Debates in the 1990s about American foreign policy in Bosnia, Somalia, and Haiti have more Republicans than Democrats calling for "the boys to be brought home," or not to be sent in the first place. That has partly been a partisan matter, given a Democratic president, but it also reflects the absence of the Soviet threat.

Furthermore, although some Jews remain wary, any incipient peace process in the Middle East, such as that initiated in 1993, if successful, will presumably reduce the need for concern about pockets of Palestinian Arab sympathy within the Democratic Party. The Democratic Party and Bill Clinton are still seen by Jews as political friends of Israel.

Part of the Jewish devotion to the Democratic Party is a matter of momentum. In their historical eye, many Jews still see the Republican Party as "the conservative" party. They are more at ease with the kinds of people they find in the Democratic Party—their fellow ethnics with whom they grew up in America—than with the White Anglo-Saxon Protestants still predominant in the Republican Party. Despite the concern of some Jews about the apparent decline of general moral constraint in American society, they do not feel comfortable when a Republican candidate for president issues a call for a "religious war," as Pat Buchanan did at the 1992 Republican convention, to much applause. As Alan Fisher notes, "Jews identify the Democrats as friends, and, by and large, they stay with their friends. The Democratic Party is home to them."[70]

Substantive issues could eventually make a difference, but it will take an emotional wrench, or more generational distance, to eliminate the Democratic Party advantage in Jewish voting. It is at the level of cultural liberalism that we still find the deepest source of Jewish reluctance to make the change. Recent opinion surveys continue to find that Jews are significantly more liberal than non-Jewish whites in all opinion areas. Steven Cohen's many studies report that on most issues the Jewish center is well to the left of the non-Jewish center.

Clearly, the numerical decline projected for the Jewish community at the beginning of the next century will have consequences for its political profile. The smaller group of cohering and affiliated Jews (the remnant) will probably be more religiously conservative—and, as a result, also more politically conservative—than the larger population is presently. We have seen a correlation between the religious and political conservatism of Jews on a range of issues. That considerable number who will have moved away from serious identification with the community will predictably still be heavily involved politically for some generations out of sheer cultural momentum, and because of residual differences in educational status, in intellectual and verbal pro-clivities, and in sense of foreboding. For these reasons also, they will still be disproportionately supportive of liberal groups and agendas. Consequently, there might well be a substantial political division be-tween the organized or affiliated Jews and the larger body of peripheral Jews, many of whom, because of the mixed marriages of their parents, will not be considered Jews by the religious communities.

Conclusion

The political arena is a showcase for the ways in which American exceptionalism has provided both unparalleled opportunity for Jewry as well as hazards to its continuity. The United States has enabled Jews to secure advantages in policy and office as a result of their extra-ordinary level of participation, their achievement orientation, the so-ciety's political openness, and a coalitional political system which re-sponds to and absorbs diversity.

Both Jewish political liberalism and activism are compounds of tribal values and defensive perceptions. That liberalism has shown no signs of flagging in America, partly because Jewish defensive needs, domestic and foreign, have been so congruent with the nature and program of the more liberal party as well as with the perceived national interests.

Insofar as "liberalism" is defined by the fundamental values of both civil freedom and government-intervening social compassion, it is still a basic part of the American political scene, and to a limited but significant extent the Jewish community has helped to maintain its position. There is no contradiction in the fact that Jews are, on the one hand, prototypically American, which denotes an individualistic and meritocratic mode; yet on the other hand, as products of their Jewish culture, they retain communitarian values which lead them to petition the government for a safety net of social welfare programs for the disadvantaged. The modern American political disposition that now approves of communitarian concerns also promotes those values that most resist hostility toward Jews.

Marginal and unidentified Jews increasingly have the opportunity to express their liberalism through channels other than Jewish organizations. They are no longer deterred from doing so by special defensive needs. As such concerns, domestic or Israel-connected, are reduced by circumstance, and as tribal connections are diminished by intermarriage, low birth rate, and other erosions, both liberalism and political activism will decrease as a cohesive characteristic of the core Jewish community. If that happens, it remains to be seen what will happen to the political effectiveness of a smaller Jewish community, what the effect of an increased proportion of religious conservatives will be, and what the consequences might be for the American political scene.

$\sim 7 \sim$

The Fragile Remnants

An Irish immigrant, Agnes Kelley, writing in the 1870s to her family, expressed the positive side of the American integrative experience with these words: "When we left [Ireland], we left the old world behind, we are all American citizens and proud of it." Another, Jane Crowe, wrote, "It is home to us now." Yet at the same time some immigrants were voicing the downside of the tribal dilemma. As still another Irish American put it in 1872: "How shall we preserve our identity? How shall we preserve our faith and nationality, through our posterity?"[1]

Around the turn of this century, W. E. B. Du Bois wrote about "the two unreconciled strivings" and the "double consciousness" that affected American blacks. African Americans have been a special case in our national history, but those terms nevertheless have meaning for most immigrant groups and Native Americans. Among all tribal groups, the two unreconciled strivings have been the same: a desire for the personal fulfillment provided by group identity, and a simultaneous desire for integration into the American mainstream.

Unless ancestral and birthright groups in America follow the abhorrent and basically impossible option of isolating themselves physically or intellectually, or unless the society turns against them in a new wave of intolerance, all of them will inevitably dwindle. We hope a new wave of intolerance will not happen, and we believe separatism runs against the cultural grain. Only those from black Africa, marked by skin color and still rejected for intimate contact by many white Americans, have not been accepted into, nor themselves chosen to accept, the "melting pot," although even for them the situation has changed considerably. Many blacks react to their history of oppression at the hands of white Americans by emphasizing the virtues of separateness. And many whites, though favoring equal educational and economic opportunity, are led by the ideology of some militant African Americans and by the news media's relentless focus on the pathologies of the ghetto to believe that the majority of blacks live wretched existences which produce high rates of crime and drug addiction, low commitment to education and other middle-class values, and intense hatred of whites.[2] Hence, a negative cycle of mutual suspicion and fear is perpetuated which keeps blacks further from the mainstream than most tribal groups.

The Jews, by contrast, are in many ways the best case to illustrate the tribal dilemma, because of their history of group oppression *outside* of the United States which motivated their immigration, and because of their subsequent experience of individual acceptance and achievement in the New World. But if Jews' historically unprecedented participation in America's economic, intellectual, political, and social life continues, then the Jewish community will massively lose numbers over the next few generations despite the gravity of the historical experience that binds them together. If American society continues its integrative course, then the scions of East European Jewry will follow the path of their German American co-religionists—they will assimilate, intermarry, and ultimately decline in numbers.

Marshall Sklare, the doyen of American Jewish sociology, entitled his 1976 book *American Jewry: The Ever-Dying People.* In so doing, he consciously was continuing a theme set earlier by Simon Rawidowicz in an essay, "Israel, the Ever-Dying People."[3] Rawidowicz and Sklare both noted that "no group has seen itself so incessantly dying as the Jews."[4] And the fear has not been of dying at the hands of an anti-Semitic enemy, but rather of demise through assimilation. This concern about continuity led to learned investigations a quarter of a century ago, sponsored by the Council of Jewish Federations and Welfare

Funds, and to similar surveys and studies of Jewish attitudes and be-havior that continue today.

For European immigrant groups, tribal cohesion is already a lost cause. The double strivings to which Du Bois referred have been rec-onciled for most of them; integration has virtually obliterated group identity. But if ethnic identity has eroded for most of the population, how do we explain the fact that 90 percent of Americans supplied at least one ancestry to the 1990 census? Twenty-one different European national origins were reported by at least a million people apiece. About 58 million Americans listed German, 39 million Irish, 33 million English, 15 million Italian, 10 million French, 9 million Polish, and so on.[5]

The fact that so many Americans of European origin are still quite conscious of their national background challenges our emphasis on the decline of ethnic identity. But there is a crucial difference between an ethnic population and a tribal group. Among ethnic populations, there are degrees of nostalgia and vestigial traces of what Herbert Gans calls "symbolic ethnicity," ranging from knowledge of the mother tongue to special food tastes. After an in-depth study of one multicultural metropolitan area, Richard Alba, an Italian American sociologist, con-cluded that despite these symbols, "ethnic experience is shallow for the great majority of [American] whites."[6]

That shallowness is what qualitatively differentiates a waning ethnic population from a durable tribal group. Increasingly absent is group solidarity, common purpose, communal loyalty, and even cultural si-militude. The group as a unit is progressively discounted as a player in the society, and individuals are deprived of the personal meaning they derived from group membership. Vestigial "identity" and remi-niscences of familiarity may persist for generations, and some voters may continue to be attracted to a political candidate because of the ethnic sound of his or her name. But the group will not act as a serious interest group, with a common agenda in the political arena.

In his study of European ancestry groups, Richard Alba found that "ethnic identities are bound up in the minds of many with family history. For many whites ethnicity is inseparable from their notions about their families, and a larger social group is only hazily discerned at best."[7] By itself, the family connection finally becomes nostalgic in nature, and even that will be generationally attenuated by intermarriage. Using 1980 data, Alba found that among women who had at least some Italian background, 66 percent of those over age 65 had married men with some Italian background, while only 23 percent of women with Italian background under the age of 25 did. The disparity was similar among most European groups, particularly the smaller ones, less so but still growing among the larger English, German, and Irish populations. The in-marriage rate was never much more than 50 percent.[8]

In recent years there has also been a breakdown in the "triple melting pot" hypothesized by Will Herberg and others, whereby ethnicity is supposed to be contained within broad religious lines, that is, Protestant, Catholic, Jewish. According to recent data, about half of young Catholics have married non-Catholics, almost the same percentage that applies to young Jews.[9]

Despite all denial and gnashing of teeth, the unromantic fact is that the European immigrant populations are becoming ethnically attenuated and are no longer seriously operating as tribal groups. Some analysts suggest that a new population group is forming called "unhyphenated whites," or simply "Europeans." A majority of American-born non-Latino whites now have ethnically diverse ancestry.[10] While some mixed-ancestry organizations have been created to address immigration and other administrative complexities, and perhaps to exhibit some pride, it does not seem likely that such heterogeneous background groups, or even the growing segment called European Americans, will take on the cohesive qualities of a tribal community, except perhaps in defensive reaction to the pressures from groups of non-European origin.

Non-European Communities

To the extent that such a pan-European or non-Latino white defensiveness develops, it may reflect the fact that by the year 2050, close to half of the American population could be non-European in origin, owing to dramatic infusions of Latino and Asian populations.[11] More than half (55 percent) of the American public agreed in 1993 with the statement that "the increasing diversity that [the new, non-European] immigrants bring to this country mostly threatens American culture."[12]

That response certainly includes some who are simply prejudiced against non-Anglos and some who are uncomfortable with social change, believing that tribal cultures should submerge themselves in the dominant one for all but the most nostalgic details. For many, however, and notably for Jews, the fear is not of a multicultural society per se—indeed the Jewish community would be comforted by the existence of groups which prove to be both integrated and cohesively tribal. The fear is of excessively separatist political and institutional tendencies that would significantly upset the integrative nature of American society.

In many societies, a contiguous rather than integrative pluralism has prevailed. The Ottoman Empire was marked by an institutional framework known as the millet system, in which numerous ancestral and religious groups governed themselves, to one degree or another, with their own internal laws, their own languages, and even their own somewhat self-contained societies. In Canada, the rise of French Canadian nationalism and Quebec separatism has frightened Jews and other nonfrancophones, many of whom have moved to Ontario or elsewhere to escape living in such a highly solidaristic ethnic enclave. Québecois, with their heightened self-consciousness, are perceived as much more xenophobic and anti-Semitic than anglophone Canadians (opinion polls confirm this impression). Jews have lived under some forms of contiguous pluralism—in the Middle East, for example, under the Turks and sometimes under the Arabs, as well as in pre-World War II Poland and Lithuania. They understand it as a system whereby subordinate groups are given—or loaned—certain autonomous rights by the dominant society. Individuals are recognized only through their groups.

No one seriously believes that such an extreme contiguous pluralism can take hold in modern America. But there are fears that some tribal communities—notably Latinos, Asian Americans, and African Americans—will grow so large, and remain so clustered, group-centered, and generally separatist, that the society will not only be riven by continuous conflict but that America's emphasis on individualism will be adversely affected.

The great quota controversy of recent decades partly reflects that fear. The majority of American Jews and their agencies have consistently favored affirmative action in hiring and education—that is, special consideration for members of groups that have been discriminated against in the past or present. But they have opposed quotas—predetermined numerical outcomes for groups in hiring and admissions, based on group proportions in the population regardless of the comparative qualifications of individuals. Even when Jews are not directly affected by programs that use quotas, they oppose them on grounds that these tend to replace the principle of individual achievement with that of group ascription.

Gerrymandering of legislative boundaries to increase minority representation has raised a similar specter. In Los Angeles County, for example, Mexican American groups, with the aid of the Justice Department, succeeded in having the courts fashion a supervisorial district in which Latinos were the majority, and from which a Mexican American was elected in 1993. In 1992 a federal court agreed to redistrict Dade County, Florida, to create more explicit Latino constituencies. Some Jewish agencies formally opposed that decision as excessively group-oriented. And then there is the famous gerrymandered congressional district that meanders, thin and winding, along a railroad track across African American sections of North Carolina. The courts continue to deal with these cases.

The use of quotas has not been as pervasive as is often advertised, and gerrymandering is an old American tradition; the strangely shaped North Carolina district is a device that serves Republican political purposes as well as those of African Americans. But both controversies have provided a focus for those concerned about an excessive group separatism altering the individualistic nature of America.

LATINOS

A 1993 Yankelovich *Time* survey found that almost a third of all Americans were unfavorable to the immigration of Latinos and Caribbeans, a larger number than looked with disfavor on any other immigrant group; this can be compared with but 2 percent who were so hostile to Chinese immigration, for example.[13] The Latino population is often singled out as posing a separatist danger because of the language difference and the threat of massive immigration owing to geographical contiguousness. Latinos in the United States numbered about 20 million in 1990, and that figure is expected to double by 2025. (For practical purposes, "Latino" and "Hispanic" are interchangeable terms; the former will mostly be used for this discussion, referring mainly to those whose origin is Latin America.)

To better appreciate the situation of Latinos, we would compare them with that of a European group, Italian Americans. About four million Italians came to America between 1891 and the early 1920s, when Italian immigration was abruptly cut by law. These immigrants were pervasively poor and little educated. Speaking a foreign language and fresh from a distinctive culture, they were compressed in ghettoes and subjected to severe discrimination. Eventually, however, they responded to the same forces that have loosened the cohesion of other ancestral groups in America: timely dispersion from the ghettoes and integration into an open society. The early-generation Italians, though typically poor, were able to start their way up the economic ladder in an industrial economy that required little education. Second- and third-generation Italians, dispersed from the ghettoes in which they grew up, have intermarried, have been accepted into the mainstream, have lost their sense of defensiveness, and have generally experienced a substantial loss of ancestral identity.

The current atmosphere for minorities is different from that which faced the Italian immigrants. For one thing, earlier newcomers such as the Southern Italians had been abused and denied educational and job-training opportunities by their nation of origin, not by this country. They could not righteously petition America for redress. Today, most Mexican immigrants also cannot claim that their lives are depressed because of centuries of vile treatment by Americans, but they are not about to adopt the earlier passive stance of the Italians. They have a new model of political activism for the excluded which was set by the black power movement of the 1960s and 1970s. It emerged among a group which, like Native Americans, had been abused and discriminated against by *this* country.

Following the success of black advocacy, Latino leaders, functionaries, politicians, and intellectuals have sought to create agencies and institutions dedicated to speeding up the processes of achievement. As in the case of the African Americans, part of their advocacy calls for repairing a sense of damaged worth, building and organizing around "brown pride" and identity.

Such organized efforts to foster cultural and political group identity were largely unavailable to immigrants in an earlier era. The current movements reflect a genuine concern for tribal continuity, although in part their demands are simply organizing mechanisms. These efforts by Latino leaders have often been built around legitimating use of the Spanish language, much like French in Quebec. In areas of high concentration, such as the Southwest and Florida, some Latino organizations have even mounted campaigns to establish Spanish alongside English as an official language. In Miami, where Cuban refugees now dominate, public signs and documents are in Spanish as well as English. In 1982 a mayor of Miami said that in his city "within ten years, there will not be a word of English spoken."[14] He was off in his prediction by a considerable margin.

The experience of Québecois immigrants in New England has implications for Latinos in the Southwest. As Lansing Lamont pointed out, over a million Québecois settled south of the Canadian border, "their leaders dreaming of another Nouvelle France: Quebec grouped with New England under the banner of Catholicism. It was an illusion . . . America's melting pot experience . . . eroded the Frenchness of the expatriate Québecois . . . French became the dying language of the old generation."[15] Geographical propinquity to their home province and French-language parochial schools did not serve to preserve the solidarity of the Franco-Americans. There are now more than six million English-speaking Americans descended from French Canadians. A third of New Hampshireans report a north-of-the-border ancestry.

Certainly Latino tribal identities will not soon dissipate in this way, but the evidence indicates that geographical proximity to their homelands will not prevent Latinos from eventually going the way of most American tribal groups—for better or for worse, sooner or later, they will become English speaking and will be integrated into the mainstream. If Latinos are to succeed in a technological economy, they must know English well, and polls have shown that most of them recognize this.[16] California, Florida, and Texas will not become American Quebecs.

"Latino" is a term of convenience that covers a number of disparate Spanish-speaking groups whose socioeconomic positions are significantly different. In 1990 about 19 percent of Cubans 25 years or older had four years or more of college, compared with 10 percent of Puerto Ricans and 6 percent of Mexicans. The median income of Cubans was about $31,000, in contrast with $23,000 and $18,000 for Mexicans and Puerto Ricans.[17] Many of the Cubans, of course, emigrated as middle-class refugees; they are unlike the impoverished, relatively uneducated Puerto Ricans and Mexicans. Hence, as Earl Shorris notes, "Some political leaders have argued that Latinos can come together around a few issues: bilingual education, entitlements, concern for newcomers, and so on. But they are dreaming. The matrix includes those who favor language maintenance, another segment that favors a transitional curriculum, and a third that opposes anything but the teaching of English ... Economic differences will cause a deep, debilitating split in the national Latino population ... [who will then] be divided again and again, according to beliefs, dreams, and histories."[18]

But most threatening of all to Latino group cohesion and continuity is the overwhelming willingness among most Latinos of every national origin to succumb to melting-pot forces whenever they are able to get out of the depressed ghetto. According to one report, "As more Latinos move out of the barrios and into the suburbs ... they marry Anglos, open businesses, move into middle-class occupations ... the language dies in the suburbs, in the intermarriages."[19] In 1987 about two thirds of Latinos in New York and Los Angeles said that a major goal of bilingual education should be to ensure that their children learn English and not fall behind in school.[20] According to a Rand Corporation study, fewer than half of second-generation Latinos use Spanish at all, and in 1988 over half of the Latinos in California, largely Mexican American, said they favored making English the state's official language.[21] The 1989–1990 Latino National Political Survey found that the overwhelming majority of Latinos, 92 percent, agreed that "all citizens and residents of the U.S. should learn English." In a 1990 poll 87 percent of Latinos in Houston felt it was their duty to learn English, and a majority, like the Californians, thought that English should be the official language.[22]

Some of the leadership and agencies in the newer tribal groups foster a separatist mood alien to these integrative aspirations of the group members at large for political, institutional, or ideological reasons. Arthur Schlesinger Jr. commented of such leaders in Latino and other tribal groups that "they have thus far done better in intimidating the white majority than in converting their own constituencies."[23] While they have not changed the integrative aspirations of most Latinos, they have tapped into the anger which results when the desired integration is frustrated, notably within the poverty-stricken and swelling barrios. As Peter Skerry has pointed out, "Mexican-American politics has fixed on race consciousness and resentments." It is not cultural values or differences that will primarily sustain any separatist tendencies of Latino groups, but defensive concerns about achieving integration.

Intermarriage, the "archway of assimilation," is the ultimate antagonist not just of cultural differentiation but of meaningful tribal endurance. It is not the original cause, of course. Intermarriage rates rise only after separatist conditions diminish—chiefly, reduction of ethnic population density and increased integration into the economic and educational marketplace. At times, other factors such as unbalanced proportions of men and women have operated to similar effect. One researcher determined that among each of the earlier European groups, except Jews, intermarriage rates started out at about 20 percent for first generation immigrants and reached well over 50 percent by the third generation.[24]

The pace has been different for Latinos, and the findings have not always been consistent, perhaps because of the vagueness of the ancestral category. But the normal integrative effect of the American society is apparent, varying with regional density and openness. The outmarriage rate for first-generation Puerto Ricans in metropolitan New York was 11 percent in 1970, compared with 32 percent for their children.[25] Among Albuquerque's Mexican Americans, the intermarriage rate was 13 percent between 1940 and 1955, and 31 percent in 1967.[26] In 1974 the intermarriage rate for Mexican Americans in Los Angeles was 34 percent, more than twice that in San Antonio, a society which then offered less hospitability and economic opportunity for the group.[27] One examination of the data found that the intermarriage rate of Mexican Americans in Los Angeles County doubled from 20 to 40 percent between the 1920s and the 1960s; and that in California as a whole more than half of all Mexican Americans were marrying non-Hispanics by the 1980s.[28] Numbers apart, if upward mobility prevails, the futures of the Latinos and the Jews are not very different.

ASIAN AMERICANS

The example of the smaller but growing population of Asians has also been cited in support of some concerns about America's integrative future, based on their rate of immigration and their even more exotic language and cultural differences. However, "Asians"—Chinese, Japanese, Koreans, Vietnamese, Filipinos, Cambodians, Thais, and so on—are divided even more radically than Latinos as to cultural background and even language. And there is an additional integrative factor: because of the history and culture of those Asians who come here, their achievement drive and desire to join the American mainstream is notably high, approaching that of the Jews. Consequently, most Asian groups manage to escape poverty more quickly than do Latinos. In 1990 about 40 percent of Chinese Americans 25 years of age or older had at least four years of college, compared with 12 percent of blacks, 10 percent of Hispanics as a whole, and 22 percent of whites.[29] In 1989 the mean Scholastic Achievement Test score in mathematics was 525 for Asians, 491 for whites, and 386 for blacks.[30] At the University of California at Berkeley in the 1990s, serious consideration was given to imposing quotas on Chinese Americans so that they would not so dominate admissions based on high school grades and achievement test scores. In 1993 a *Los Angeles Times* poll found that in southern California 83 percent of Asians rated their ability to get adequate housing, education, and jobs as "good," compared with 77 percent of whites, 55 percent of Latinos, and 33 percent of blacks.[31]

Despite their being non-white, mating patterns for the different Asian groups are similar to those of European groups. The intermarriage rate for immigrant Japanese was estimated as 2 to 5 percent; for the second generation, 5 to 15 percent; for the third generation, 30 to 45 percent.[32] In 1993 the rate as reported by *Time* magazine was 65 percent for Japanese Americans. Like the Jews, they have become well-integrated and have experienced no recent rushes of newcomers.[33] Among the Chinese, perhaps because of massive immigration and therefore more eligible marriage partners of Chinese ancestry, the intermarriage rate has increased more slowly, from 10 percent in the 1950s to 18 percent in the 1970s.[34] But overall, as of 1992, according to Arthur Schlesinger Jr., about half of marriages involving Asian Americans are with non-Asians.[35]

Asian tribal qualities and cultural identities will dissipate more gradually than did those of most European groups, not only because of defensiveness but also because of the strength of age-old cultural and community institutions. But despite differences of culture, there is a fundamental congruence between the major family and work values and aspirations of most Asian newcomers and those of American society.

NATIVE AMERICANS

Two tribal populations in the United States—Native Americans and African Americans—are distinct from the rest of the population in that they did not arrive here as immigrants escaping harsh conditions in their homeland and seeking opportunities in the New World. White

America itself created the hardships to which the defensiveness of these groups was a reaction.

The Native Americans number about two million, more than half of whom now live outside the reservations. Most of their migration to urban areas took place during and following World War II and was in large part the result of a deliberate Bureau of Indian Affairs effort between 1953 and 1972 to relocate and integrate Native Americans.

Although the condition of the relocated Native Americans in the cities has remained depressed, the Bureau of Indian Affairs has continued to support integration, and by the end of the 1980s some measures had begun to show evidence that Native Americans could be integrated into the mainstream. For example, by 1990 the percentage enrolled in college came close to their proportion in the population.[36] The interracial marriage rate has also been high in the cities, depending as always on the density factor. In 1970 the proportion of Native Americans marrying outside the group was under 10 percent for those living on the reservations, about 20 percent in cities near Indian concentrations, and between 45 and 60 percent in distant urban centers like New York, Chicago, and Los Angeles.[37]

Nevertheless, the tribal identities of some Native American groups will endure into the foreseeable future, not primarily as a consequence of prejudice and defensiveness but because of the strength of their traditions and the isolation of the reservations.

AFRICAN AMERICANS

The African American population, however, remains a group apart. Racism and the cultural and institutional residues of slavery and segregation have fostered a level of tribal separatism for many blacks greater than anything found among Latino, Asian American, and Native American groups. But despite the vicious treatment to which they have been subjected, black Americans have been among the most prototypical Americans with respect to meritocratic aspirations. Their traditional agenda has been to join the mainstream as equal participants. "Integration" was the keyword of the black-led civil rights movement of the 1960s.

As of the 1990s, a sizable corps of African Americans have moved into the mainstream. Occupational mobility for disadvantaged groups usually depends on an expanding economy. Partly for that reason, occupational progress for blacks as a group has not been linear, but it has been considerable in the civil rights decades. In the 1950s a little over one out of ten black workers was in a white-collar occupation. By the 1990s four out of ten held such positions, compared with five out of ten whites. In 1990 the median income of African American married couples was a little under $40,000, a figure which represented 84 percent of the income of white married couples. In 1967 the comparable figure was 60 percent. This increase is startling, given the recency with which blacks have been allowed to compete in the economy. In 1990 the median earnings of black college graduates had reached 90 percent of that of white college graduates.[38]

White acceptance of "de-ghettoized" blacks has radically changed for the better. As another signal of change, an increasing number of new black officials have been elected by heavily white constituencies, leading one black congressman to comment that "there isn't a new generation of black politicians; there is a new generation of white voters."[39] In 1985, documenting the "important and pervasive changes" that have taken place in relations between blacks and whites, academic pollster Howard Schuman suggested that "only because so much of the population of the United States is now too young to remember race relations circa 1940 can there be any doubt about the magnitude of the change."[40] This largely peaceful reform is unprecedented in the history of dominant societies and subjugated minorities. As belated and incomplete as they are, these changes demonstrate the integrative potential of American society.

However, it became apparent early on that a tragically schizoid situation was developing. While a substantial part of the African American population was improving their lot by escaping from the ghetto and entering the middle-class mainstream, a substantial segment was becoming even more deeply mired in disorganized hopelessness. The Kerner Commission on Civil Rights in the 1960s had warned of the emergence of "two nations," one black and one white. As of the 1990s it has become more apparent that two different black populations are emerging, one "making it," the other constituting an inconsolable underclass. In 1988 Carl Zinsmeister estimated that a third of the African American population was comfortably middle class, definitely above the national median in family income, while another third was lower middle class, working and mostly owning their own homes. The final third, however, was ghettoized in deep and apparently hopeless poverty. Of the eight million in this bottom third, most received government benefits, but half of them, during a period of prosperity, were still below the poverty line. A quarter were involved in or suffering from the effects of criminal activity; the other three quarters of the impoverished were primarily nonworking single mothers and their children.[41]

The gap between lower and higher income blacks has become greater than the difference between lower and higher income whites.[42] As early as 1969, noting the progress being made, a Census Bureau official said that the "deterioration" also taking place in the ghettoes "may reflect the migration of the more successful families from the slums, leaving behind widows, deserted wives and children, the aged and the uneducated—those least able to cope with their social and economic problems."[43]

The situation has worsened since this comment. In the 1960s— notably at the time when the black middle class began to seriously grow—the overall family structure of the African American population began to crumble. In 1950, 78 percent of black households featured a married couple, comparing closely with 88 percent of white households. In 1990, only 48 percent of black households had a married couple, compared with 83 percent of white households.[44] The proportion of black children born in female-headed households was 23 percent in 1960 and 62 percent by the end of the 1980s.[45] There is a direct relationship, of course, between family structure and both the education and income of parents. In 1988 the majority, 56 percent, of single-parent black households with children were living in poverty, compared with 12.5 percent of two-parent families with children.[46]

In one way, the situation may not be quite as bad as these numbers suggest. Christopher Jencks calculates that if married black women had borne the same number of babies in 1987 as they did in 1960, the proportion of black infants born to unmarried mothers would have risen from 23 percent in 1960 to only 29 percent by 1987. The figure has grown steadily because the birthrate among married blacks has plummeted, resulting in the ratio of illegitimate to legitimate going way up.[47]

The persistent economic frustration among poor African Americans understandably blunts their achievement drive and integrative impulses. According to a 1986 study by the National Bureau of Economic Research, almost a third of black inner-city males believed they could earn more from committing street crime than from working.[48] A National Academy of Sciences panel noted, "Conditions within the black community began to diverge sharply in the 1970s. By the early 1980's, black men aged 25–34 with at least some college earned 80–85 percent as much as their white counterparts . . . In terms of education, these black men represented the top one third of their age group. At the other end of the group were the one quarter of black men aged 25–34 who had not finished high school and who could not compete in the stagnant 1970s economy. An increasing number dropped out of the labor force altogether."[49]

One might simply say that a substantial number of African Americans have been upwardly mobile during the postsixties era, recession periods apart. It could be argued that if the trend re-emerges, if there are job opportunities, then the African American future will resemble the past of other tribal groups: a cycle of integration, intermarriage, and dissolution of birthright ties. In such an optimistic scenario, the ghetto-dwellers would just be expected to enter the mainstream much more slowly. But that would be a serious misreading of the situation. To a singular degree, even those African Americans who have escaped from the ghetto are caught by the uniquely perverse historical relationship between black and white Americans which sustains negative cross-racial stereotypes among both groups.

Studies of metropolitan areas have found that the poorest Latinos are less segregated than most affluent blacks. Both Latinos and Asians are more likely to inhabit integrated neighborhoods with whites than areas of ethnic concentration; the same is not true of blacks.[50] Even the new suburbs in which more affluent blacks live tend to be segregated.

Intermarriage rates reflect this special African American situation. The overall ratio has risen only slightly, in sharp contrast to that of Asians and Latinos, despite significant progress by many African Americans in college education and economic integration. One study of 1980 data concluded that among blacks who were not of Latino background, only 2 percent had married nonblacks.[51]

Highly visible, acutely negative conditions helped sustain tribal separatism. Some black intellectuals, notably on university faculties, have stressed separatist themes and the need for segregated institutions. Newspapers occasionally report on the use of African rituals in the weddings or in rites of passage for young American blacks. The growing use of the term "African American" is itself a case in point. Self-segregation among black students on college campuses has become highly publicized, including calls for separate black graduation ceremonies. A *Doonesbury* cartoon in 1993 depicted black militant students demanding "separate water fountains," the despised symbol of segregation in the South a generation earlier.

Tribal cohesion of the black population as a whole does not derive from cultural ties to Africa. Du Bois said that "there is nothing so indigenous, so 'made in America' as we," and Martin Luther King Jr. once said, "The Negro is an American; we know nothing of Africa."[52] Two polls of the black population in 1990 and 1991 found that most blacks preferred to call themselves "blacks" rather than "African Americans."[53]

The African American drive for "black pride" preceded and inspired the other ethnic revivals of the 1960s and 1970s, but very often served as a platform for the achievement of political and economic equality. Today, there are distinctive and positive cultural group attributes to which American blacks are pridefully attached, but their tribal cohesion is now driven primarily by what some observers call "oppositional social identity," that is, defensive considerations. To some extent, the defensive posture has been held most emphatically by the black leadership. In the mid-1980s three fifths of black leaders told pollsters that the situation of blacks was "going backward," while two thirds of a national black sample said that they were "making progress." The proportion of blacks who expressed optimism has apparently declined slightly since the mid-1980s, owing to the economic recession, but it is still greater than black leaders perceive it to be.[54] But, not surprisingly, African American defensiveness is high relative to that of other tribal populations, having been created by a particularly egregious history of bigotry and pervasive ghettoized poverty. Attitudes of mutual hostility or wariness between whites and blacks, including the most affluent blacks, have been repolarized by the pathologies created within the ghettoes.

Since those black ghettoes have also been uniquely "made in America," it seems obvious that the majority group owes moral and civil rights obligations to the African Americans beyond what are due to Latinos—and that the consequences for ethnic separatism will also be different. By the middle of the next century, there will still be sizable Asian and Latino groupings in America, but to the extent that the American open reward system persists, they will be much more integrated, and their tribal cohesion will be much looser. But until the American society can find some way to hasten the dissolution of black ghettoes, there will always be the possibility that separatist tendencies will harden within the black community.

Louis Farrakhan and his Nation of Islam, concentrating heavily on the campuses, have denigrated the idea of integration. He told the *Washington Times* in 1990 that "we have no hope that we can effect true reconciliation between blacks and whites in this country ... The answer ultimately is going to be separation."[55] Significantly, Farrakhan's call for separatism is based primarily on oppositional and defensive grounds. He wrote in a Nation of Islam publication that "the Caucasian is born by nature to be the enemy of the original man ... This is why the Honorable Elijah Muhammad called them a race of devils ... They have never established justice, equity or freedom."[56]

Tribal Dissolution

We predict that the melting pot will continue to dissolve tribal cohesion among those of Asian, European, and Latino origins, and ultimately, assuming economic growth, among Native Americans and African Americans as well, although blacks will make the slowest progress. America will then be in a qualitatively new situation.

Ancestral groups once provided the majority of Americans with a specific sense of rootedness, of community. Most Americans are no longer tribally connected, and yet they are still not ready to acknowledge the direction in which the society is headed. They are often reluctant to accept the reality of the melting pot because a comfortable and romantic image of America has centered around ethnic cultural survivals, even among some of the non-European groups, particularly with respect to their kitchens. Film and television feature ethnic groups as an integral part of the American scene, and certain tribal customs and characteristics—once considered negative stereotypes—are now fondly recalled. Third generations remember their grandparents, and they resist the idea of numerical decline. And, of course, there are also the group-connected functionaries and intellectuals who have an additional stake in resisting the disappearance of these groups.

However, one can imagine the new American scene in a different light. In the new century of the coming millennium, America may finally approach the destiny Ralph Waldo Emerson once saw for it, the construction of "a new race . . . as vigorous as the new Europe which came out of the smelting pot of the Dark Ages." His comment reminds us that the ancestry groups of this nation do not date back to Adam, or even to the Tower of Babel, but were themselves created in the crucible of history. America may just outgrow the tribal dilemma. Its historic role may have been to demonstrate a new political idea which allows associational diversity to flourish within an integrated, achievement-oriented society—but neither that diversity nor the communities to which humans typically aspire need to be based on ancient national backgrounds. America may absorb those ancestral origins much as

England and France did. After all, who in England remembers the Germanic, Latin, and Nordic tribes that once divided that country?

That might seem like the most fantastic proposition of all, in light of the contemporary tribal explosions on the world scene. In Yugoslavia, for example, during the half-century of totalitarian freeze, ethnic as well as religious differences were repressed, and a substantial amount of intermarriage took place. When the freeze melted, ethnic consciousness again took over, with tragedy for the intermarrieds and no place for Yugoslavs. But the countervailing qualities of American society have been different from the ethnically heterogeneous parts of Europe, have indeed been exceptional.

This does not mean that cultural diversity will end in America or that other communities will not emerge, much as the various categories of Latinos and Asians have since World War II. But, sentiment aside, the evidence does insist that, for better and for worse, we can anticipate the virtual end of most ancestral tribal groupings now in America. The future of American Jewry must be weighed in that context.

The Jews in America's Future

The same group dissolution factors that affect most of America's tribal units have been dramatically changing the Jews. A basic dwindling cycle is evident. American Jews steadily are becoming more thoroughly integrated into the intellectual, economic, and public life of the society. Their social and geographic mobility is increasing, as is their interaction with other Americans and their cultures. The level of mingling with other Jews is decreasing. Jews express greater acceptance of other Americans and their cultures, just as other Americans express greater acceptance of Jews and their culture. The rate of intermarriage, already above the halfway mark, is still accelerating. More than eight out of ten intermarriages result in mixed households, without conversion of the non-Jewish spouse. The tribal connections, including the religious identification of the children of mixed households, are diminishing.

Some researchers have demurred from this bleak picture, but they have been more likely to question the total and runaway aspects of this model than the model itself. The dwindling pattern is unmistakable—not for all Jews, but for the Jewish population as a whole. Much of Jewish leadership is either "in denial" about this downward cycle, or has some romantic and unrealistic notions about how to reverse it. The denial, ironically, is often based on a negativity: a belief that some historical intervention will increase hostility to the Jews, and thereby rebuild a defensiveness which will bring many Jews back to the fold. (A French Rothschild once commented to us that he believed God had sent a disproportionately Jewish New Left to stimulate anti-Semitism, which in turn would cause Jews to remain identified.)

The evidence indicates that if current trends are not interrupted, the socioeconomic status of American Jews will be even more secure by the year 2050. Most of the obstacles having disappeared, the Jews will be even more thoroughly integrated into America's economic main-stream.[57] Partly because of that integration, the levels of expressed anti-Semitism will recede even further.

Such a prophecy would have raised eyebrows on that morning in 1993 when the newspapers reported the arrest of a few young men in Los Angeles who had planned—and, in some cases, had executed—the bombing of Jewish and black targets. It was a small gang, but a dangerous one for those it intended to bomb, not to be laughed away. But neither was it a starter-group for some large or influential anti-Semitic or racist movement. Its behavior was met with universal horror and speedy law enforcement. In the years ahead, there will undoubtedly still be a fraction of activist but generally rejected anti-Semites—about 5 percent of the population. A larger portion of the mainstream American population will still passively hold some package of those anti-Semitic attitudes and stereotypes which have been imbedded in our culture for so many centuries—but they will comprise a much lower proportion than the 20 percent who are assessed as holding such beliefs today.

The fading of the Jews as a target factor in the dynamics of anti-Semitism will be further aided by continuing changes in their occupational pattern. Jews once owned a disproportionate number of the shops where the consumer met the economy, sometimes disagreeably. But in the future, with more Jewish professionals and executives and fewer exposed middlemen, the visibility of Jewish participation in America's business and financial life will be blurred in the anonymous corporate structure.

Meanwhile, indices of the acceptability of Jews in the American culture continue to grow. During and after the 1992 campaigns in which Californians elected Jews to both U.S. senatorial vacancies, not a voice was raised publicly to mark the fact. The Republican nominee for one of these seats was also Jewish. Highly Germanic Wisconsin has two Jewish senators, and Scandinavian Lutheran Minnesota chose a Democratic Jew to replace a Republican co-religionist in 1990. As noted earlier, neither Ruth Bader Ginsburg's nor Stephen Breyer's appointment to the Supreme Court caused any public comment about their being Jews, although Bader made a point of that fact in her presentation to the U.S. Senate. The same could not have been said when Louis Brandeis was appointed to the Supreme Court in 1916, Benjamin Cardozo in 1932, or Felix Frankfurter in 1939.

Israel-connected problems in America have been considered by Jews to be the greatest potential source of an anti-Semitic revival. Such a trigger factor could presumably emerge if relations between the United States and Israel deteriorated, and if support for Israel was perceived by American policymakers and the American public as counter to the interests of America while American Jews continued to vehemently lobby for Israel. Not being able to anticipate history, we cannot entirely dismiss that possibility. However, it seems highly unlikely. While the menace of Soviet adventurism in the Middle East has disappeared, American national interest in that area has not, and the unique political stability of a friendly Israel remains attractive. Meanwhile, Israel's image as a Western society remains firm. If the Middle East peace process initiated in 1993 is largely successful, it might reduce the American public's level of suspicion toward Arabs in general. But the animosity toward the West held by many of the extremist political forces of the Muslim-Arab world—punctuated by acts of terrorism in the United States such as the 1993 bombing of the World Trade Center in

New York—will not quickly depart from the American public's consciousness.

Also, while the perception of American national interest is a determinative factor, the social and political integration of American Jews is a strong deterrent to any American break with Israel. It is ironic that in a 1993 survey, six out of ten American Jews agreed that "the criticism of Israel that we hear derives mainly from anti-Semitism," but the evidence suggests that the reverse is more likely to be true.[58] Many non-Jews in America are favorable toward Israel because they identify it with American Jews, toward whom they have favorable feelings and with whom they have ties. The columnist Richard Reeves, who is a Protestant, has suggested that Americans support Israel not because of its security value or the political activity of the Jewish community, but because they like the Jews they know. He believes that realizing how dedicated American Jews are to Israel, non-Jewish Americans give them the issue.

The consciousness that favorable trends can be reversed and that there are many "indifferents" in the society will keep a sense of foreboding alive, even among Jews who do not personally feel the presence of hostility in this country. Referring to Pat Buchanan's strong showing in the 1992 presidential primaries, the political scientist Benjamin Ginsberg recently warned that "as in the case of Louisianians voting for David Duke, the voters of New Hampshire and the other primary states did not give their votes to Buchanan *because* he was an anti-Semite. On the other hand, the fact of his anti-Semitism *did not prevent* . . . roughly 30% of the Republican electorate in a number of other states from supporting Buchanan."[59]

The existence of so many indifferents legitimates some level of foreboding. However, if Buchanan is an anti-Semite, he assiduously avoids any overt expressions of such a sentiment—behavior which signals that the crucial constraints are still in place. In June of 1993, a small newspaper outside of St. Louis noted unhappily that a large number of President Clinton's advisors are Jewish. But more significant than this newspaper's anti-Semitic attitude are two facts: that a large number of Clinton's advisors *are Jewish,* and that the region's cultural spokespersons, including the Bishop of St. Louis and commentators in the mainstream newspapers, took vigorous and indignant exception to the offensive editorial.

The official constraints against active bigotry show no signs of breaking down. Significantly, the politics behind that reality lies in the fact that the groups traditionally thought of as ethnic targets—Latinos, African Americans, Asians, and Jews—will soon make up half of the American population. Since ethnic identities, including those of non-Europeans, will endure long after cohesion vanishes from the tribal communities—and bigotry only strengthens such identities—the constraints imposed by massive heterogeneity will continue to deter the development of generally intolerant political movements on a national scale.

Anti-Semitism, after all, has been shown to be a cultural phenomenon. All things equal, it is transmitted by the societal culture and can be diminished in the same way. The "law of longevity" proposes that if the culture of anti-Semitism is muted long enough by constraints, it can atrophy. The lower the reservoir of anti-Semitic attitudes, the less available is anti-Semitism for exploitation by a demagogue, the less easily can the fringe bigot influence the mainstream.

Despite many reasons for optimism, there is continuing concern among some Jews about a religious *kulturkampf,* resulting in a Christian fundamentalist domination of American public policy. The concern has centered around Protestant evangelicals, those fundamentalists who report themselves as "born again" and are conversionary. About a third of Americans so describe themselves. But their potential as a right-wing force is frequently exaggerated because a higher percentage of blacks than whites, and of low-income than high-income people, fall into this category. Consequently, evangelicals are at least as likely to declare themselves Democrats as Republicans, since only the middle-class whites are identified with the GOP.[60] Although some white evangelical leaders have periodically entered the national political arena—mainly on the Republican and economically conservative side—they have not been able to mobilize a dominant national constituency. Jerry Falwell tried and lost support for his religious activities.

And certainly fundamentalists have not been able to garner majority support in the Republican Party, although they have been gaining strength in a number of states, to some degree because they are much more likely to take part in the low-turnout primaries and open conventions than moderates.

Furthermore, as we have seen, efforts to impose a sectarian bias on federal public policy—that is, to reverse the principle of separation of church and state—have largely failed throughout American history. And since the federal government has thoroughly preempted the issue in the latter part of this century, congressional and judicial constraints have demonstrated that such efforts will continue to fail, again partly for reasons of heterogeneity. As in the case of civil rights, the courts and legislatures will continue to wrestle with such refining questions as how far religious practices can be accommodated in public life—and some Jewish groups will make demands for further accommodation—but the basic laws invalidating any official sectarian preference are irreversible for the foreseeable future.

Some American Jews are nervous about the apparent rise of anti-Semitism in Eastern and even Western Europe. Aside from tribal concern, they remember the importation of anti-Semitism into America from Nazi Europe during the 1930s. While it is true that, for all the reasons cited, levels of xenophobia and even of anti-Semitism are still much higher in most of Europe than in the United States, the constraints have been generally growing there also. And one source of those constraints has been the United States itself, in an increasingly interlocked international society.

It is not yet time for American Jews to abandon some degree of misgiving. The above considerations do not guarantee the absence of danger forevermore, but they do shift the odds considerably against anti-Semitism or prejudicial disadvantage becoming a serious problem for Jews in the next couple of generations. Even the stubborn sense of foreboding—a historically understandable defense mechanism—must diminish as newer generations of American Jews perceive that their civil status is basically assured and protected, as all indications suggest it will be. In any case, in an open and option-rich America, negative defensiveness is not the quality on which to build a durable cohesive consciousness, for the Jews or any other group.

The Continuity of the American Jewish Community

Just as special Jewish factors provided an unusual fit between Jews and America, leading to acceptance and assimilation, so special *positive* factors will predictably slow any dissolution of the Jewish community. To begin with, an unparalleled network of strong communal institutions has been developed to serve and promote the association of Jews. Upwards of two hundred Jewish communities have established formal Federations in order to raise funds for a variety of local services, as well as for Israel. Depending on size, those communities typically encompass such traditional services as burial societies and loan associations, as well as community centers, family agencies, public affairs committees, and others. There are thousands of synagogues in those and other communities. About 250 national organizations include some large membership groups as well as institutions and coordinating agencies. Many of these organizations have local branches.

The Jewish organizational network is so dense, as the hyperbolic joke goes, that every Jew who is connected can look forward to being president of a Jewish group at some time in his or her life. This unusual network intensifies the attractive communal aspect of Jewish life and maintains a level of interaction among Jews—cohesive factors which will defer tribal departure for those families that are affiliated.

Also, because Jews share certain occupational and educational similarities to a unique degree, they will remain interactive in social, professional, and political arenas, even if Jewish neighborhoods continue to decline. The unexceptionable premise is that the more spheres of such activity in which members of the same group interact, the stronger the group cohesion.

The various deterrent factors cited—insecurity, institutional depth, structural similarities—will certainly prevent any precipitate disappearance of American Jewry. However, foreboding is likely to thin eventually. Moreover, much of the non-Jewish population is gradually coming to resemble the Jews educationally and even occupationally.

And about half of American Jews are not affiliated with that dense organizational network.

As the Jews spread out, the organizational connections become more crucial for cohesion. In 1927, when over 40 percent of all American Jews lived in New York City and were residentially segregated within that city, it did not much matter that their level of organizational and synagogue affiliation was much lower than in smaller cities. The communal atmosphere in the neighborhoods and in the city was itself so dense that formal affiliation was not necessary for group solidarity. But now that density within neighborhoods, even in New York City, is much less common, Jews who are unconnected to Jewish organizations have little to reinforce their tribal identity.

Given the inexorably integrative forces of American society and the resultant parallel trends among Jews, it is reasonable to predict that the Jewish community as a whole will be severely reduced in numbers by the middle of the next century. The extent to which the remaining core will endure, or even possibly recoup, will depend on more intrinsic factors than defensiveness, structural similarities, or even institutional depth.

The prospect of a much-reduced Jewish community has caused great consternation among community leaders. "Jewish continuity" is the prime item on the community agenda. The rhetoric is often tautological: Jews would be better and stronger Jews if only they would be stronger and better Jews. Research projects have been multiplied in an effort to find the social engineering that will fix the problem. But, for the most part, the problem is beyond social engineering, as it is for other tribal groups; it is rooted in the dynamics of the American society.

Charles Liebman suggests a more pertinent question than whether American Judaism will survive: Is it *worthwhile* for American Judaism to survive? He then comments that "anyone who can seriously pose such a question to himself is unlikely to answer that survival is worthwhile."[61] But the "worthwhileness" of Jewish existence is essential to the survival and durability of Jewish life; it is the elusive "intrinsic" factor, beyond defensiveness and other external qualities.

Too often, the primary search for that quality is for a unique social or political ideology. As we have indicated, there are special ideologies related to Jewish life, but for the most part they are only of interest to those who are already Jewish. Options for social action can be found outside the Jewish community, such as in the political parties, the American Civil Liberties Union, the Sierra Club, and other liberal and conservative public interest groups. The primary reason for consciously engaging in such public activity *as a Jew* is the sense of tribal community from which such ideology flows; and that is exactly the source which is under attack by the integrative American society.

It is not unreasonable to believe that the existence of Israel has intrinsic tribal reverberations, not only for the peripheral Jews but for the "shadow Jews," the uncounted numbers who have some vestigial sense of Jewish identity. However, for reasons earlier explored, there is evidence that intrinsic emotional attachments between American Jews and Israel are becoming somewhat weaker rather than stronger, and may be further reduced by a successful Middle East peace process. There has even been the suggestion that the existence of Israel, with its total Jewish life, threatens the authenticity of most American Jews and their compartmentalized Jewish lives.

So finally, many analysts have pointed to religion as the intrinsic *sine qua non* of American Jewish durability. However, as we have seen, religious beliefs, or adherence to religious practice, are not simply matters of will—for most people—and those who do not adhere to the beliefs or practices are not just willful defectors.

There is a body of Jews—Conservative and Reform as well as Orthodox—who are "devoutly religious" in the sense of a more scrupulous commitment to religious doctrine or practice, such as regularly attending synagogue services. But such Jews will be a fractional and smaller part of the population in the future. However, those defined as devout do not sum up the religious dimension of the Jews. A much larger number of Jews, while not as devoutly or scrupulously religious in ideology or practice, clearly find some range of spiritual meaning in Jewish practices. A dominant theme in the 1993 biennial convention of the Union of American Hebrew Congregations—the Reform federation—was the need to fulfill the "spiritual" needs of young Jews.

There is evidence that a pervasive sense of anomie is driving some of the American population back to a "spiritual yearning" that can be fulfilled in religious institutions which offer traditional sources of community—perhaps partly in the place of lost tribal identities. In a nationwide survey of the baby-boomer generation, one sociologist of religion, Wade Clark Roof, found that while almost half had left and never returned to church or synagogue, millions of them remain active "seekers," although identifying themselves as spiritual rather than religious. Many of them tend to draw from a cafeteria of religious traditions.[62] In California, admittedly the vanguard of "New Age seekers," anecdotes abound of Christmas trees whose ornaments include a Mogen David and ceremonies presided over by a Buddhist priest and a rabbi.

That image is not comforting for those concerned about Jewish continuity and raises the chicken-and-egg question of what comes first for much of the Jewish population, religious or communal attachment. While there is a strong need among most humans for some spiritual expression, it is the tribal attachment that makes that expression feel *Jewish*. There are, especially in America, many perceived alternatives. About three quarters of American Jews do *something* that has a Judaic tinge, even if it is only sometimes attending a Passover seder. The source of much of this practice is the impulse for a particular communal connection. However, since the record indicates that the particularistic tribal attachment will continue to be eroded by the open American society, there will be fewer Jews whose communal connections are Jewish to begin with. For those, Steven Cohen's image would seem to apply: an "artichoke syndrome," whereby "the encounter with America gradually strips away, layer by layer, distinctive Jewish practices."[63]

On the other hand, Jewish life does offer unusually deep, historically based tribal traditions, presented in a religious framework and grounded in a set of explicit and life-organizing personal values. For most Jews, as Charles Liebman argues, these traditions bear some relationship to the definition of "folk religion," which "tends to accept the organizational structure of the elite religion, but to be indifferent to the elite belief structure," although not indifferent to the structure of personal values.[64] That mode would encompass the many religious fellow-travelers who engage in minimal ritual practice primarily as a means of tribal identity, but nevertheless personally sense a gratifying spiritual and even transcendent quality in those particular tribal traditions. Their attachment might not always qualify as "religious" in the minds of some of the more devout or learned, but it is certainly religion-connected.

This religion-connected aspect of Jewish life provides the strongest deterrent to the swift or complete dissolution of American Jewry. It also is the most credible basis for the prediction that while the Jewish community will be much reduced in size by the middle of the next century, it will not have disappeared and may even have reached some relatively stable plateau.

More than that, it is not beyond the realm of possibility that conditions could change, bringing marginal Jews back to the community. Even if the process of deracination proceeds, a general counter-reaction among Americans is possible. For the most part, human nature abhors rootlessness. Most people eventually seek the fulfillment of a cohesive community, especially one which will provide their lives with some felt measure of form, continuity, and personal or spiritual meaning, beyond familiarity.

Such a resurgent communalism may already be appearing. In the widely used terms of sociological art invented by the German scholar Georg Simmel, the attractions of *Gemeinschaft* (meaning community) are again coming to the fore as distinct from those of *Gesellschaft* (meaning the mass, unmediated society)—for reasons not only of personal satisfaction but of perceived social health. But whatever the results of a renewed search for community, they do not denote an "ethnic" renaissance. The new yearners are not notably returning to their ancestral communities whose distinctive qualities have been strained in the open and mobile marketplace of integrative America.

Looking at suburban evidence, Richard Alba has suggested that "nationality differences tended to diminish under the homogenizing influences of suburban life, leaving religion as the primary form of ethnicity."[65] But as we noted earlier, the ranks of the mainstream or religiously liberal Christian denominations have been thinning, while the more fundamentalist denominations, often regionally concentrated, have gained some strength. Andrew Greeley has pointed out that the parish concept, even in the suburbs, has served to maintain neighborhood communities among Catholics. Even though dispersion from neighborhoods and parishes is an American fact of life, religion-connected groups, with their distinctive rituals and practices, are in a better position than ancestral groups per se to establish lines of community beyond geographical boundaries.

After the dispersion of Jews from ancient Jerusalem, the rabbis came to recognize that the Jews required a wall of distinctive rituals, practices, and laws to keep them cohesive in far-flung places, especially where conversion was an easy option. As we have seen, that separatist wall has been crumbling in an integrative America.

Even in cross-ethnic or non-ethnic religious populations, approval of denominational intermarriage has risen to once unimaginable heights. By 1983, nine out of ten Catholic respondents to a Gallup poll expressed their "approval" of marriages between Catholics and Protestants, and, indeed, between Catholics and Jews; seven out of ten Protestants expressed the same agreement on both counts.[66] Such figures have some significance, even if they only reflect a bowing to the inevitable. Nevertheless, for the reasons which have been indicated, not only have the religious properties of communities proved more durable than their ancestral ones, but a community based on strong religion-connected qualities has a better chance of renewal—if its peripheral communicants have not become thoroughly disconnected.

The most commonly proposed solution for the problem of diminishing Jewish ranks is "Jewish education." That makes sense in that the research reports that the longer and more intensive the Jewish training, the more likely people are to practice Judaism.[67] On the other hand, the prescription for Jewish education is a cliché which does not in itself provide a very sharp or actionable focus. As the entire American society has learned to its sorrow, providing access to education is not enough. We can only educate those who are already motivated to take advantage of the access. In the case of the Jews, the prior motivation lies in a strongly held or remembered sense of tribal connection.

But where do we get on this merry-go-round? The strategists of Jewish continuity may be too concentrated on the quantitative aspects. The evidence indicates that educational "inreach" may turn out to be more important than "outreach," not just for keeping the core of Jews, but for the possibility of expanding it in the future. While the cohesive Jewish community will become smaller, for generations many peripheral and "shadow Jews" who are no longer tribal in practice or affiliation will retain some sense of Jewish identity or at least some knowledge of their ancestry. A vibrant "core" which is strongly and visibly committed to the tribal and religious depth of Jewish tradition could be the magnet that draws back some of those who eventually may find themselves spiritually or communally hungry, including people who only have a partial Jewish ancestry.

Against that day of possible return, however, it would be helpful if the more ragged edges of "Jewish identity" were prolonged to the extent possible. Most patterns of sheer association—structural, social, philanthropic, defensive, service-connected, and even Israel-connected—are themselves not enough to maintain cohesion indefinitely, but the longer those associations persist, on any basis, the better the possibilities.

The new place of women in Jewish life is the most dramatically promising example of a change that will contribute to continuity. Once virtually excluded from the *bimah,* the platform from which religious ceremonies are led, women are increasingly welcome to leadership. In recent years, for the first time, women are being trained and employed as rabbis to serve in Reform and Conservative congregations. The proportions of women in lay and religious leadership are still relatively small but are visibly growing every year.

Such a development is important not only because women have always tended to have a strong role in committing families to religious practice, but because it is a signal that much of the Jewish community is open to new forms of association. The formation of *havura*—small, independent groups of worshippers—has been encouraged, and these groups have often eventually associated themselves with established congregations.

Familiar questions have been raised about whether some of the new openness is counter-productive. Because of the intermarriage rate, for example, some Jewish religious institutions have laid out a new welcome mat for non-Jewish spouses. Programs for making members of mixed marriages more comfortable in the community have multiplied, but may have reduced the conversionary pressure. In general, however, the new openness is calculated to keep more Jews associated with the community in some way.

After all, the majority of Jews want to be Jews, as indicated by their adherence to *some* Jewish practice into the fourth generation. In the spirit of his time, John Adams wrote that "once ... no longer persecuted, [Jews] would soon wear away some of the asperities and peculiarities of their character, possibly in time become liberal Unitarian Christians."[68] Since American Jews are no longer persecuted, Adams would find it less remarkable that many Jews are leaving the fold than that so many are stubbornly staying in. Like many of his—and our—contemporaries, Adams may have underestimated the force of certain communal and spiritual impulses.

Nevertheless, the force of the unique society which Adams helped to initiate has countered those impulses, at least as far as they have been historically manifested in ancestral groups. Given the theoretical possibility of one of Nathan Glazer's "surprises," the pursuit of strategies to stem the diminution of the American Jewish population is certainly warranted, if it is geared to reality rather than to nostalgia, defensiveness, or guilt. But despite the educational and associational programs that are brought to bear, the American tribal dilemma will continue to press on even the remnant of committed Jews in a society no longer seriously characterized by the major presence of tribal groups.[69]

The nub of the dilemma is that even most of those Jews who would like to maintain their identity will not relinquish their place in an integrated society. At the turn of the twenty-first century, they are not that far from Rebecca Samuels, who, at the close of the eighteenth century, wrote her parents about "what a wonderful country this is"; or from the characters of Abraham Cahan who, at the turn of the twentieth century, "rose like one man" to applaud the national anthem, "as if they were saying," in astonishment, "we are not persecuted under this flag."

No one recognized the nature of the dilemma more clearly than a small group of Hasidic Jews, numbering about 12,000 in 1994, who attempted to establish an insulated political enclave, including their own school district, in upper New York state. Their remedy was starkly separatist. As one spokesman said: "We want isolation . . . we don't want to expose our kids to the entire society, to the entire world . . . We want to keep to our tradition."

"We are not like the Amish," he pointed out. "We have electricity. We have cars and other things the modern world gives. But we want to live like our forefathers did—dress like them, speak the same language." Toward that end, the children are isolated from other groups, from the cultural influences of television, and, after age eighteen, their marriages are arranged by parents.[70]

Such imposed isolation could conceivably work for a small group, especially if it could manage somehow to avoid the integrative hazards of college and the economic marketplace. But a thoroughly separatist solution is not likely to sustain even an appreciable remnant of American Jews.

"Fragile remnant" is a term Benjamin Disraeli applied to Jews in the nineteenth century. "Remnant" is a relative term, and American Jewry will almost certainly qualify. If there are no big historical surprises, the cohesive body of Jews will not only be a smaller portion of the American population by the middle of the next century, it will be smaller in absolute numbers. However, the remnant—both the more devout and the fellow-travelers—will tend to be those who feel somehow connected to the religious core of their tribal identity. As a result, unlike most ancestral groups whose defensive need has waned, the remaining body of American Jewry may well be significantly less "fragile" than it is now. Yet, even that religious core cannot be durably nourished by isolationist remedies. The tribal dilemma in America is not to be solved for most Jews—or most members of this country's ancestral groups—by requiring them to forego those exceptional qualities of American society that have so beneficently created that dilemma.

~ Notes ~

Introduction: America's Tribal Dilemma

1. Abraham Cahan, *The Rise of David Levinsky* (New York: Harper and Brothers, 1917; Harper Torchbook edition), p. 424.
2. For an elaboration of this analysis, see Seymour Martin Lipset, *Exceptionalism: The Persistence of an American Doctrine* (New York: W. W. Norton, forthcoming).
3. Seymour Martin Lipset, *The First New Nation: The United States in Historical and Comparative Perspective* (New York: W. W. Norton, rev. ed. 1979), pp. 110–113.
4. Ibid.
5. Edward A. Tiryakian, "American Religious Exceptionalism: A Reconsideration," *The Annals of the American Academy of Political and Social Science*, 527 (May 1993), pp. 51–52.
6. Todd M. Endelman, *The Jews of Georgian England, 1714–1830: Tradition and Change in a Liberal Society* (Philadelphia: Jewish Publication Society of America, 1979), p. 31.

1. An Old People in a New Land

1. Jacob R. Marcus, *The American Colonial Jew, 1492–1776* (Detroit: Wayne State University Press, 1970), p. 267 (emphasis in original); and "Jews and the American Revolution: A Bicentennial Documentary," *American Jewish Archives*, 27: 2 (November 1975), p. 210.

2. Mary Antin, *The Promised Land* (Boston: Houghton Mifflin, 1912), p. 202.

3. Richard Hofstadter, *America at 1750* (New York: Alfred A. Knopf, 1971), p. 139.

4. Stanley Feldstein, *The Land That I Show You* (Garden City, NY: Doubleday-Anchor, 1978), p. 14.

5. George Mason, in *Reminiscences of Newport,* cited in Ibid., p. 4.

6. Henry L. Feingold, *A Midrash on American Jewish History* (Albany: State University of New York Press, 1982), p. 189. For excellent discussions of this congruence see Arnold M. Eisen, *The Chosen People in America: A Study in Jewish Religious Ideology* (Bloomington: Indiana University Press, 1983), pp. 25–52, and Joseph L. Blau, *Judaism in America: From Curiosity to Third Faith* (Chicago: University of Chicago Press, 1976), pp. 7–20.

7. Max Weber, *The Protestant Ethic and the Spirit of Capitalism* (New York: Scribner, 1958), pp. 54–55.

8. Max Weber, *Economy and Society* (Berkeley: University of California Press, 1978), vol. 1, pp. 622–623. For an elaboration of the links between Puritanism and Judaism, particularly in America, see Edward A. Tiryakian, "American Religious Exceptionalism: A Reconsideration," *The Annals of the American Academy of Political and Social Science,* 527 (May 1993), pp. 51–52.

9. Tiryakian, "American Religious Exceptionalism," pp. 48–50. In elaboration of the relationship of the achievement drive of Jews to the Protestant ethic, see Fred Strodtbeck, "Family Interaction, Values and Achievement," in David C. McClelland et al., *Talent and Society* (Princeton: D. Van Nostrand Co., 1958).

10. Hillel Levine, personal communication. Anita Libman Lebeson, *Pilgrim People* (New York: Minerva Press, 1975), p. 178; Blau, *Judaism in America,* p. 113; Nissan Waxman, "A Neglected Book" (Hebrew), in *Shana Beshana: Yearbook of Heichal Shlomo* (Jerusalem: 1969), pp. 303–315.

11. Naomi W. Cohen, *Encounter with Emancipation* (Philadelphia: Jewish Publication Society of America, 1984), p. 8.

12. Leon Harris, *Merchant Princes* (New York: Harper & Row, 1979), pp. 92–114.

13. Cohen, *Encounter,* p. 20.

14. Harris, *Merchant Princes,* p. 263.

15. Feldstein, *The Land,* p. 53.

16. Naphtali J. Rubinger, *Albany Jewry of the Nineteenth Century* (Ph.D. Dissertation, Yeshiva University, 1970), p. 190.

17. Francis Gregory and Irene D. Neu, "The American Industrial Elite in the 1870s," in William Miller, ed., *Men in Business: Essays in the History of Entrepreneurship* (Cambridge: Harvard University Press, 1952), p. 200.

18. Floyd S. Fierman, "Reminiscences of Emanuel Rosenwald," *New Mexico Historical Review,* 37: 2 (1962), p. 110.

19. Feldstein, *The Land,* p. 37.

20. Rubinger, *Albany Jewry,* p. 198.

21. "In Praise of the Jews," in Morris U. Schappes, ed., *A Documentary History of Jews in the United States, 1654–1875* (New York: Schocken Books, 1971), pp. 557–558.

22. Editorial in the *Philadelphia Sunday Dispatch* (April 21, 1867), "Excluding Jews From Insurance," in Schappes, ed., *Documentary History,* p. 514.

23. Cohen, *Encounter,* p. 24.

24. Henry L. Feingold, *Zion in America* (New York: Twayne, 1974 edition), p. 114.

25. Quoted in Moses Rischin, *The Promised City* (New York: Corinth Books, 1964), p. 30.

26. Feingold, *Zion,* p. 114.

27. Cohen, *Encounter,* p. 29.

28. U.S. Bureau of the Census, *Historical Statistics of the United States* (Washington, DC: U.S. Bureau of the Census, 1960).

29. Gerald Sorin, *A Time for Building: The Third Migration, 1880–1920* (Baltimore: The Johns Hopkins University Press, 1992), p. 74.

30. Howard M. Sachar, *A History of the Jews in America* (New York: Alfred A. Knopf, 1992), p. 141.

31. Michael Gold, *Jews Without Money* (New York: Carroll & Graf Publishers, 1985), pp. 159–160. Originally published in 1930.

32. Abraham Bosnio, "Chicago," in Charles S. Bernheimer, ed., *The Russian Jew in the United States* (Philadelphia: John C. Winston Co., 1905), p. 135.

33. Rischin, *Promised City,* pp. 52–54.

34. Isaac M. Rubinow, "New York," in Bernheimer, ed., *The Russian Jew,* p. 103.

35. Nathan Glazer, "Social Characteristics of American Jews, 1654–1954," *American Jewish Yearbook, 1955,* 56 (Philadelphia: American Jewish Committee and Jewish Publication Society, 1955), p. 15.

36. Rubinow, "New York," pp. 106–107.

37. Sachar, *History of the Jews,* p. 341.

38. Rudolf Glanz, *Jew and Italian, 1881–1924* (New York: Shulsinger Bros., 1971), p. 67, citing Bruno Roselli, *Our Italian Immigrants: Their Racial Background* (New York, 1927), p. 113.

39. Richard W. Fox, "The Paradox of Progressive Socialism: The Case of Morris Hillquit," *American Quarterly*, 26 (March 1974), p. 136.

40. Ibid.

41. Charles E. Silberman, *A Certain People: American Jews and Their Lives Today* (New York: Summit Books, 1985), p. 137.

42. Feingold, *Zion*, p. 160.

43. Arthur N. Holcombe, *The Middle Classes in American Politics* (Cambridge: Harvard University Press, 1940).

44. Seymour Martin Lipset and Reinhard Bendix, *Social Mobility in Industrial Society* (New Brunswick, NJ: Transaction Books, 2nd edition, 1992).

45. Lewis Corey, "The Middle Class," *Antioch Review*, 5 (Spring 1945), pp. 1–20.

46. U.S. Bureau of the Census, *Historical Statistics*, p. 74.

47. Glazer, "Social Characteristics," p. 20.

48. Steven M. Cohen, *The Dimensions of American Jewish Liberalism* (New York: American Jewish Committee, 1989), pp. 28–29. A decade earlier, Andrew Greeley concluded from National Opinion Research Center data that Jews are "the most successful group in American society." Andrew M. Greeley, *Ethnicity, Denomination and Inequality* (Beverly Hills: Sage, 1976), p. 39. See also David C. McClelland, "Issues in the Identification of Talent," in McClelland et al., *Talent and Society*, pp. 19–21.

49. Data from Gerald Bubis as reported in Barry A. Kosmin, "The Dimensions of Contemporary American Jewish Philanthropy," in Barry A. Kosmin and Paul Ritterband, eds., *Contemporary Jewish Philanthropy in America* (Lanham, MD: Rowman and Littlefield, 1991), p. 24.

50. Barry A. Kosmin and Seymour P. Lachman, *One Nation under God: Religion in Contemporary American Society* (New York: Harmony Books, 1993), p. 260. Calvin Goldscheider and Alan S. Zuckerman, *The Transformation of the Jews* (Chicago: University of Chicago Press, 1984), p. 183.

51. Richard D. Alba and Gwen Moore, "Ethnicity in the American Elite," *American Sociological Review*, 47 (June 1982), p. 377. Stanley Lieberson and Donna K. Carter, "Making It in America: Differences between Eminent Black and White Ethnic Groups," *American Sociological Review*, 44 (June 1979), pp. 349–352.

52. For an overview and references on intellectual and artistic activities, see Charles E. Silberman, *A Certain People: American Jews and Their Lives*

Today (New York: Summit Books, 1985), pp. 143–156; for the top intellectuals, see Charles Kadushin, *The American Intellectual Elite* (Boston: Little, Brown, 1974), pp. 19–32; on American Nobel Laureates, see Harriet Zuckerman, *Scientific Elite: Nobel Laureates in the United States* (New York: Free Press, 1977), p. 68. The data for professors are from Seymour Martin Lipset and Everett Carl Ladd, "Jewish Academics in the United States: Their Achievements, Culture and Politics," *American Jewish Yearbook*, 71 (1971), pp. 92–93.

53. The references for these findings are in Lipset and Ladd, "Jewish Academics," p. 99.

54. Nathan Reich, "The Role of the Jews in the American Economy," *YIVO*, Annual 5 (1950), pp. 197–205; Nathan Glazer, "The American Jew and the Attainment of Middle-Class Rank: Some Trends and Explanations," in Marshall Sklare, ed., *The Jews: Social Patterns of an American Group* (Glencoe, IL: Free Press, 1958), pp. 138–146; Sidney Goldstein, "Socioeconomic Differentials among Religious Groups in the United States," *American Journal of Sociology*, 74 (May 1969), pp. 612–631; Simon Kuznets, *Economic Structure of the Jews* (Jerusalem: Institute of Contemporary Jewry, Hebrew University, 1972); Marshall H. Medoff, "Note: Some Differences between the Jewish and General White Male Population in the United States," *Jewish Social Studies*, 43 (Winter 1981), pp. 75–80.

55. Lucy S. Dawidowicz, *On Equal Terms: Jews in America 1881–1981* (New York: Holt, Rinehart and Winston, 1982), p. 51. See also Arthur A. Goren, *The American Jews* (Cambridge: The Belknap Press of Harvard University Press, 1982), pp. 73–76.

2. The Promise of Double Freedom

1. A letter from Naphtali Philips to John A. McAllister, quoted in Jacob Rader Marcus, "Jews and the American Revolution," *American Jewish Archives*, 27 (November 1975), p. 249.

2. Edmund Burke, *Selected Works*, ed. E. J. Payne (Oxford: Clarendon Press, 1904), pp. 180–181.

3. Seymour Martin Lipset, "The American Jewish Community in Comparative Perspective," in *Revolution and Counterrevolution: Change and Persistence in Social Structures* (New Brunswick, NJ: Transaction Books, 1988, 3rd edition), pp. 141–153; Joseph L. Blau, *Judaism in America: From Curiosity to Third Faith* (Chicago: University of Chicago Press, 1976), pp. 51–72.

4. See Arthur A. Goren, *New York Jews and the Quest for Community: The Kehillah Experiment, 1908–1922* (New York: Columbia University, 1970).
5. Ibid., p. 252.
6. "Washington's Reply to the Hebrew Congregation in Newport, Rhode Island," *Publications of the American Jewish Historical Society,* no. 3 (1895), pp. 91–92.
7. John A. Hardon, *American Judaism* (Chicago: Loyola University Press, 1971), pp. 32–33; Anita Libman Lebeson, *Pilgrim People* (New York: Minerva Press, 1975), pp. 165–167.
8. Samuel Rezneck, *Unrecognized Patriots: The Jews in the American Revolution* (Westport, Conn.: Greenwood Press, 1975), p. 165.
9. "Washington's Reply to the Hebrew Congregation of the City of Savannah," in Joseph L. Blau and Salo W. Baron, eds., *The Jews of the United States, 1790–1840: A Documentary History,* vol. 1 (New York: Columbia University Press, 1963), p. 11.
10. "Jefferson to Jacob De La Motta, 1820," in ibid., p. 13.
11. "James Madison to Jacob De La Motta, 1820," in ibid., p. 14.
12. Morton Borden, *Jews, Turks and Infidels* (Chapel Hill, NC: University of North Carolina Press, 1984), p. 28.
13. Robert Baird, *Religion in America* (New York: Harper and Brothers, 1844), p. 188. See also Seymour Martin Lipset, *The First New Nation: The United States in Historical and Comparative Perspective* (New York: W. W. Norton, 1979), pp. 141–150.
14. Philip Schaff, *America: A Sketch of the Political, Social and Religious Character of the United States of North America* (New York: C. Scribner, 1855), pp. 94, 118.
15. Borden, *Jews,* p. 60.
16. Ibid., p. 101.
17. "Newport Inhabitants Ask for More Equitable Proportioning of Taxes, 1762," in Jacob Rader Marcus, ed., *American Jewry: Documents, Eighteenth Century* (Cincinnati: Hebrew Union College Press, 1959), p. 211.
18. Borden, *Jews,* pp. 108–109.
19. Ibid., p. 41.
20. Cohen, *Encounter,* p. 80.
21. James R. Rohrer, "The Sunday Mails and the Church-State Theme in Jacksonian America," *Journal of the Early Republic,* 7 (Spring 1987), p. 74.
22. Richard M. Johnson, "Sunday Observance and the Mail," in George E. Probst, ed., *The Happy Republic* (New York: Harper Torchbooks, 1962), pp. 250–254.

23. Borden, *Jews,* p. 63.

24. Cohen, *Encounter,* p. 82.

25. "Jacob Henry's Speech, 1809," in Blau and Baron, eds., *Jews of the United States,* pp. 29–31.

26. "Naval Hero Vindicated," in Morris U. Schappes, ed., *A Documentary History of the United States, 1654–1875* (New York: Schocken Books, 1971), p. 376.

27. Seymour Martin Lipset and Earl Raab, "The Election and the Evangelicals," *Commentary,* 71 (March 1981), pp. 25–31.

28. Michael Shannon, "GOP: The God Party," *San Francisco Examiner,* June 12, 1994, p. A15.

29. Allison Mitchell, "Musing on Religion, Giuliani Extols His Vision of Tolerance," *New York Times,* April 21, 1994, pp. B1–2.

30. Abraham Cahan, *Rise of David Levinsky* (New York: Harper and Brothers, 1917), p. 528.

3. The Downside of Exceptionalism

1. Jacob R. Marcus, "Jews and the American Revolution: A Bicentennial Documentary," *American Jewish Archives,* 27: 2 (November 1975), p. 211; Jacob Rader Marcus, *American Jewry: Documents; Eighteenth Century; Primarily Hitherto Unpublished Manuscripts* (Cincinnati: Hebrew Union College Press, 1959), pp. 52–53.

2. Sidney Goldstein, *Profile of American Jewry: Insights from the 1990 Jewish Population Study* (New York: North American Jewish Data Bank, Council of Jewish Federations, 1993), pp. 121–124.

3. Ibid., p. 124.

4. Drora Kass and Seymour Martin Lipset, "Jewish Immigration to the United States from 1967 to the Present," in Marshall Sklare, ed., *Understanding American Jewry* (New Brunswick, NJ: Transaction Books, 1982), pp. 272–294.

5. Howard M. Sachar, *A History of Jews in America* (New York: Alfred A. Knopf, 1992), p. 113.

6. National Jewish Population Study of 1990. See Goldstein, *Profile of American Jewry,* pp. 82–86, for description of the methodology of the study. Findings designated NJPS are derived or extrapolated from that study, through our own analyses of the data tapes.

7. For this modern definition, see *The Random House Dictionary of the English Language* (New York: Random House, 1987). For earlier definitions,

see *Webster's Universal Dictionary* (Cleveland: World Syndicate Publishing Co., 1937), or *The Shorter Oxford English Dictionary* (Oxford: Oxford University Press, 1950).

8. Nathan Glazer and Daniel Patrick Moynihan, *Beyond the Melting Pot* (Cambridge, Mass.: MIT Press, 1970), p. 254.

9. Herbert Gans, *The Urban Village: Group and Class in the Life of Italian Americans* (New York: Free Press, 1982), p. 33.

10. Morris Raphael Cohen, "Zionism: Tribalism or Liberalism," *New Republic*, March 8, 1918, p. 182.

11. Richard Gambino, *Blood of My Blood: The Dilemma of the Italian Americans* (Garden City: Doubleday and Company, 1974), chap. 1 and p. 341; Andrew Greeley, *The Irish Americans: The Rise to Money and Power* (New York: Warner Books, 1981), p. 10.

12. Ibid., p. 10; Gambino, *Blood,* chap. 1.

13. Steven Cohen, *National Survey of American Jews, 1986* (New York: American Jewish Committee, 1986). Respondents were allowed multiple choices. Nine out of ten chose both "It is my culture," and "I was born Jewish." Eight out of ten chose both "It provides me with a tie to other Jews" and "It is my way of life." Five of ten chose both "It gives me a sense of being special" and "It is the foundation for Israel's existence." Only four of ten chose "God wants me to be Jewish," four of ten disagreeing. Seven of ten chose "Judaism is a major source of liberal and humanitarian values" (a subject for later discussion).

14. Russell Jacoby, *Dogmatic Wisdom: How the Culture Wars Divert Education and Distract America* (New York: Doubleday, 1994), pp. 152–159.

15. Richard D. Alba, *Italian Americans: Into the Twilight of Ethnicity* (Englewood Cliffs, NJ: Prentice-Hall, 1985), chaps. 6 and 7.

16. Milton Gordon, *Assimilation in American Life* (New York: Oxford University Press, 1964), p. 81. See also Mary C. Waters, *Ethnic Options: Choosing Identities in America* (Berkeley: University of California Press, 1990).

17. Lawrence H. Fuchs, *The American Kaleidoscope* (Middletown, CT: Wesleyan University Press, 1990), p. 327.

18. Alba, *Italian Americans,* p. 147.

19. Darrel Montero, "The Japanese Americans: Changing Patterns of Assimilation over Three Generations," *American Sociological Review,* 42 (April 1977), pp. 829–839.; Eric Woodrum, "An Assessment of Japanese American Assimilation, Pluralism and Subordination," *American Journal of Sociology,* 87 (July 1981), pp. 157–169.

20. *Los Angeles Times,* "Israel and the Palestinian Problem," study no. 149, fieldwork March 26 to April 17, 1988.

21. Calvin Goldscheider and Alan S. Zuckerman, *The Transformation of the Jews* (Chicago: University of Chicago Press, 1984), p. 184. See also Chaim I. Waxman, *America's Jews in Transition* (Philadelphia: Temple University Press, 1983).

22. Will Herberg, *Protestant, Catholic, Jew: An Essay in American Religious Sociology* (Garden City, NY: Anchor Books, 1955).

23. Rabbi Hertzberg told this story at a Brandeis University conference in 1990, as recorded in Arthur Hertzberg, "The Jews in America: an Uncertain Future," in Earl Raab, ed., *American Jews in the 21st Century: Brown University Studies on Jews and Their Societies* (Atlanta, GA: Scholars Press, 1991), p. 30.

24. Joseph L. Blau and Salo W. Baron, eds., *The Jews of the United States, 1790–1840: A Documentary History,* vol. 1 (New York: Columbia University Press, 1963), pp. 110–111.

25. Stanley Feldstein, *The Land That I Show You* (Garden City, NY: Doubleday-Anchor, 1978), p. 37.

26. *Israelite,* vol. 6 (1859), p. 226, cited in Rudolf Glanz, "The Spread of Jewish Communities through America," *Yivo Annual of the Jewish Social Sciences,* 15 (1974), p. 11.

27. "Sketches from the Seat of War by a Jewish Soldier," February 1862, in Morris U. Schappes, ed., *A Documentary History of Jews in the United States* (New York: Schocken Books, 1971), p. 465.

28. Naomi W. Cohen, *Encounter with Emancipation* (Philadelphia: Jewish Publication Society of America, 1984), p. 20.

29. Jonathan D. Sarna, *Jacksonian Jew: The Two Worlds of Mordechai Noah* (New York: Holmes and Meier, 1981), p. 138.

30. *The Proceedings of the Conference of Reform Rabbis,* Philadelphia, November 1969, as translated by Sefton D. Temkin, *The New World of Reform* (London: Leo Baeck College, 1971), p. 39.

31. *Yearbook of the Central Conference of American Rabbis,* 45 (1935), pp. 198–200.

32. Cited in Nathan Glazer, *American Judaism* (Chicago: University of Chicago Press, 1957), pp. 56–57.

33. Marcus, *American Jewry,* pp. 136–137.

34. Marttila and Kiley, Inc., *ADL Antisemitism Survey,* Tabular Report #2 (Boston: May 1992).

35. NJPS and *Los Angeles Times,* "Israel and the Palestinian Problem."

36. Jack Wertheimer, "Recent Trends in American Judaism," *American Jewish Yearbook, 1989,* vol. 89 (New York: American Jewish Committee, 1989), pp. 86 ff.

37. Ibid., pp. 85–86; and assorted surveys conducted by Gallup and Jewish groups.

38. Arthur Hertzberg, "America Is Galut," *Jewish Frontier,* July 1964, pp. 7–9.

39. Marshal Sklare and Joseph Greenblum, *Jewish Identity on the Suburban Frontier* (New York: Basic Books, 1967), p. 57.

40. See Seymour Martin Lipset, "The Study of Jewish Communities in Comparative Context," *Jewish Journal of Sociology,* 5 (1963), pp. 157–166.

41. R. L. Bruckberger, "The American Catholics as a Minority," in T. T. McAvoy, ed., *Roman Catholicism and the American Way of Life* (Notre Dame: University of Notre Dame Press, 1960), pp. 45–47.

42. William V. Shannon, *The American Irish* (New York: Macmillan Company, 1966), p. 116.

43. Benton Johnson, Dean R. Hoge, and Donald A. Luidens, "Mainline Churches: The Real Reason for Decline," in *First Things,* 11 (March 1993), p. 18.

44. Herberg, *Protestant, Catholic, Jew,* p. 260.

45. Albert Gordon, *Jews in Suburbia* (Boston: Beacon Press, 1959), p. 98.

46. Glazer, *American Judaism,* p. 132.

47. Emile Durkheim, *The Elementary Forms of the Religious Life* (Old Woking, Surrey: George Allen and Unwin Ltd., 1976, first published in 1915), p. 419.

48. Jacob Katz, *Tradition and Crisis, Jewish Society at the End of the Middle Ages* (New York: Schocken Books, 1971), p. 182.

49. Ibid., p. 191.

50. Ibid., p. 235.

51. Ibid.

52. Mordecai Kaplan, "An Approach to Jewish Religion," in Simon Noveck, ed., *Contemporary Jewish Thought* (Clinton, MA: Colonial Press, 1963), p. 345.

53. Arnold Eisen, "The Rhetoric of Chosenness," in Seymour Martin Lipset, ed., *American Pluralism and the Jewish Community* (New Brunswick, NJ: Transaction Books, 1990), p. 66.

54. NJPS data.

55. Charles S. Liebman, "The Religious Life of American Jewry," in Marshall Sklare, ed., *Understanding American Jewry* (New Brunswick, NJ: Transaction Books, 1982), p. 107.

56. Jack Wertheimer, *A People Divided: Judaism in Contemporary America* (New York: Basic Books, 1993), p. 66.

57. Six out of 10 respondents perceived a general increase in anti-Semitism, while 2 perceived a decrease; in government action, 3 perceived an increase in anti-Semitism, 1 a decrease; in physical violence, 5 perceived an increase, none a decrease. These figures come from a survey of Jewish Federation members in nine Jewish communities across the country, conducted in December 1990 by the Cohen Center for Modern Jewish Studies and Perlmutter Institute at Brandeis University.

58. Some relevant figures interpolated from NJPS Survey: 82 percent of those who observe none of the three home rituals (Yom Kippur fast, Passover seder, Hannukah celebration) have none of the three community connections (synagogue membership, organizational affiliation, Federation contribution); 72 percent of those who observe only one home ritual have no community connections; 50 percent of those with no community connections observe no home ritual; 24 percent have no community connections and observe no home rituals; 36 percent have no community connections and observe only one home ritual; 27 percent have no community connections and do not strongly agree that anti-Semitism is a serious problem in the U.S. today; 16 percent do not observe any home rituals and do not strongly agree about the danger of anti-Semitism; 26 percent observe fewer than two home rituals and do not strongly agree about the danger of anti-Semitism.

59. Seymour Martin Lipset, *The Power of Jewish Education* (Boston and Los Angeles: The Wilstein Institute, 1994).

60. NJPS extrapolation. While age is an overall factor in the expressed intention of further educating children, the differential between mixed and entirely Jewish households remains dramatic. See Lipset, *The Power of Jewish Education.*

61. Barry A. Kosmin and Ariela Keysar, "The Demography of the Jewish Child Population in the U.S.: The Impact of Changing Patterns of Jewish Identity" (paper prepared for the 2nd International Conference on Jewish Demographic Policies, Jerusalem, February 1992), p. 2.

62. NJPS extrapolation. "Mixed" households consist almost entirely of intermarrieds where spousal conversion has not taken place.

63. Simon Rawidowicz, "Israel, the Ever-Dying People," in his *Studies in Jewish Thought* (Philadelphia: Jewish Publication Society, 1974), pp. 210–224.

64. Nathan Glazer, "New Perspectives in American Jewish Sociology," *American Jewish Yearbook, 1987*, vol. 87 (New York: American Jewish Committee, 1987), p. 19.

4. The Riddle of the Defensive Jew

1. The regional figures are from a survey done by the San Francisco Jewish Community Relations Council in 1981; the national figures are from the 1990 Jewish Public Opinion Survey of the Perlmutter Institute and the Cohen Center for Modern Jewish Studies at Brandeis University.

2. Lev Pinsker Semenovich, *Auto-Emancipation* (New York: Federation of American Zionists, 2nd edition, 1916; first published, 1882), pp. 4–5.

3. See Peter Mark Roget, *Thesaurus of English Words and Phrases* (New York: Grosset and Dunlap, 1937).

4. Charles Herbert Stember et al., *Jews in the Mind Of America* (New York: Basic Books, 1966), p. 69; Harold E. Quinley and Charles Y. Glock, *Anti-Semitism in America* (New York: Free Press, 1979), p. 8; Yankelovich survey group, July 1981; Marttila and Kiley, Inc., *ADL Antisemitism Survey*, Tabular Report #2 (Boston: May 1992).

5. The 1937 Gallup poll was reported in "Census Shows Minorities Are Gaining in Big Cities," *New York Times*, April 16, 1981, pp. A1 and B14. The 1983 figure was in *The Gallup Report* of September 1983.

6. Quinley and Glock, *Anti-Semitism*, p. 13.

7. Stember et al., *Jews in the Mind of America*, p. 56; NORC survey reported in Seymour Martin Lipset, "Blacks and Jews: How Much Bias?" *Public Opinion*, 10 (July/August 1987), p. 4.

8. Floris W. Wood, ed., *An American Profile: Opinions and Behavior, 1972–1989*, derived from the General Social Survey conducted by the National Opinion Research Center (Detroit: Gale Research, Inc., 1990), pp. 352–360; Tom Smith, *What Do Americans Think about Jews?* (New York: American Jewish Committee, 1991); Smith, *Anti-Semitism in Contemporary America* (New York: American Jewish Committee, 1994). Ninety-one percent rated Protestants above the "sixty degree" mark, as compared with 89 for Catholics and 85 for Jews.

9. Marttila and Kiley, Inc., *ADL Antisemitism Survey,* Tabular Report #2.

10. Ibid.

11. Lipset, "Blacks and Jews," p. 5.

12. Seymour Martin Lipset and Earl Raab, *The Politics of Unreason: Right-Wing Extremism in America, 1790–1977* (Chicago: University of Chicago Press, 1978), pp. 485–487.

13. John Higham, *Strangers in the Land* (New Brunswick, NJ: Rutgers University Press, 1955), p. 27; Leonard Dinnerstein, *Antisemitism in America* (New York: Oxford University Press, 1994), pp. 39–40.

14. Bertram W. Korn, *American Jewry and the Civil War* (Philadelphia: Jewish Publication Society, 1951), pp. 122–155.

15. John Higham, *Send These to Me: Immigrants in Urban America,* 2nd edition (Baltimore: Johns Hopkins University Press, 1984), p. 143.

16. Joakim Isaacs, "Ulysses Grant and the Jews," in Jonathan D. Sarna, ed., *The American Jewish Experience* (New York: Holmes and Meier, 1986), pp. 62–64.

17. Dinnerstein, *Antisemitism,* pp. 35–57.

18. Goldscheider and Zuckerman, *The Transformation of the Jews,* p. 166. For details see Glazer, "Social Characteristics," pp. 9–10, and Goren, *The American Jews,* pp. 34–36.

19. Barry E. Supple, "A Business Elite: German-Jewish Financiers in Nineteenth Century New York," *Business History Review,* 31 (Summer 1957), pp. 143–178; Vincent P. Carosso, "A Financial Elite: New York's German-Jewish Investment Bankers," *American Jewish Historical Quarterly,* 66 (September 1976), pp. 67–87.

20. John Higham, "Social Discrimination against Jews in America, 1830–1930," *American Jewish Historical Society,* 47 (1957), p. 10; "Anti-Semitism in the Gilded Age: A Reinterpretation," *Mississippi Valley Historical Review,* 43 (1957), p. 566. For these and other essays see Higham, *Send These to Me.*

21. "People's Platform of 1896," in Kirk H. Porter and Donald B. Johnson, eds., *National Party Platforms, 1840–1964* (Urbana: University of Illinois Press, 1966), p. 104.

22. "Platform of 1896," in ibid., p. 98.

23. C. Vann Woodward, *Tom Watson, Agrarian Rebel* (New York: Oxford University Press, 1963), p. 419; Gustavus Myers, *History of Bigotry in the United States* (New York: Capricorn, 1968), p. 195.

24. Lipset and Raab, *Politics of Unreason,* pp. 98–99.

25. Benjamin H. Avin, *The Ku Klux Klan, 1915–1925: A Study of Religious Intolerance* (Ph.D. Dissertation, Department of History, Georgetown University, 1952), p. 85.

26. Dinnerstein, *Antisemitism*, pp. 128–149.

27. Leo P. Ribuffo, "Henry Ford and the International Jew," *American Jewish History*, 69 (June 1980), p. 437; Gallup Poll, December 1938; Lipset and Raab, *Politics of Unreason*, pp. 167–189, esp. pp. 172–173.

28. Morton Keller, "Jews and the Character of American Life since 1930," in Stember et al., *Jews in the Mind of America*, pp. 260–263; Dinnerstein, *Antisemitism*, p. 127.

29. Quoted in Leah Garchik, "Personals," *San Francisco Chronicle*, June 1, 1994, p. D8.

30. CBS/*New York Times*, October 6, 1986; Roper Report 74–3, April 1974; Roper Report 79–3, April 1979; Gallup, March 16, 1981.

31. Gertrude Jaeger Selznick and Stephen Steinberg, *The Tenacity of Prejudice: Anti-Semitism in Contemporary America* (New York: Harper & Row, 1969), p. 54.

32. Ibid.

33. Lipset and Raab, *Politics of Unreason*, p. 171–189.

34. Jacob Rader Marcus, *The Colonial American Jew, 1492–1776*, vol. 2 (Detroit: Wayne State University Press, 1970), p. 888.

35. E. E. Schattschneider, *Party Government* (New York: Rinehart and Co., 1942), pp. 65–98.

36. Selznick and Steinberg, *Tenacity of Prejudice*, p. 157.

37. Richard Rovere, *Senator Joe McCarthy* (New York: Meridian, 1960), p. 125.

38. Joseph R. McCarthy, "America's Retreat from Victory," *Congressional Record* (June 14, 1951), 9A Reprint, p. 1.

39. Lipset and Raab, *Politics of Unreason*, pp. 239–245.

40. *Historical Statistics of the United States, Colonial Times to 1970* (Washington, DC: Bureau of the Census, U.S. Department of Commerce, 1970), part 1, p. 139.

41. Ibid., pp. 379, 381.

42. The report on incidents and on the skinheads are both found in *Audit of Anti-Semitic Incidents, 1993* (New York: Anti-Defamation League, 1994), pp. 1–3, 15.

43. Edward D. Rogowsky, "Intergroup Relations and Tensions in the United States," *American Jewish Yearbook 1969*, vol. 70 (New York: American Jewish Committee, 1969), p. 84.

44. Ibid., p. 78.

45. Dinnerstein, *Antisemitism,* pp. 197–227.

46. Speech by Leonard Jeffries on July 20, 1991, in Albany, New York, to the Empire State Black Arts and Cultural Festival. Reported by Jacques Steinberg in *New York Times,* August 6, 1991, B, 3:1.

47. *The Final Call,* editorial, May 27, 1988.

48. Paul Berman, "The Other and the Almost the Same," *New Yorker,* February 28, 1994, pp. 61 ff.

49. Yankelovich poll of February 16–17, 1994, reported in "How African-Americans See It," *Time,* February 28, 1994, p. 22.

50. Sylvester Monroe, "Doing the Right Thing," *Time,* April 16, 1990, p. 22; ADL Research Report, *Louis Farrakhan: The Campaign to Manipulate Public Opinion* (New York: Anti-Defamation League, 1990), p. 7.

51. Cornel West, "How Do We Fight Xenophobia?" *Time,* February 28, 1994, p. 30.

52. Steven M. Cohen, *1984 National Survey of American Jews* (New York: American Jewish Committee, 1985). He asked a sample of Jews, "In your opinion, what proportion of each of the following groups in the U.S. is anti-Semitic, Most, Many, Some or Few?" Over half, 54 percent, of the respondents indicated that "most or many" of the blacks were anti-Semitic, a higher figure than ascribed to any other group. Fundamentalist Protestants came next, with a figure of 46 percent.

53. Marttila and Kiley, Inc., *ADL Antisemitism Survey,* Tabular Report #2.

54. Ibid.

55. Seymour Martin Lipset, "The 'Socialism of Fools': The Left, The Jews and Israel," *Encounter,* December 1969, pp. 24–35; "The Socialism of Fools," *New York Times Magazine,* January 3, 1971, pp. 6–7, 26–27, 34.

56. San Francisco Jewish Community Relations Council, poll of affiliated Jews, 1981.

57. 1990 Jewish Public Opinion Survey, Perlmutter Institute and Cohen Center for Modern Jewish Studies, Brandeis University.

58. Simon Rawidowicz, "Israel, the Ever-Dying People," in his *Studies in Jewish Thought* (Philadelphia: Jewish Publication Society, 1974), pp. 220–221.

59. Judith Levine, "A Swastika in Vermont," *New York Times,* July 10, 1993, p. 19.

60. For an analysis of the ways that acceptance makes for decline in the United States, see S. N. Eisenstadt, "The Incorporation of the Jews in the United States," in his *Jewish Civilization: The Jewish Experience in a Com-*

parative Perspective (Albany: State University of New York Press, 1992), pp. 119–139.

5. Israel, the X-Factor

1. An overwhelming majority, 68 percent, of an American Jewish sample agreed with that statement in the American Jewish Committee survey of 1993. Similar proportions were found in Steven M. Cohen's *National Survey(s) of American Jews* (New York: American Jewish Committee, 1983, 1986, 1988, 1991).

2. Mordechai Manuel Noah, *Call to America to Build Zion (Discourse on the Restoration of the Jews)* (New York: Arno Press, 1977). The ceremony is described in Jonathan D. Sarna, *Jacksonian Jew: The Two Worlds of Mordechai Noah* (New York: Holmes and Meier, 1981), p. 66.

3. "Judah Touro's Will," in Morris U. Schappes, ed., *A Documentary History of the Jews in the United States, 1654–1875,* 3rd edition (New York: Schocken Books, 1971), p. 337.

4. "American Jews and the Damascus Affair," in ibid., p. 211.

5. Peter Grose, *Israel in the Mind of America* (New York: Alfred A. Knopf, 1984), p. 29.

6. *Yearbook of the Central Conference of American Rabbis,* 45 (1935), p. 199.

7. *Yearbook of the Central Conference of American Rabbis,* 7 (1897), pp. x–xii.

8. C. Levias, "The Justification of Zionism," *Hebrew Union College Journal,* 3 (April 1899), pp. 165–175.

9. Grose, *Israel,* p. 56.

10. Ibid., p. 74.

11. *Proceedings of the Central Conference of American Rabbis,* 47 (1946), pp. 97–99.

12. Marshall Sklare and Benjamin B. Ringer, "A Study of Jewish Attitudes towards the State of Israel," in Marshall Sklare, ed., *The Jews: Social Patterns of An American Group* (Glencoe, IL: Free Press, 1958), p. 444.

13. Reuben Fink, *America and Palestine* (New York: Arno Press, 1977), p. 20.

14. Frank E. Manuel, *The Realities of American-Palestine Relations* (Washington, DC: Public Affairs Press, 1949), p. 72.

15. Richard N. Lebow, "Woodrow Wilson and the Balfour Declaration," *Journal of Modern History,* December 1968, p. 521, cited in Stephen L.

Spiegel, *The Other Arab-Israeli Conflict* (Chicago: University of Chicago Press, 1985).

16. Howard M. Sachar, *Europe Leaves the Middle East, 1936–1954* (New York: Alfred A. Knopf, 1972), p. 454.
17. Spiegel, *The Other Arab-Israeli Conflict,* pp. 51, 54.
18. *The Cambridge Report,* Summer 1975, p. 180.
19. Charles Herbert Stember et al., *Jews in the Mind of America* (New York: Basic Books, 1966), p. 179; Eytan Gilboa, *American Public Opinion Toward Israel and the Arab-Israeli Conflict* (Lexington: Lexington Books, 1987), pp. 47, 90, 127.
20. Martilla and Kiley, Inc., *ADL Antisemitism Survey* (Boston: May 1992).
21. Stember et al., *Jews in the Mind of America,* p. 178.
22. Gilboa, *American Public Opinion,* p. 145.
23. Ibid., p. 226.
24. Ibid., p. 220.
25. *The Palestinian Autonomy Agreement and Israel-PLO Recognition: A Survey of American Jewish Opinion* (New York: American Jewish Committee, 1993).
26. Ibid.
27. Earl Raab, "Attitudes Toward Israel and Attitudes Toward Jews: The Relationship," in Michael Curtis, ed., *Antisemitism in the Contemporary World* (Boulder: Westview Press, 1986), pp. 289, 299.
28. Marttila and Kiley, Inc., *ADL Antisemitism Survey.* On the relationship between the anti-Semitic index and the belief that pro-Israel lobbies have too much influence, 23 percent of the least anti-Semitic respondents believe that pro-Israel lobbies have too much influence, and 54 percent of the most anti-Semitic respondents believe it.
29. William A. Henry III, "Buchanan the Biter, Bitten," *Time,* 136 (October 1, 1990), p. 80.
30. Gore Vidal, "The Empire Lovers Strike Back," *The Nation,* 242 (March 22, 1986), pp. 350, 353.
31. Ahad Ha-Am, "A Spiritual Centre," in Simon Noveck, ed., *Contemporary Jewish Thought: A Reader* (Clinton, MA: Colonial Press, 1963), pp. 45–51.
32. Max Schloessinger, "Reform Judaism and Zionism," in *Jewish Comment,* 24 (Baltimore: January 4–11, 1907), p. 26.
33. In the 1993 American Jewish Committee survey, 79 percent of Jews agreed with that sentiment. Earlier agreements with the same statement

varied from 68 percent to 81 percent in Steven Cohen's surveys and NJPS.

34. Cohen, *1991 National Survey*, p. 38.
35. Perlmutter Institute and Cohen Center for Modern Jewish Studies, Brandeis University, 1990.
36. Cohen, *1983 National Survey*, p. 32.
37. Cohen, *1991 National Survey*, p. 38.
38. *Los Angeles Times*, "Israel and the Palestinian Problem," Study #149, March 26 to April 7, 1988.
39. *1990 Jewish Public Opinion Survey*, Perlmutter Institute and Cohen Center for Modern Jewish Studies, Brandeis University, 1990.
40. Cohen, *1986 National Surveys*, p. 51; Cohen, *1988 National Survey*, p. 5; Cohen, *1991 National Survey*, p. 39.
41. Cohen, *1991 National Survey*, p. 51.
42. Charles S. Liebman, *The Ambivalent American Jew: Politics, Religion, and Family in American Jewish Life* (Philadelphia: The Jewish Publication Society of America, 1973), p. 94.
43. NJPS data.
44. Benjamin Halpern, *The American Jew* (New York: Theodor Herzl Foundation, 1956), p. 129.

6. Still on the Left

1. Estimate from personal communication from Herbert Alexander, the leading academic authority on campaign finance.
2. Jacob Rader Marcus, *American Jewry: Documents; Eighteenth Century; Primarily Hitherto Unpublished Manuscripts* (Cincinnati: Hebrew Union College Press, 1959), pp. 232–233.
3. Samuel Rezneck, *Unrecognized Patriots: The Jews in the American Revolution* (Westport, CN: Greenwood Press, 1975), p. 24.
4. *Asmonean*, December 19, 1851, cited in Naomi W. Cohen, *Encounter with Emancipation* (Philadelphia: The Jewish Publication Society of America, 1984), p. 140.
5. Hasia R. Diner, *A Time for Gathering: The Second Migration, 1820–1880* (Baltimore: The John Hopkins University Press, 1992), p. 146.
6. *Occident*, February 12, 1855, pp. 561–563, cited in Cohen, *Encounter*, p. 138.
7. Peter Wiernik, *History of the Jews in America* (New York: Hermon Press, 1972, 3rd edition), pp. 128–134.

8. Henry L. Feingold, *Zion in America* (New York: Hippocrene Books, 1974), pp. 89–90.
9. Frederic Cople Jaher, *A Scapegoat in the Wilderness: The Origins and Rise of Anti-Semitism in America* (Cambridge: Harvard University Press, 1994), p. 177. On Civil War generals see Feingold, *Zion*, p. 91.
10. Diner, *Time for Gathering*, p. 144.
11. *Tageblatt*, English page, November 23, 1914. Reprinted in Mordecai Soltes, *The Yiddish Press* (New York: Teachers College, Columbia University, 1925), pp. 211–212.
12. Charles A. Madison, *Eminent American Jews* (New York: Frederick Ungar, 1970), p. 94.
13. Leonard Dinnerstein, "Jews and the New Deal," *American Jewish History*, 72 (June 1983), p. 464.
14. "Our State Department and the Damascus Affair," in Morris U. Schappes, ed., *A Documentary History of the Jews in the United States, 1654–1875* (New York: Schocken Books, 1971), p. 209.
15. Wiernik, *History of the Jews*, pp. 345–346. For a detailed account of such interventions, see Cyrus Adler and Aaron M. Margalith, *American Intercession on Behalf of Jews in the Diplomatic Correspondence of the United States 1840–1938* (New York: American Jewish Historical Society, 1943).
16. Feingold, *Zion in America*, pp. 239–249.
17. David Biale, *Power and Powerlessness in Jewish History* (New York: Schocken Books, 1986), pp. 124–125; Bertram W. Korn, *The American Reaction to the Montara Case 1858–1859* (Cincinnati: The American Jewish Archives, 1957), pp. 88–92.
18. "The Lobby with a Lock on Congress," *Newsweek*, October 19, 1987, p. 46; Robert Pear and Richard L. Berke, "Pro-Israel Group Exerts Quiet Might as It Rallies Supporters in Congress," *New York Times*, July 7, 1987, p. A8.
19. Steven L. Spiegel, *The Other Arab-Israeli Conflict* (Chicago: University of Chicago Press, 1985), p. 160.
20. Beverly and Wesley Allinsmith, "Religious Affiliation and Political Economic Attitudes," *Public Opinion Quarterly*, 12 (1948), pp. 577–589.
21. Alan Fisher, "The Myth of the Rightward Turn," *Moment*, 8: 10 (1983), p. 25.
22. Steven Cohen, *1988 National Survey of American Jews* (New York: American Jewish Committee, 1988), p. 3.
23. William B. Helmreich, "American Jews and the 1988 Presidential Elections," *Congress Monthly*, 56 (January 1989), pp. 3–5; Peter Steinfels,

"American Jews Stand Firmly to the Left," *New York Times*, "News of the Week," January 8, 1988, p. E7; and table, "Portrait of the Electorate," *New York Times*, November 5, 1992, p. B9.

24. Lawrence H. Fuchs, "Jews and the Presidential Vote," in Lawrence H. Fuchs, ed., *American Ethnic Politics* (New York: Harper & Row, 1968), pp. 50–76.

25. Lawrence H. Fuchs, *The Political Behavior of American Jews* (Glencoe, IL: Free Press, 1956), pp. 180–182, 187–188.

26. Thorstein Veblen, *Essays on Our Changing Order* (New York: Viking Press, 1934), pp. 221, 223–234. The essay on the Jews was first published in 1919.

27. See Seymour Martin Lipset and Richard B. Dobson, "The Intellectual as Critic and Rebel: With Special Reference to the United States and the Soviet Union," *Daedalus*, 101 (Summer 1972), p. 147.

28. Charles S. Liebman, *The Ambivalent American Jew: Politics, Religion, and Family in American Jewish Life* (Philadelphia: Jewish Publication Society of America, 1973), pp. 149–150.

29. See Jerrold S. Auerbach, *Rabbis and Lawyers* (Bloomington: Indiana University Press, 1990), esp. chap. 3.

30. Steven M. Cohen, *1983 National Survey of American Jews* (New York: American Jewish Committee, 1984 and 1986), p. 56.

31. "A Letter to the Printer of the *Gazette*," cited in Schappes, ed., *A Documentary History*, p. 95.

32. Fuchs, *Political Behavior*, p. 26.

33. National Jewish Community Relations Advisory Council, *Joint Program Plan, 1992–1993* (New York: National Jewish Community Relations Advisory Council, 1993), p. 2.

34. E. Merton Coulter, *The South during Reconstruction, 1865–1877* (Baton Rouge: Louisiana State University, 1947), p. 202.

35. Cyrus Adler, *Jacob A. Schiff: His Life and Letters* (Garden City, NY: Doubleday, Duran & Co., 1928), vol. 1, p. 315.

36. Steven A. Holmes, "A Rights Leader Plays Down Racism as a Poverty Factor," *New York Times*, July 24, 1994, pp. 1, 15.

37. Earl Raab, "The Black Revolution and the Jewish Question," *Commentary*, 53 (January 1972); Louis Harris and Bert E. Swanson, *Black-Jewish Relations in New York City* (New York: Praeger Publishers, 1970), pp. 131–158.

38. Earl Raab, "Quotas by Any Other Name," *Commentary*, 47 (January 1969), p. 44.

39. Sam Roberts, "The Tide Turns in Voter Turnout," *New York Times*, November 4, 1992, p. B6. The data are from the Voter Research and Survey's 1992 Exit Poll.

40. Cohen, *1983 National Survey*, p. 15. See also Cohen, *1991 National Survey*.

41. Perlmutter Institute and Cohen Center for Jewish Studies, Brandeis University, 1990.

42. *The Palestinian Autonomy Agreement and Israel-PLO Recognition: A Survey of American Jewish Opinion* (New York: American Jewish Committee, 1993); Cohen, *1983 National Survey*, p. 13. See also Cohen, *1991 National Survey*, p. 28.

43. See Seymour Martin Lipset, *Continental Divide: The Values and Institutions of the United States and Canada* (New York: Routledge, 1990).

44. J. A. Laponce, "Left or Center: The Canadian Jewish Electorate, 1953–1983," *Canadian Journal of Political Science*, 21 (December 1988), pp. 694–696.

45. See Geoffrey Alderman, "Not Quite British: The Political Attitudes of Anglo-Jewry," in Ivor Crewe, ed., *British Political Sociology Yearbook*, vol. 2: *The Politics of Race* (London: Croom Helm, 1975), pp. 188–211; "Jews and Socialism: The End of a Beautiful Relationship?" symposium, *Jewish Quarterly*, 35: 2 (1988), pp. 7–19; Peter Y. Medding, "Factors Influencing the Voting Behaviour of Melbourne Jews," in Medding, ed., *Jews in Australian Society* (South Melbourne: Macmillan, 1973), pp. 141–159; Bernard Wasserstein, "The Jews, the Left and the 1973 Elections in France," *Midstream*, 19 (August/September 1973), pp. 41–54.

46. See W. D. Rubenstein, *The Left, the Right and the Jews* (New York: Universe Books, 1982), pp. 77–173.

47. Stephen D. Isaacs, *Jews and American Politics* (Garden City, NY: Doubleday, 1974), p. 153; Fuchs, *Political Behavior*, pp. 41–57; Nathaniel Weyl, *The Jew in American Politics* (New Rochelle, NY: Arlington House, 1968), pp. 63–76.

48. Fuchs, *Political Behavior*, pp. 55–57; Isaacs, *Jews and American Politics*, pp. 153–155.

49. Werner Cohn, "The Politics of American Jews," in Marshall Sklare, ed., *The Jews: Social Patterns of an American Group* (Glencoe, IL: Free Press, 1958), pp. 615–618.

50. Ronald Sanders, *The Downtown Jews* (New York: Dover Publications, 1987), pp. 56–180; Melech Epstein, *Jewish Labor in the U.S.A.* (New York: Trade Union Sponsoring Committee, 1950).

51. Arthur Liebman, *Jews and the Left* (New York: John Wiley and Sons,

1979), p. 1, also pp. 20–33; Irving Howe, *World of Our Fathers* (New York: Harcourt, Brace, Jovanovich, 1976), pp. 287–324.

52. Isaacs, *Jews and American Politics,* pp. 151–152; Fuchs, *Political Behavior,* pp. 151–169. On the Jews and the American Communist Party, see Nathan Glazer, *The Social Basis of American Communism* (New York: Harcourt Brace and World, 1961), pp. 130–168.

53. Cohn, "Politics of American Jews," p. 621.

54. Fuchs, *Political Behavior,* pp. 71–81, 129–130.

55. Isaacs, *Jews and American Politics,* p. 152.

56. Stephen J. Whitfield, "The Jewish Vote," *Virginia Quarterly Review,* 62 (Winter 1986), pp. 1–20. See also Seymour Martin Lipset and Earl Raab, "The American Jews: The 1984 Elections and Beyond," in Daniel J. Elazar, ed., *The New Jewish Politics* (Lanham, MD: University Press of America, 1988), pp. 35–50.

57. Martin Hochbaum, *The Jewish Vote in the 1984 Presidential Election* (New York: American Jewish Congress, 1985), p. 6.

58. "Portrait of the Electorate," *New York Times,* November 5, 1992, p. B9.

59. American Jewish Congress, Commission on National Affairs, *The Jewish Vote in the 1992 Presidential Election* (New York: American Jewish Congress, 1993).

60. Isaacs, *Jews and American Politics,* pp. 151–153; *Statistical Abstract of the United States, 1970* (Washington, DC: U.S. Bureau of the Census, 1971); and "Portrait of the Electorate," p. B9. Jewish voting figures in early years, and even in later years as the product of exit polls, are approximations.

61. Leonard Fein, *Where are We? The Inner Life of America's Jews* (New York: Harper & Row, 1988), pp. 227–241.

62. American Jewish Congress, *The Jewish Vote.*

63. Seymour Martin Lipset and Earl Raab, "The Message of Proposition 13," *Commentary,* 66 (September 1978), pp. 42–46.

64. Cohn, "Politics of American Jews," p. 620.

65. Irving Kristol, "The Liberal Tradition of American Jews," in Seymour Martin Lipset, ed., *American Pluralism and the Jewish Community* (New Brunswick, NJ: Transaction Books, 1990), pp. 109–116.

66. Robert Lerner, Althea K. Nagai, and Stanley Rothman, "Marginality and Liberalism among Jewish Elites," *Public Opinion Quarterly,* 53 (Fall 1989), pp. 335, 338–339.

67. Ibid., pp. 339–340.

68. Seymour Martin Lipset, "Neo-conservativism: Myth and Reality," *Society,* 25 (July, August 1988), pp. 29–37.

69. For examples, see Rob Kroes, ed., *Neo-Conservatism: Its Emergence in the USA and Europe* (Amsterdam: Free University Press, 1984).
70. Fisher, "Myth," p. 26.

7. The Fragile Remnants

1. Reported from different sources in Ronald Takaki, *A Different Mirror: A History of Multicultural America* (Boston: Little, Brown and Company, 1993), pp. 163–164.
2. Seymour Martin Lipset, "Two Americas, Two Value Systems, Blacks and Whites," *Tocqueville Review*, 13: 1 (1992), pp. 159–164.
3. Marshall Sklare, *Observing America's Jews* (Hanover, NH: University Press of New England/ Brandeis University Press, 1993), pp. 262–274.
4. Ibid., p. 265.
5. Sam Roberts, *Who We Are: A Portrait of America Based on the Latest U.S. Census* (New York: Times Books, 1994), p. 283.
6. Richard D. Alba, *Ethnic Identity: The Transformation of White America* (New Haven: Yale University Press, 1990), p. 297.
7. Ibid., p. 299.
8. Ibid., p. 47.
9. Ibid., p. 15.
10. Ibid., p. 5.
11. "The Numbers Game," *Time Magazine*, Fall 1993 Special Issue, p. 15.
12. Gallup Poll, July 9 and 11, 1993, reported in *San Francisco Chronicle*, July 23, 1993, p. A26.
13. "The Numbers Game," p. 15.
14. *Tampa Tribune*, November 2, 1982.
15. Lansing Lamont, *Breakup: The Coming End of Canada and the Stakes for America* (New York: W. W. Norton, 1994), p. 210.
16. Richard Rodriguez, *Hunger of Memory* (Boston: David Godine, 1982), pp. 19–27; Earl Shorris, *Latinos: A Biography of the People* (New York: W. W. Norton, 1992), pp. 73–74, 181–183.
17. Census Bureau, *Statistical Abstract of the United States 1992* (Washington, DC: Bureau of the Census, Department of Commerce), p. 41.
18. Shorris, *Latinos*, pp. 428–429.
19. Ibid., p. 426.
20. Peter Skerry, *Mexican Americans: The Ambivalent Minority* (New York: Free Press, 1993), p. 285.
21. Kevin F. McCarthy and R. Burciaga Valdez, Report R-3365-CR (Santa

Monica: Rand Corporation, 1986), pp. 61–62; see also Skerry, *Mexican Americans,* p. 285.

22. Rudolfo O. de la Garza, Louis De Sipio, F. Chris Garcia, John Garcia, and Angelo Falcon, *Latino Voices: Mexican, Puerto Rican, and Cuban Perspectives on American Politics* (Boulder: Westview, 1992), p. 98. JoAnn Zuniga, "87% in Poll See Duty to Learn English," *Houston Chronicle,* July 12, 1990, p. A19.

23. Arthur M. Schlesinger Jr., *The Disuniting of America: Reflections on a Multicultural Society* (Knoxville: Whittle Books, 1991), p. 79.

24. Paul R. Spickard, *Mixed Blood: Intermarriage and Ethnic Identity in Twentieth-Century America* (Madison: University of Wisconsin Press, 1989), p. 344.

25. Ibid.

26. Ibid.

27. Skerry, *Mexican Americans,* p. 68.

28. Linda Chavez, *Out of the Barrio* (New York: Basic Books, 1991), p. 81.

29. Census Bureau, *Statistical Abstract of the United States 1992,* p. 41.

30. Louis Winnick, "America's 'Model Minority,'" *Commentary,* 90 (August 1990), p. 25.

31. Carla Rivera, "Asians Say They Fare Better than Other Minorities," *Los Angeles Times,* August 20, 1993, p. A20.

32. Spickard, *Mixed Blood,* p. 344.

33. "The Numbers Game," p. 14.

34. Spickard, *Mixed Blood,* p. 345.

35. Schlesinger, *Disuniting,* p. 80.

36. *Statistical Abstract of the United States 1992,* p. 164.

37. Spickard, *Mixed Blood,* p. 348.

38. These figures can be found in *The Black Population of the United States,* Current Population Reports, Population Characteristics, pp. 20–464 (Washington, DC: U.S. Bureau of the Census, March 1991), pp. 16, 33; in Robert Staples, "The Illusion of Racial Equality: The Black American Dilemma"; in Gerald Early, ed., *Lure and Loathing* (New York: Penguin Press, 1993), p. 229; and in Census Bureau, *Statistical Abstract of the United States 1992,* p. 94. See also Bart Landry, *The New Black Middle Class* (Berkeley: University of California Press, 1987).

39. In Paul Ruffins, "Interracial Coalitions," *Atlantic,* June 20, 1990, p. 4. For survey evidence on increasingly favorable attitudes overall toward African Americans, see Howard Schuman, Charlotte Steeh, and Lawrence Bobo,

Racial Attitudes in America (Cambridge, MA: Harvard University Press, 1985).

40. Schuman et al., *Racial Attitudes,* p. 202; Lipset, "Two Americas," pp. 160–163.

41. Carl Zinsmeister, "Black Demographics," *Public Opinion,* 10 (January/February 1988), pp. 41–44.

42. Census Bureau, *Statistical Abstract,* p. 444.

43. Statement of Herman Miller, director of the Census Bureau's population division, reported in *Chronicle,* monthly report of Urban America, Inc., March 1969, p. 5.

44. *The Black Population of the United States,* p. 7.

45. Gerald D. Jaynes and Robin M. Williams, eds., *A Common Destiny: Blacks in American Society* (Washington, DC: National Academy Press, 1989), pp. 279–286.

46. David Ellwood and Jonathan Crane, "Family Change among Black Americans: What Do We Know?" *Journal of Economic Perspectives,* 4 (Fall 1990), p. 70.

47. Christopher Jencks, "Is the American Underclass Growing?" in Christopher Jencks and Paul E. Peterson, eds., *The Urban Underclass* (Washington, DC: The Brookings Institution, 1991), pp. 86–89.

48. Zinsmeister, "Black Demographics," p. 41.

49. Jaynes and Williams, *Common Destiny,* p. 275.

50. Douglas S. Massey and Nancy A. Denton, *American Apartheid: Segregation and the Making of the Underclass* (Cambridge: Harvard University Press, 1993), pp. 67 and 85–87.

51. Alba, *Ethnic Identity,* p. 13.

52. Schlesinger, *The Disuniting,* p. 46.

53. Ibid, p. 88.

54. Lipset, "Two Americas," p. 159.

55. Jerry Seper, "Leader Urges Black Exodus," *Washington Times,* February 28, 1990, p. A1.

56. Louis Farrakhan, "The Black Man: An Endangered Species," *Final Call,* May 9, 1988.

57. For a general evaluation to this effect, see S. N. Eisenstadt, "The Incorporation of the Jews in the United States," in his *Jewish Civilization. The Jewish Historical Experience in Comparative Perspective* (Albany: State University of New York Press, 1992), pp. 119–139.

58. Survey conducted for the American Jewish Committee by Market

Facts, September 20–26, 1993 (New York: American Jewish Committee, 1993).

59. Benjamin Ginsberg, *The Fatal Embrace: Jews and the State* (Chicago: University of Chicago Press, 1993), p. 235.

60. *Religion in America,* Gallup Report, April 1987, Report #259.

61. Charles S. Liebman, *The Ambivalent American Jew* (Philadelphia: The Jewish Publication Society of America, 1973), p. 177.

62. Wade Clark Roof, *A Generation of Seekers: The Spiritual Journeys of the Baby Boom Generation* (San Francisco: Harper, 1993), pp. 182–212, 241–262.

63. Steven M. Cohen, *American Assimilation or Jewish Revival* (Bloomington: Indiana University Press, 1988), p. 46.

64. Charles S. Liebman, "The Religious Life of American Jewry," in Marshall Sklare, ed., *Understanding American Jewry* (New Brunswick, NJ: Transaction Books, 1982), p. 47.

65. Richard D. Alba, *Italian Americans: Into the Twilight of Ethnicity* (Englewood Cliffs, NJ: Prentice-Hall, 1985), p. 89.

66. George Gallup Jr. and Jim Castelli, *The American Catholic People* (Garden City: Doubleday, 1987), pp. 59–60.

67. Seymour Martin Lipset, *The Power of Jewish Education* (Boston and Los Angeles: The Wilstein Institute, 1994).

68. Peter Grose, *Israel in the Mind of America* (New York: Alfred A. Knopf, 1984), p. 6.

69. Sklare, *Observing America's Jews,* pp. 234–247, 262–263. Chaim I. Waxman, "Heightening Ideology, Diminishing Community: A Review Essay," *Shofar,* 12 (Winter 1992), pp. 102–103.

70. Don Lattin, "Church-State Conflict in a Jewish Town," *San Francisco Chronicle,* March 25, 1994.

~ Index ~